JUST LIKE, ANY OTHER DAY IN, THE LIFE OF ME

JUST LIKE, ANY OTHER DAY IN, THE LIFE OF ME

HEATHER CHICONELLA

LitPrime Solutions
21250 Hawthorne Blvd
Suite 500, Torrance, CA 90503
www.litprime.com
Phone: 1 (209) 788-3500

© 2021 Heather Chiconella. All rights reserved.

No part of this book may be reproduced, stored in a retrieval system, or transmitted by any means without the written permission of the author.

Published by LitPrime Solutions   03/05/2021

ISBN: 978-1-954886-21-6(sc)
ISBN: 978-1-954886-23-0(hc)
ISBN: 978-1-954886-22-3(e)

Library of Congress Control Number: 2021904920

Any people depicted in stock imagery provided by iStock are models, and such images are being used for illustrative purposes only.

Certain stock imagery © iStock.

Because of the dynamic nature of the Internet, any web addresses or links contained in this book may have changed since publication and may no longer be valid. The views expressed in this work are solely those of the author and do not necessarily reflect the views of the publisher, and the publisher hereby disclaims any responsibility for them.

CONTENTS

Chapter One: The birth of my unwanted sidekick................. 1

Chapter Two: Then suddenly, the dreaded curse of the go
between days...came true!"..................... 54

Chapter Three: "The day that, Time...Stood Still" part 1 & 2....... 97

Chapter Four: "Untangling it's "mysterious," Web of last "dreams" 173

Chapter Five: My eight grade discovery........................214

Chapter Six: "Talks the easy part 226

CHAPTER ONE

The birth of my unwanted sidekick

Eventhough, I wouldn't begin exhibiting the symptoms of having. The neurological disorder known as, epilepsy. Until I was, 11 years and 28 days old. That's definitely "not" when or how it began.

As for, the real reason that, I'm now epileptic? Well apparently, it's the consequence as the result of, my own actions. From being hit by a car four years earlier.

Hi, I'm Heather Lynn Jensen and here's what I like to call. My from "within the realm" version as to, how everything came to, play itself out. On the afternoon of. 3/12/74.

When I first left for school that morning. I'd had absolutely no reason to suspect that, the day. Held any potential to become, anything more or less. Than, "just ordinary."

That is, until our classroom teacher, "Mrs. Fitly". Began prepping us for the 3:00 dismissal bell and I'd found myself. Stepping into an episode of, my life. That would make what was usually, just a normal, everyday, put and dry, routine. The least of, anyone's worries!

In fact, since, Mrs. Fitly would always begin. What all of us kids considered to be, "Her usual end of the day lecture. To stress the importance of, us doing our homework.

After that, the last five minutes of, teach???. Would always play out like, this.

As soon as I'd finish my daily 3 minute round of, rummaging through my locker. For necessities such as, homework assignments...ect. I'd immediately return to my desk. Where I'd attempt to preoccupy my overly inquisitive mind. With one of the two following options at, our disposal. For almost after school entertainment.

1.) Enjoying the official shifting of, the classroom's usual ABC's and 123's aura. As it changed back into, kid's mode.

2.) The exchanging of daily thoughts that, directly concerned. What we'd considered to be, "our must do after school list."

Both in which, at that time of day. Seeming to be the only topics of conversation. That we'd interestingly enough, had all agreed were worthy of discussion.

Since my buddy, "Mike Pratton." Didn't live any further than 100 yards from our house. He'd always meet me at mine. At exactly 8:45 am. and after the 3:00 dismissal bell rang. We always are the 2½ block traveling distance between home and school. For exchanging and comparing our daily kid observations. In what we'd considered to be, an "adult free" atmosphere.

Although, most of what we'd discuss in the AM, would usually just consist of, basic "Kid Talk". Such as, "How to trigger your mind into, a working mode. Without becoming addicted to, caffeine"...ect.

We'd always survive our five minute return trips. For what we'd believed to be, more sophisticated topics. Such as, "Which one of us would walk away. With the daily title. For having the "Weirdest day at school."

Heck, we even went as far as to, take the scout oath of silence. Just to make sure that, it stayed that way!

Then, just like, I'd do after any other ordinary day at school. As soon as I'd get back home. I'd always follow what I'd considered to be, "Mom's Rules."

1.) Make her aware of, my presence.

2.) Kick my shoes off over by, the front door.

And

3.) Find something to preoccupy myself. Until dinner... "No Exceptions!"

Well at least, there were have usual expectations when executing. What most people would just consider to be. A normal, day to day, put and dry, after getting home from school, routine...No biggy!

Which is why, just to be on, the safe side. That is, if such a place even exists in my world. I should probably offer you a what kind of "Unscheduled disadvantages". Were about to, introduce themselves into, my daily lifestyle. Through a level of perspective and insight that, couldn't've been obtained or observed. From outside my "Within the realm" interpretation of, the following events.

Things like, it's one and only rule...for example.

1.) Never ignore details that, seem to fall. Beyond the boundaries of, what you'd consider to be. A rational threshold for one's imagination. Because your denial. Won't make them any less true!

The key participants

1.) Hindsight: The perception of the nature and demands related to a specific event. "After" it's taken place."

2.) Foresight: "The act or power of, focusing the future". In other words, it's supposedly just a theory. Based strictly on the concept of, having psychic premonitions.

Something that because it hadn't happened yet. I've always been led to believe...wasn't possible!

It was just a temporary misunderstanding. That as soon as, brother "Foresight". Decided to formally introduce himself into, my world. Personal experiences wouldn't hesitate to resolve by, proving otherwise.

And

3.) Myself

Yea, I'm sure there will be those amongst you. Of whom, not unlike, back in, 1974. Would rather went to whopping themselves up in skepticism. Than to except the probability that, brother "Foresight" held any form of significance. Beyond that of, the imaginary. Where as, I...know better!

But hey since nothing's ever been that easy. Especially, when you're about to, discover. Exactly how wide the gap between.

1.) Being able to, pick up on, the aura of, it's presence.

2.) Attempting to visually zero in. An exactly, when it's "unfamiliar" lingering within our dining room's mojo. Was coming from!

3.) Trying to understand why it made me feel as though, it'd held. The "unlocked potential to become, something more than... Just these!

Really is! Allow me to explain in, further detail!

Eventhough, no can't deny being, caught a bit off-guard when I'd got home from school that day and since. The add imbalance in, our dining rooms usual mojo.

But, that all changed rather rapidly when my mother, "Sybil Alexandrea Jensen." Began redirecting my point of focus by, filling me in. On what every kid under the age of ten. Would consider to be, "Need to know" details. When executing a long awaited "Childhood Adventure.

In fact, according to my mother's brief summary of, the days events. She'd taken my little brother, "Walter Allen Jensen II and sister, "Hanna Karen Jensen". To a little neighborhood store known as, "Harts Market." Just a few hours prior to, me getting home from school. So, they could have the luxury of picking out. what she'd referred to as being, "Aa candy bar of, their own choose," and was offering me. The opportunity to, do the same.

So, naturally. Just like, you'd expect any other kid my age to be done. I didn't hesitate to snatch the offer right up. As soon as, she'd presented it. But hey, what do you expect? I was seven and a half...not stupid!

Now here's the part. Where trying to distinguish both, the significance and magnitude of, each detail. None in which, couldn't've been witnessed from anywhere else. Than a realm of perspective that, I'd not only manage to keep from my mother but, everyone else.! Until I'd set my pen to paper 41 years later. Starts to get complicated!

Heck, I've been able to recognize moms "unmistakable inability" to, co-divert amongst other. Without strutting her stuff like, she was all that and a box of chicken. For what it really was. Since, I've been two.

I mean, yea! My efforts may've came off as being, of the frivolous. Especially, during the beginning stages of, their experimentation and developmental process.

But, rest assured. Because, by the time I'd reach seven and a half. I will've had plenty of time to, perfect my craft. Enough to pursue explorations of more advanced, Top Secret, investigations. Not made available outside an atmosphere. That'd so far, managed to restrain levels of curiosity. To those that only feel within the boundaries of, Jefferson Elementary and my Aunt Karen's house. Or, even better yet. Our own front yard.

So, now that I've given you a little background. As to, what kind of significance. That it'd held in, my life. Let's get back to reviewing those of, the "Non-visible" kind which were still way too soon to label as being, anything more. A pigment of, my own imagination.

One that for a lack of having a much better comparison to describe it. Was a feeling but, not being able to. Visually zero in on, the location of, it's aura. Was like, receiving a very unwelcomed visit from, "The Invisible Man" himself. On one of his, less than cooperative days!

The only difference will be that in my version. Our brief visit wouldn't be limited to, the bindings of, a 100 year old "Sci Fi" movie. But, running freely in, real life! By arousing circumstances so intense that, I'd actually find myself. Having to rely on, what little info I'd managed to acquire. With my uncanny ability to read mom's "Till signs. As a fall back plan!

While I can't deny that, at the time. This particular procedure was relatively in, it's experimental stages. Just judging from my own personal observations of, mom's past exhibition of, behavioral patterns. Only meant one thing in, my mind! Especially, when it came "to dealing with mom's self made, illusion fetish!

"That it was time to start envisioning the image of, my mother. Stepping up to veto her own ruling. Before it became, an issue of, the less than favorable...Towards herself!

But, surprising by enough and trust me. When it came to decoding my mom's tell signs. I surely was! I did find it rather odd. When after skid spent the next fifteen minutes driving me on, "The do's and don'ts when crossing the street." Without exhibiting any visible symptoms of either, self-distracting or aborting my mission altogether!

What'd originally started out to be, a sudden jolt of surprise on, her part. Would rapidly turn into, a huge sigh of relief...on mine! Or perhaps, I should say, "Temporary fix!"

Besides where as, now...for example. I just know better! For some reason, I'd always envisioned the hardest abstain that, I'd find myself having to overcome. While executing my first time venture without mom. As involving, the choice of getting her to let me leave the house. So, I could make it happen!

But, even though, I'd never inverted either, any time or effort. Towards confirming this exact measurements as to, footsteps wise. I still didn't need a measuring tape to realize that, I'd hadn't made it any further than fifty feet from our front porch. Before, my mother began insisting upon having me recite 'The do's and don'ts when crossing the street "back to her. For the thirst freaking time in, a row!

Which is when, I used my quick nod of reassurance maneuver . To coax my mother's sudden form of uneasiness. Back into it's battle. With what'd already struck me as being, a coy the rapidly dissolving offer.

No, I'm not trying to deny the small twinge of frustration. That I'd felt running through my veins. Especially, when my mother insisted upon having me do both, listen to and quotes. "The rules when crossing the street back to her face. The third freaking time in a row.

However, since due to past experience when reading mom's tell signs. That, I'd never be able to read the full benefits from them. Until without playing a successful sound of, a "not-so-well" known game. That I pace..."Virtual Modd Wrestling" with mom.

Only this round, was one that I'd had absolutely no intension of, letting my mom's. Usual method for performing interrogation tactics. Suppress my rather acute appetite to obtain. What she'd already declared to be, rightfully mine!

Which by the way, is just one of the many reasons as to, why. I can't continue any further with how my version of, how these events would play themselves out. Or, even better yet. Attempt to walk you through them from, "Within the realm of my perspective". Until I'll made you aware of, which ones would really count. So you can distinguish the difference between. The intense interrogation tactics that, mom insisted upon, drilling me with. From those that'd sun at a "very place" second place.

After all, I may've been able to pick up on the aura of it's presence. But, invalidated hunches alone. Wouldn't provide enough evidence for me to either, confirm or dismiss. The events that I'd witnessed taking place during, my accidental discovery into, a world. That clearly possessed the makings of an undetectable to everyone else but, me mystery. Seemingly designed to rapidly establish the makings of, a 180° turn around in my daily lifestyle pattern. Of which, I'd later come to recognize as being, "The Birth of my unwanted sidekick."

However, with that thought in mind. May I just suggest that, if you still feel interested in learning. The location of the key that lies deeply hidden within this mystery. That you give serious consideration to, listening to. Each and every word I'll use to describe it clearly. When I attempt to, recreate a "Non-visual image of several different occurrence. That I'd personally witnessed through, the same level of existence responsible. For bringing the likes of, my "first time venture"... Straight to it's freaking knees!

While, to most people. My home town may sum like, nothing more than just another dot on a map. I was raised in what's known as being, a one house, one traffic light, seven bar town. Located in, Northern Hancock Co. W.Va. Called..."Newell."

Which is why, the last thing I'd expected to find myself encountering. When I reached the other side of the intersection between", Second and Washington Street. Was another sensing of, the very same vibe. That'd only minutes before, had seemed a lot more like, a calling card. From, "The "Invisible Man" himself.

As for the miscellaneous rush that, I'd receive as, a result? Well, all and all. I'd say that it couldn't've lasted any longer than, ten seconds...tops!

But apparently, that's all of the time it needed. To spark the beginning stages of, what was about to, become. Alot more like, an activity that just couldn't be savored. From any where else other than, from a jurisdiction. Only made accessible by way of, my own imagination.

However, since the following theory as, I'm about to explain it. May present itself as being, a little further beyond. What most people would consider to be of, the rational.

Where as, to myself? I'd use to create a background worthy of, furthering my secret investigations into a world. In which, no one else but, me. Held any access to!

Plus, taking into account that, this isn't anything. That I'd consider to be, practiced amongst todays youth. I should probably mention how back, when I was a kid. The privilege of getting opportunities such as, first time ventures." Just didn't face into one's hop everyday. But, trust me. When they did. It was considered to be, nothing less than, a freaking privilege!

In fact, now that it's been mentioned. Up until the afternoon of, 3/12/74. I'd never had one land in mine! Which, needless to say. Is just part of what made mom's offer to grant me one. Sum even more irresistible than, it'd already sounded!

So in interest of, keep you to create. An accurate image of, what something like this was to experience. I'm willing to take the risk by, walking you through the dreaded process of each detail. In the manner they'd surrendered themselves to me on the afternoon of, 3/12/74. Without arousing any unwanted detection of it's presence...from other!

Then again, as I'm sure you're already quite aware. Just the states of one's age and attitudes. Ain't the only thing that change. Once they've been subjected to the scrutiny, impact, wrath and elements of time.

Which brings me back to our original discussion concerning as to, exactly where and when. I'd find myself experiencing my second encounter with what'd only minutes before. Seemed like, a very unexpected and beyond that of the rationally plausible visit. From, "The Invisible Man" himself.

There may only be a mess shell of a building. Left to symbolize the area of it's former location today. But, back in 1974. It was the home of a little town establishments known as, "The Jewell Box".

To sum it up. It was the kind of place that, from the street. Appeared to have, no windows offering a view inside. That I'd only noticed those of, the adult flinted either, entering or exiting and finally. How people would pretend to ignore and disapprove of it's presence. Every time they'd walk by it.

So, of course. Myself being one of, the overly inquisitive breed. Felt the need to rely on, my only made available resource for info. Which was, my mother. To acquire information as to, it's purpose amongst society.

A woman of whom, only once. Did make the resistant effort to, answer me. In mid field trip distance between "Hart's Market" and our house. With, "That place is nothing more than, a tourist attraction for misfits. Such as, Waterford Park track rats...for example!"

But by, other than to request my mother's rather speedy briefing as to, it's supposed standing in society. I'll never felt any need or desire. To pay it any mind!

Which explains why, it didn't make any sense. When it'd caught my attention as easily as, it did. By arousing a distraction within me. That'd actually made me feel as though, I was being alerted. To some kind of "Non-visual" warning that, something really big. Was about to happen...right there!

With a sensation so strong that, I'd actually feel this need. To halt my long awaited quest in mid-path, just so I could check out my surrounding's. For anything that'd even came close to, capturing my attention as being of, the unusual sort.

But, once I'd reached my destination/AKA. "Harts Market." I didn't hesitate to head straight for the Candy Counter. So, I could begin immediate investigations and evaluations for, "My bar of choice."

Although, just between us. I'd personally always forerun the delicate process of illumination in this case. As one that would've taken a lot longer than it did. After only a few brief minutes of careful consideration. Between such things as, what kind of taste that, I was in the mood for and which ones had caramel, nuts...eat.

I'd finally reached the conclusion that, this specific occasion. Required a slightly different taste than usual to properly celebrate. Otherwise known as, "The Chocolate bar." Something that I'd ironically enough, had never once considered the idea of trying before them and now... Never will again!

As for, what'd put me in the sudden mood to experiment "Taste wise," on that, specific afternoon? Well, that parts still being questioned. But, if you're really interested in hearing my opinion in, this matter. Then personally, I think my taste wise set, theory. Probably had a lot more to do with me knowing the ratio of success level. For celebrating newly acquired ventures. When it came to not having the proper supplies. To make it happen!

So, with the urgency of my current interest. In need of being sufficed. I'd decided to go ahead and make an exception!

Which is why, as soon as I was sure that, I'd made the proper selection. For celebration purposes. I walked over to the check out counter and proceeded to follow. The exact same routine as I'd observed from watching my mother in this case. By approaching, the dude who was working the cash register. So, I could square my purchase. Up with him!

However, with myself being only, seven and a half. Not to mention, still fairly new as to, how this specific procedure. Was supposed to play itself out. I guess, I'd just assumed that, the practice of exhibiting proper store conduct. Automatically meant, speaking to the cashier as, they rung you up!

Therefore, taking extra care not to embarrass my mother by, appearing rude. I stepped up to the check out counter and nervously attempted to fulfill. What I'd gathered to be either, a test or unspoken obligation. By bringing up the only topic that, my seven and a half year old brain. Was either, willing or prepared to humor at the time. AKA "My first big adventure" without the worry of, dodging mom's looming effect.

But, I could tell just by the way. The cashier smiled and agreed with me. When he attempted to portray my little "Childhood Newsflash" as being, of the interesting. That the chance of him grasping the significance behind my achievement. Was beyond his reach.

While the only difference would be that, this time. It would be even stronger. Accusing a bigger suspicion as to, it's actual existence within me. I first began to pick up on, what'd turned out. To be, vibe number there from, "The Invisible Man" himself. As soon as, the cashier started to, do his thing. Causing the previous ones to elevate themselves onto, a different level of intensity. With access to humor both, the extremely weird and creepy.

Now, keeping in mind that, back in the year, 1974. Just the idea of knowing someone. Claiming to have experienced this type of sensation. Let alone, them suggesting that, it'd held some kind of significance in, their lives. Seemed way too ridiculous to by, anything more. Than a complete fabrication within anyone's imagination!

In fact, if I hadn't been right then to overhear my mother. When she'd asked the clerk to confirm it's accurate???. Only, a few days earlier. I probably wouldn't've so much given that, stupid clock on the wall at, "Hart's Market" A second thought that afternoon either!

But because, I'd found myself experiencing the very same sensation lingering in my gut. When I glanced up at it as, when I'd worked past "The Jewell Box" establishment. Only a few minutes earlier. It'd almost made me feel. Almost, as though, it was literally trying to distract my attention. Away from disguising what I'd considered to be, the need to know details. Concerning, my "first big adventure"...without mom!

So instead of, barking in what should've been, the benefits. From executing a well trained but, slightly skilled technique. Like I'd planned!

I'd find myself in, a position. Where I'd almost feel as though, I was silently fending off. My "third" bought of what was still at, a medium level of paranoia...by ear!

When I kept experiencing this overwhelming urge to glance up at their clock. You know, the one my mother asked the cashier to confirm. Only a few days earlier. Just to realize that it's hands hadn't moved from 3:35 p.m. During the entire five minutes, I'd been there!

As for, my own opinion towards my basic instincts method of choice. For making me aware of it's presence? Or perhaps, I should say...It's attempt to!

Well, from my perspective. It'd never seemed to qualify as being, anything less. Than of the annoying!

As to, whether or not they'd have the ability to alert me of, the still unknown whims and why's. Belonging to, the warning signs concerning, our first crossing of paths. Or, even better yet how to interpret them for, what they really were...was irrelevant! Because, the circumstances them self. Not to mention, their day, time and place they'd go down. Where about to enlighten me!

However, instead of just letting this off vibe that, I'd kept picking up on. Mess with my head...So to speak. You know, like most people, would've probably done! I merely glanced up at, what I'd suspected to be, it's source, "this time!".. No pun intended! Shrugged my shoulder in question and...left the store!

Plus, once you overlook my brief thirsty second long self debate. As to whether or not I should devour my candy bar of choice. Right there in Hart's parking lot. I'd have plenty of other things that, I'd still hadn't been made aware of. Left to deal with!

Such as, the "Strad's Beer" truck that'd been parked right in front of, the town's little establishment. Known as, "The Jewell Box" During the short five minutes. I'd been at the store.

But hey! It was also a Friday. Which meant, weekly deliveries!

So, in interest of, fulfilling the expectation that, my mother'd laid down for me. By having me quote "the do's and dont's when crossing a street" Back to her. More than once! I'd eagerly made my way back to, the intersection between, second and Washington Street.

Personally, I don't know what'd made me think that, the view there. Would be any better! Esp. with, that stupid beer truck being in, the way!

So, as a spur of the moment attempt to, avoid allowing this situation to become. A bigger problem than it'd already had. I decided to walk around to the back of the truck. In hopes of getting a better view of what from the intersection. Was otherwise obstructed!

Which is why, when I didn't see any oncoming traffic coming from, that angle. I immediately headed back around to the front of it. To recheck my options from, the four way.

But since, I wasn't having any luck seeing past that stupid truck from either, the four way or the curbs. I decided that it was time to take things to the next level. By walking out to the edge of, the front driver side fender. To investigate possible alternative plans from there!

But, I guess with myself being, the age I was. I'd just readily assumed when I couldn't see any cars passing by. That there was, no traffic! Which needless to say. Didn't end up being one of, my, "Most intelligent theories!"

Heck, I can even remember seeing this flash of white coming towards me from, my left side. As soon as, I'd stepped out from in front of that truck. Which was immediately followed by, this extremely loud "thud!"

From there, my entire body suddenly felt as though, it'd been suddenly overcame. With the most excruciating pain that, I've ever felt before in my life and hopefully...Never will again! But after that, any rounds that, I may or may not've heard only seconds before them. Were rapidly drowned out by, a deafening ring!

One that'd forever make anyone else's desires to share their input. Be it by way of voluntarily or otherwise. Permanently pale in comparison to, everything "I'd witnessed. "From within the realm of only my perspective. On the afternoon of, 3/12/74.

But, trust me. They were just more problems that, I'd be adding. To a very long fist of miscellaneous questions. From what was about to, become, a rapidly accumulating pile of several! In order to, possibly fill in the blanks. Belonging to whatever'd clearly happened. But, I'd apparently...missed!

Especially when I'd realized that, their "so called" stray opinions concerning, what they'd believed they'd witnessed. Didn't coincide with mine! As far as, how the actual act of, watching how I'd received the emotional impact from there injuries had effected me. In either, a mental or emotional way. But...physical! Which, in all dire fairness. Pretty much spoke for itself!

Yea, I'm sure that their where those amongst us. Of whom, would've much rather preferred that, I'd believed otherwise. But, I don't. Because in what couldn't've taken any longer. Than it would for you to blink your eyes.

I'd find myself standing in front of, a recycling company. Which was located right across the street from, "The Jewell Box". Without any recollection "what-so-ever" as to, how I'd came to be there!

While being trapped inside a state of mind. That'd seriously seeked with the untanned stench of nothing less. Than that of, the extremely disoriented and confused.

But, even with everything that'd seemed to be finding pleasure. In the idea of, going down around me. I couldn't help but to, become distracted. By a small crowd of people that'd just began to accumulate. In the exact same spot where I'd ironically enough, had just crossed the street. The real question, was...why?

So, since my level of curiosity. Had clearly already been provoked more than just a few notches above, it's usual status. I'd decided to take full advantage of, my temporary fascination with, immediate situation as hand. By pushing the terms belong to it. A bit further than any of, my previous investigative procedures. Would've normally, permitted me to go.

By trying my hand at, my newly acquired but, definitely not perfected art form. For "visually scrounging together" the still unrevealed missing link. That was apparently, responsible for triggering this specific chain reaction of events. With what few fun facts that, I'd had working in my favor. But, before now. Could never share!

Things such as, how easily this seven and a half year old kid. Was able to do both, recognize and interpret the intensity as to, how much the flow of traffic. Which between the hours of, 3:00 and 4:00 pm. Were usually pretty busy....had slowed.

As, even better yet. How the stupid beer truck. Which, for as wild as, this probably sounds. Was now, parked conveniently on, the other side of, the street. Had left me looking at it. From what'd struck me as being, a visual angle completely different than before.

As for, how it'd came to be there? Well, interestingly enough, that's a very good question. One that, I've asked myself several times over the years. But am prepared to answer to the best of, my abilities. "Even though, a certain someone. Of whom, shall remain nameless. Would refuse to consider it to be, anything more or less. Than merely just, a ridiculously fabricated story made on, my behalf!

In order to, justify the things that, I'd claimed to have witnessed going down. When my usual everyday lifestyle. Made it's extremely swift change from being that of, a calm, cool and collected like state. To one that humored the type of atmosphere adjustment. Destined to become, just a tad bit on, the scary side!

Personally, I don't know what I'd expected to as being, the source of the problem. That'd apparently, captured everyone's immediate attention. But, I'm pretty sure that, it wasn't myself. Just lying there motionless on, the pavement.

Yea, this may've been just an innocently made assumption on, my part. One that'd allow me to create a relevant sense of doubt within myself. Which wouldn't hesitate to prove me wrong in, it's beginning stages.

By forcing me to ride out one of the most messed up dreams. Something in which, wise all guilty of having from time to time. That I've ever experienced in, my entire life. You know, like a nightmare... you example!

Although, it's definitely not how this situation would end up, slaying itself out. At first, it'd almost made me feel as though, I'd actually wake up. Just to find everything as, it should be.

So, when they didn't. My options would remain as follows.

1.) I could either, attempt to convince myself that this. Was all just the makings of, a really messed up dream. By performing further investigations towards. What'd supposedly captured everyone's attention.

Or,

2.) Allow myself to be completely overwhelmed by my fears. Towards an, invalidated experience.

But, rest assured. Because the events that, I'd witness taking place during them. Would be right there to pick up the unwanted slash. With something that, only I'd been made aware of concerning key factors. Belonging to, a specific sequence of events. Which, thanks to my "discretely made" observational studies towards people's behavior. I'd rapidly conclude were details that'd only been made available. For "my eyes" to visualize.

You know, such things as, what'd really taken place. After the, flash of white, the extremely loud "Thud" and deafening ring...ect.

Or, even better yet. Why after all of the various attempts I'd made to, get the paramedics attention. From an angle of perspective, that'd clearly, only permitted me to observe everything going down within it. I'd still find the time to secretly reach for an insight. That'd actually let me reassemble and decode it's mysteries. Down to every last milispec!

So if the fact that, I'd been given no other choice. But to view the circumstances of this situation from, a completely different angle than everyone else. Wouldn't be enough to create this "rude awakening" I'd be dealing with. Then the numerous abilities that I'd find myself running into, along the way...would!

As for whom'd be left with the extensive choice of ironing out. All of the "Non-visual" wrinkles that, it'd leave behind? Well, apparently that'd also turn out to be, my job.

To tell the truth, if I'd hadn't been right there to witness it happening. I would've never believed such things to be of, the rationally plausible.

Which is when, everything I'd already qualified as being, more than just a little missed up. Decided to elevate it's official status. Up to the level of, the seriously extreme!

Besides, even though I've personally. Always looked at what would happen next as being. Alot more along the lives of a reflex action. I even jumped out of the way. To avoid getting run over by, the E.M.T.'s gurney.

In fact, because this memory is so, etched into mine. I can even remember what the lounge from the EMT's bodies felt like. "When" they'd ran past me.

Besides, just judging by what I could tell from their reactions. They'd never showed any signs of sensing my reaction towards their presence. So apparently, they'd never even knew that, I was there!

Which is why, even though the answer that. I'd hoped for and the one received. Wouldn't even come close to falling under the same category standards. I'm not going to pretend that I didn't at least, expect to see them jump in surprise. When the saw me standing right behind them!

Then right before everything just went black. I stood there and watched as my entire hand. Passed clear through the E.M.T's shoulder and out his chest.

That is, until I arrived at, the hospitals emergency room. But even then, any occur I'd towards my medical statis. Would have to remain of, the extremely limited, a bit muffled and non-visual kind.

Yea, I heard my mother's voice calling out to me. "Heather Lynn! Can you hear me? Heather Lynn!"

To tell the truth, it even sounded like, she was inserting upon an answer. One that, I couldn't give her. But, it was abruptly interrupted by, a male voice. Of whom, kept telling her that, "It didn't matter how many times she'd tried to get me to answer her. Because, I was in shock, and didn't have the ability to either, hear or respond.

While in, all due fairness to both, him and myself. I could hear them discussing my condition, just fine.

I mean, yea. He may've been only "half-right. But the concept of me not being able to respond. Well, that part. Seemed to be a lot more along the lines of, "not having a choice."

Plus, as I'm sure your already quite aware. Medical Science isn't perfect within anyone's imagination! Because just like anything else in life. The act of practicing it, comes with it's own share of errors.

Which is why, in it's own way. It's not just useful when drawing conclusions as to, how the "Human Body" should work. But how it reacts when supposed to certain forms of stimuli. Such as, viruses...ect.

However, since unlike them. The challenge of drawing my conclusions. Didn't require the assistance of Medical Science. Because, unlike them. I could tell just by the decibels in their voices that, they wasn't very far away.

I mean, yea. I may've been able to tell that much about, the circumstances them self. But my soul felt as though, it'd been thrown between two completely separate plains. Then, stuck into a state of limbo until, it'd decided. Which side it'd favored most!

As for, the extent of my injuries as, a result. Well, it ended up costing me a cracked pelvis, collar bone, two major concussions and finally. A bruised kidney and spleen.

As for, my spleens condition? Well, it'd swollen to the point of being, almost two times it's normal size, which just for the record. If it would've ruptured could've very possibly requires "Emergency Survey." Just to save my life!

However, even though the stress and strain it'd caused on my body. Would never actually become, an issue. It didn't keep everything that, the next 48 hours would teach me. From becoming "very crucial" information. When it came to learning the "real" answers. Or be enough to block my acknowledgement of stray comments. Made by both, familiar and unfamiliar voices.

Which interestingly enough, beings me to another "Well hidden" tidbit of information. That specifically involved, my grandmother doing.

My grandmother had a habit of telling me this little story. Every time I'd spend the night at her house. Or at least, that's how I'd presumed it to be at, the time.

One that, she'd specifically based on, this "incredibly bright" light. Which according to her, wasn't viable until, "after" you've passed on to, the next world. In fact, I believe she'd referred to it as being, "The gateway to the heavens".

Therefore, making in it exactly what it'd seemed like was going on. When I'd saw it!

Although the wildest part about, this experience. Would be that up until then, I've never so much as once considered gram's story. To be anything more than...just that!

Explaining why, when I'd found myself regaining consciousness. Under what'd appeared to be of, the same circumstances and nature. My grandmother's "story" was, "The first thing." That'd came to mind.

Besides, the fact that, my "lack of vision." Had me trapped inside a level of existence that'd only seemed to humor. The concept of, complete darkness and muffled voices. The probability of getting any confirmation as to, it's states. Not an option?

Yes, I recognized the excruciating pain part. But, clearly my eyes, needed a little time to readjust themselves.

So, when it came to figuring out. What was destructing it and my other "five basic instincts. Which consist of your ability to, taste, touch, smell, hear and see. It didn't take me very long to reach the conclusion. That I'd only had two left and in working order. At my disposal.

But before, I can trust myself to freely describe. These events in, any further detail. To either you or, anyone else! I need to ask you to, invasion yourself in, the some position. Are you ready? Then let's begin our reassembly of, the "For my eyes only picture. That I've personally, gathered and constructed. Strictly by way of, miscellaneous puzzle pieces, sound, memory and a very blurred visual aid.

Although at first, it'd sounded muffled and faint like, the other. I distinctly remember hearing a voice off to my sight. Saying something about, me coming out of it. Followed by, a single set of footsteps. Which,

I'd soon come to learn. Was the sound of my mother. When she'd went out. To alert those at the nurse's station of, the sudden change in my current "Medical Statis."

In which, about ten seconds later. When accompanied by several other voices and sets of footsteps. Countering the room, and judging by the amount of weight they used to take them. Well made by one male and four females...To be more precise!

Therefore, just to make sure that, your details of this event accurately coincide. With the one's I'd witnessed from, 'My side of the fence". I'd first like to take a few last minutes seconds. To briefly review "What we've already discussed about, the extent of the limitations. Involved with, taking this side.

1.) The unasked for benefit of knowing what I'd witnessed taking place. From, "Within the realm of, only my perspective. But for the life of me. Couldn't explain to myself or anyone use. Let alone...Prove!

And

2.) My grandmother's story concerning, "How to find, The gateway into, "Heaven".

Yea, I suppose that I'd could've been a little, "Blinded by the light"...So to speak. Experiment with, everything I'd just been through. Or perhaps I should say, had "unknowingly" survived. But I could tell by the level of decibels in their voices. That the male was not only the closest to me. But had a habit of changing it's location within the room. About, every five to ten seconds.

Therefore, when the images refused to humor my simple request. Or, even better yet. Attempt to, volunteer any useful information as to, what was going on. I decide to push my quest to learn it's answers even, one step further. By opening the conversation with, "Am I in Heaven."

But, when all they gave in return was, a mere gesture. In which, after being blinded by the light...so to speak. I could barely see! So, their insistent lack of cooperation in this matter. Quickly turned into, an excuse for this to act in a manner. That I'd personally, found to be of, "the rudely insulting," on, their part.

Besides, even though their lack of response. Towards my line of questioning then, wasn't a lot to go on, at the time. I think it's safe to say that, what made this line of questioning. Been so intense from, my end. Had a lot more to do with how easily and quickly it's words. Just fell out of my mouth, "Are you an angel?"

Although I'd definitely failed to share in their "invalidated" form of amusement. They'd apparently, considered something about, my legit question as funny. Because not only had the off atmospheric mojo that, it'd portrayed. Shifted from them just, taking up space and making me nervous. But drowned out by, the sound of them chuckling under their breath. When I...wasn't kidding!

Which is when, the male image finally decided. That, no matter how stupid my question may've sounded to them. My request, deserved a fair answer.

"No" the male voice reluctantly replied. "Your not in Heaven. Your at the East Liverpool city hospital and you've...been hit by a car!"

It was a comment that he'd quickly followed up with. "No, I'm not an angel. I'm a doctor." Then after he'd paused just long enough, to lightly chuckle under his breath. At the idea as how ridiculous my question's sounded. Decided to finish off his thought. With, "Not even close!"

A statement that was, immediately followed by, another outburst of laughter. Of which, I'd presumed to be from all of the other voices and sets of footsteps. In whom, I'd heard reentering my hospital room with mom.

But since, none of them or their attitudes. Had been willing to offer up any information. Concerning the as to, how or why my "innocently based" question. Had struck them as being, so amusing.

Once you take into account as to, exactly how brief. Our amount of communication actually was.

Which, just between you and me. Couldn't have taken any longer than, five minutes...Taps!

At least, the situation at hand had started to make a "little list" of sense. Before the terms of it began shifting from your ordinary everyday, "Am I in, Heaven' and "Are you an angel? Mode. Into on that'd require me to, reveal my name and age.

In fact, if I remember the details correctly and trust me...I do! The terms of the brief conversation held between myself and the still "visually unidentified" male voice. When something like, this...

Although I'm willing to admit that, my eyes. Still "not being" completely readjusted to, the room's lighting situation. Probably had a lot to do with, it's outcome.

When the male voice of whom, due to current circumstances. I'd felt more than just, a tad bit uncomfortable, with the thought of, being there.

Didn't so much as, "vocally or otherwise. Give me one reason to suspect that, he'd even thought twice. About how much just ignoring my request for a plausible solution. As it tested for such things as, my reflexes, pupil dilations...ect.

Made me feel every time it'd failed to, meet me half-way. I didn't see or perhaps, I should say hear. Any reasons as to, why I shouldn't be willing to, return the favor! By slyly cooping it a little further into, the conversation.

"Young lady," it calmly asked. "Can you tell me your name?"

But, from that point on. The circumstances of our little conversation would rapidly deteriorate. Into, what'd felt a lot more like, an unrehearsed exercise on both parts. Concerning how to go about determining the differences. Between, what one would strike me as seeming like. It'd belonged more on, "The rather odd" side. For example...

1.) Finding myself trapped right in the middle of, a "very awkward" situation. That'd not only force me to, stop but, think, about my answers before, giving them.

Just Like, Any Other Day in, The Life of Me | 23

Or

2.) Hearing myself say the words, "Heather! My name is, Heather!" No more than 20 seconds later.

Then just as, I'd already suspected it would. The male voice's line of questioning suddenly...changed!

"Young lady," he asked calmly. "Can you tell my your age?"

But even tough, not unlike it's first question. The words, "Seven! I'm seven and a half!" Would also just seem to pap right out. Without any forewarning. Before, I'd even have the opportunity. To "make things over" in, my mind.

Because I've taken the time to recreate a "visual image". That'll allow you the insight to both, measure and compass. As to, exactly how much. You'd consider this type of situation to be of, the "seriously annoying" breed.

Perhaps, my tip will be enough to, help you draw national conclusions as to, why mine. Included, snatching ahold of the male voices little pointing thing. So I could give myself both, the privilege and satisfaction of knowing. That I'd been the one to shave it up. His...you know what!

Yea! I may've been able to find a way to retrieve. Most of my previous replies when answering "Pathetically stupid" questions. From what I call, "The straight up and to the point pile" without alerting any suspicions as to, what was "really" going on. Inside my mind.

But, even with me being, only seven and a half. It would take alot more than the likes of, "one minute" disadvantage. To disguise the do's next remark as being, anything other than, a serious insult. Towards my "level of intelligence."

"Young lady," the male image that, I'd just recently been able to identify as "The good doctor asked. "Can you tell me exactly where it hurts? Or, you feel pain?"

While, coming from a man of, his 'claimed" profession. I myself, would've expected him to, come up with a "much better" choice of words. It'd still been the only question I'd been asked. That didn't require me to, stop and think it through. Before, answering it!

Which is why, in interest of reassuring myself that, he'd not only heard. But, seen the lame expression that, his "two-bit" request. Had left smeared all over my face. By replying with the word..."Everywhere!"

But even though, the doc may've managed to get away. With tricking "those of us" in the room from, "The less than educated" nature. Into falling for her, "I can grasp the entire concept of what'd really takes place. On the afternoon of, "3/12/74" Act.

Unlike, those nimrods, for example. I wasn't too gullible to either, see or hear the extent of, it's wrath. Radiating from places on my body that, I'd never even knew existed...Yet!

Which is why, I still to, this very day. Refuse to acknowledge the doc's, so called routine as being, anything more or less. Than just a "Shotgun diagnosis" of, my supposed, "medical states."

Making it more than enough to, prove my theory as to, why. Those in the room felt the need to, talk around. Instead of, to me.

So, prepare yourself. Because, whether you like it or not. Your about to learn "exactly why." Their neglect to just humor my request. By answering my request straight up. "Would only create a much bigger problem within itself. That'd leave me hanging with, no other option. But, to fix...my way!

Especially, when it'd "clearly" involved, "The complexed process of, learning how to spot occurrences. From what I'll always recognizes as, "Those of the less than visible to, the naked eye" details.

1.) Those that'd hadn't made themselves available. Through..."obvious obstruction."

2.) Myself trying to "single handedly find off. All of the "unnecessarily generated" vibes with, the room.

3.) What'd made the "good doctor" reach his conclusion. That, other than the injuries I'd received as, a result. I should be OK? Without running further tests?

4.) The introduction of, yet. Two more "unexplained theories into a picture that both, my mother and Aunt Caroline. Would attempt to interpret as being, "Tears of Joy"...whatever that was!

And finally,

5.) As to, why. You'll never find me trying to blame you or, anyone use. For claiming this next part. To be of..."the impossible!"

Where as, now. This may seem a lot more like, a memory in the back of, my mind. As I've stated previously. Judging by my observations as, it'd happened. I'd been the only person there. With the ability to witness the entirely of, it's details.

Unlike, my mother and everyone else for, that matter. I'd held the unknown advantage of being, "quite aware" as to, it's depth. From within what'd definitely portrayed itself as, the perspective of..."Another person's body!"

But even though, the only thing my secret comparison of, their insights to mine. Would allow me to determine is, that, they "definitely" "Weren't" even of, the..."Same breed!"

It did make the thought of, me keeping my own "personal footnotes". About, the evens I'd witnessed taking place on, the afternoon of, 3/12/74. Strictly to, myself! Sound even "better and better by, the second!

So much, in fact. That just it alone, would ironically enough, end up evolving into, my first "big insight" and drive towards decoding. The hidden mystery behind the secret details as to, exactly how. To make it happen! Allow me to explain...

While I have had a little bit of success. When it came to learning the fine art of, discreetly diversing. Workable "spin of the moment plans that'd give me. The well deserved benefit of at least, "pretending to ignore". Most of mom's foolishly flowed attempts to either, validate or excuse her desire. To send ridiculously made comments my way at random.

I can't deny that, my access of mobility had became, rather limited. Leaving me with only two plausible options to work with!

1.) I could either, allow myself to be, manipulated. By blindly submitting to mom's "less than foolish efforts. To consume my entire world with, the less than suddle" comments. That mom insisted upon using as, a face back. Every time she'd get the random urge to remind me that, "I wasn't exactly the easiest child in the world. To try to, raise! "Without requesting any form of "verbal reasoning" as to..."Why?"

Or,

2.) Follow the long awaited resurfacing of, my "basic instincts." By stepping up and calling her on, the kind of validity. Her two bit poor excuse for a "poker bluff" held. Without turning her on to, exactly how. What was, "The for my eyes only" perspective of, it's circumstances. Had portrayed themselves from...mine!

No! My grandmother's stories may've never once so much as, struck me. As holding any form of significance in my life before, that specific afternoon. But, thus was one thing she'd say during them. That's never failed to stand out from...the rest!

"That, I should never believe anything I'd heard and only half of, what I see...No exceptions!"

Or, as my grandmother'd please it. "Young lady! Just because you can't hear something. It doesn't mean that, it's not these and just because, you can't see it. Doesn't mean that, it don't exist?"

While I've personally always considered the whole concept of, having patience. As being a lot more along the lines of, an inconvenience than, a virtue.

Well, just between you, me and the lamppost outback. I'm a firm believer that, whomever decided to, come up. With this not-so-brilliant "theory...lied!

If you really interested in learning about, my opinions. As to, how this went. I've always found promise in drawing all of, my conclusions. From what's known as, the hard-cold" facts.

With the main one being. That because of, "how" my body felt. Every time I'd so much as, attempt to move. I'd just have to temporarily settle for "postponing." All investigations in, this specific manner. Until, further notice!

Leaving me with a lot of spare time and space. To devote towards the "top secret" place of, trying to sort out and revaluate. Specific "unresolved details" that would from my perspective. At least qualify as being, informational. ON a strictly "need to know" basis.

You know, as a precaution. Just in case, what I'd witnessed taking place around me. On the afternoon of, 3/12/74. Was meant to be viewed by, "my eyes only."

While this subject in general. Will hold it's fair share of, intense details. Especially as to how. Or, even better yet. Why I'd been the only person there who'd...Seen it!

I also knew that, if someone else. Would've so much as, caught a "brief glimpse of, it's presence. They would've hinted this acknowledgement. Within their "behavioral pattern" changes. During the "extremely limited" amount of time it'd taken. To play itself out!

But hey, I stood right there in the middle of, everything and that..."didn't happen!"

Which is why, I'd like to go on record as saying. That no matter how clear they'd thought it was. It'd be their "extremely limited" range of sight. That'd interestingly enough, prevent them from even coming to the equivalence of, mine and yes! You can "quote" me on that!

Yea, yea! I know what you probably thinking right now and honestly. I don't blame you for feeling that, way!

Because, even after years of, listening to myself. Repeat there details over and over again in, my mind. It all still sounds "pretty doing crazy" to, me too!

At least, they'd allow me to explain. Some of the, "This is getting me no where" speech. That kept repetitiously running through my mind at, "lightning speed."

But, just it alone. Would never be a strong enough, influence. To detour me away from literally farming my own personal opinions. Towards mom's so called "falsely illusioned" gift. To develop what I'd got the vibe she'd felt was, her "uncanny noch" for, pulling stray answers. Out of a hat like, they were some kind of, "Stupid Rabbit!"

I mean, no disrespect intended mom. But, just the idea of, having to tolerate that, "magnitude of pain." While, watching you attempt to, scold me. With your "That's what you get for defying me" stare. Just wasn't working for me...go figure!

Although, my mother's excuse to perform her daily visitations. Would seem more and more like, it was just her way of, offering me. A form of, emotional support and trust me. They were to, an extent!

Her biggest downfall would lie solely on, "What she didn't seem to understand about, the terms...it's depth!

In fact, whether or not she'd liked them, wouldn't matter. Because, if they were meant or, delivered in, an emotional, mental or, physical manner. Both it's injuries and the pain I'd received as, a result. Were mine to bare..."Not theirs!"

So, speaking for those amongst us. Of whom'd, fallen upon the consequences from it's wrath. Such as, myself..."For example!"

I was made "quite aware" that, I'd been given. All of the reasoning I'd need to begin. My own personal "mental preparations" for, the upcoming battle it'd "secretly enraged."

As soon as, the "good doctor". Decided to make his "Not-so-brilliant" call. To talk around instead of, to me. About, my "Current Health" issues.

Which, in my mind. Made it's battle "officially mine" to, fight alone. Under certain terms that, only I'd been made familiar with..."No exceptions!"

Besides, after I'd witnessed all of my requests for, "verbal input" on, his part. Bring immediately, cured and disintegrated. Right after the "good doc" decided that, asking me to, tell him. "Where it hurt." Wasn't a "good idea!"

It didn't take a lot of brains to, figure out. That this was one mistake. In which, he'd had absolutely "no intension" on repeating!

Now, please don't get me wrong. Because I'm not saying that, having my mom there to support me. During the beginning stages of, what was about to, become a "very long" healing process. Wouldn't hold it's benefits!

But unlike, her memory, for example. Mine held secrets within it that, she couldn't even fantasize about!

Things like...

1.) What'd I witnessed happening after the extremely loud "Thud" part.

2.) The process of, having to tolerate. The excruciating pain I'd been forced to endure. While mom sat by my bed and gloated at, my mistakes!

And

3.) Trying to except the reality. That I'd just been hit by of car to... name a few!

But, until I'd acquired enough facts. To actually prove them to be, of, the "legit" like. I didn't attempt to rattle anyone's chain...either way!

Because, according to every one I'd held access to and by that. Those made by my mother and the several nurses whom, were working. Everyone there seemed as though, they were going out of, their way. To make the long process of recooperation, sound a lot easier than, I'd knew it felt.

In other words, I downright refused to just lay my cards out on the table. For all to see. Until I was sure as to, what each one was worth. Yea, yea, I know...details!

Then again, when your looking at this kind of situation. Through the eyes of, someone like, myself. The words that come to mind.

Only sound good or, make sense. When your saying them to, yourself!

However, since my world had already proven itself. To be a lot more deceiving than it'd looked. Be it by way of, fate, accident, or, otherwise. Whatever it was, I'd witnessed. Wasn't exactly alot to, go on!

So, as I patiently tolerated their quest to help me recooperate "gracefully." My secret information states. Had plenty of time to excel beyond theirs!

Heck, after that. All I had to do was, come up with a way. That'd allow me to decode it's hidden mystery. Without arousing any "unwanted suspicions." That could give away my "very detailed" viewing of, it's events. As they'd fallen into play from..."my perspective!"

You know, for my own piece of mind." While killing a little "hospital recooperation time" and trust me. I'd had lot's of that, to deal with!

I decided to use this opportunity to review. The little unknown details without rational plausibility. To back them up! Such as...

1.) How I'd felt and reacted. When I'd first realized that, I was looking at myself. Just lying there motionless on, the pavement. From what'd struck me as being, another person's body.

2.) As, how I'd stood right there in the middle of, Washington Street and watched. As my hand passed clear through an, EMT's shoulder and out his chest. Without anyone other than myself to acknowledge it. Something that shouldn't've been a problem!

In fact, if you remember correctly. Just judging by what we'd discussed earlier. I was only in "Hart's Market" for a matter of, five minutes...taps!

Before, deciding what "Candy bar of choice. Worked for me! But, other than that. I'll never be able to forget exactly what I'd witnessed taking place. During the brief amount of time that, I was there!

Then as soon as, I was able to, come to terms. With that much. The rest of the miscellaneous pieces to, it's puzzle. Just started "Slowly" falling together.

You know, little things like, why the clock above, their cash register. In which, I'd never so much as, paid any mind to before them. Had succeeded at making me feel as though, it was ready. To jump off the store wall. Just to get my attention.

And

How I'd had the same feeling lingering in my gut. When I'd glanced up at it. As I did when I'd walked past "The Jewell Box" establishment.

Or, even better yet. How come even after the cashiered confirmed it's accuracy. Only, a few days earlier. It's hands never moved from the position of 3:35 per once. During the whole time I was there.

But even though, from my perspective. It'd been made quite obvious that, there particular occurrences. Held something in common.

The real share would involve the act of, finding and pulling together. All half decent theory that'd "Not only," support the numerous things. I'd experienced in such, a short amount of, time.

But, would allow me to keep myself from being, consumed. By an acute form of, boredom. During my "long" hospital recooperation period.

So, with thought in mind. I decided to "very carefully" faces. All of my unreserved" "spare time" and trust me. These was plenty of it to, go around. Towards trying to secretly decode. The numerous memories that, my "Sub-conscious" mind. Had obtained so easily during, it's struggle.

In fact, if you really that interested in learning. About, my opinions in, this matter. I think the scariest part of, having to relive this memory. As it replied itself over and over in my mind as, I'd slept. Had a lot more to do with, how it played itself out in my dreams. Compared to, the "real deal."

Because even though it's replay effect. Would never fail to start out at, normal speed. It was almost like, I was being forced. To relieve it's wrath all over again. Every night I'd face to sleep.

That is, until it'd reach the part. Where I'd see the flash of white coming towards me. But, from that point on. Everything would just appear as though, it'd switched. Into, a "slow motions" mode.

Which is when, I'd find myself. Once again becoming like, just another onlooker. From off the street.

I mean, hey! I may've only been seven and a half at, the time. But, I definitely "wasn't" stupid and just judging by, the way. I'd watched everyone react to, what they'd thought was, the "afterwards" part. I'd had absolutely no reason to believe that, anyone else had seen it!

Therefore, turning the act of, trying to solve it's mystery. That of, a "high priority" level.

But, because, I myself. Have never been the kind to settle things. By just throwing my arms up in, the air. At, the first sign of, trouble. I've never been the type of, person. To have a lot of patience with, those... who do!

Besides, even though most people don't even seem intelligence to acknowledge it's existence. Life itself, basically works like, a two way door. One that not only, has the capability to, hold you back. But, from moving forwards too! That is, if you actually "gullible enough", to let it!

Which is why, if the events I'd witnessed taking place. Right in front of, me on, the afternoon of, 3/12/74. From what'd appeared to be, a third person's point of view. Hadn't been enough to make me. "Extremely paranoid" of every little sound and movement around me.

Then, being repetitiously awakened by, the various doctors and nurses. Of whom, kept coming in and out of, my hospital room at, all hours of the night...Was!

Sure, I may've managed to get lucky enough. To squeeze in a few stray "Cat Naps" here and there. But personally, I myself didn't care what anyone else thought. Because, as far as, I was concerned. The first week of, being, sinned up in that, hospital bed. Had to have been, the worst!

So much, in fact. That just the hope of, possibly sneaking in, a full night's sleep. With everything else going on around me. Seemed, next to, impossible!

In other words. Heck, I couldn't even have the privilege of, passing out from exhaustion. Without my "sub-conscious" mind. Stepping in to, overrule my bodies decision. Without the repetitious flashbacks from the afternoon of, 3/12/74. Haunting my "REM" sleep stage.

However, since having to relieve this trauma over and over again. By way of, one's dreams. Does have the tendency to make a task. As simple as, trying to catch a few stray z's. A lot easier said than done.

I can't pretend to, overlook. The other times either! Especially, when my inability to sleep. Actually turned out to be, a good thing. But, even them. These episodes were still too far and few between!

Besides, even though I can't deny being, more than just a little bit curious as to, what those "yahoo's" thought they'd known. About, the real inside details concerning, my situation.

Until, I'd had the chance to, devise a plan that, included. A method for measuring the "true inner depth" of, their shallow mindedness issues.

I'd just have to settle for, making due. With what little facts I could. Through little tid bits of information. That I'd hear them trying to, "inconspicuously" pass back and forth. Between, each other! During their "Nightly visits."

But unlike, those idiots, for example. In whom, clearly just "assumed" that, they'd "automatically knew." What they were talking about. I'd retrieved all of, "my information". Through a source "way more" accurate. Then, they could even pretend to fantasize!

Plus, with most of my own "personal footnotes" concerning, the activities. In which, only "I'd" been capable of witnessing taking place. Still being, "too complexed" for even my insight to decode.

I decided to, create a half decent "fall back" plan. That'd offer me the luxury of both, the evaluation and comparison. Of other peoples poor excuses for "personal footnotes on, this specific subject. Next to Mine!

While, all and all. I personally, think that it's basically the same story. For anyone who's been put through a traumatic event such as, this.

Having to repeat something over and over again. By the way of, their dreams. Would've been enough to make any one more than reluctant. About the idea of, "going to sleep!

So, in hopes of, giving myself a much better perspective. Of it's events as they'd fallen into play. On the day that it'd happened. I attempted to use my "unspoken" insights about, what I did know.

In hopes that, just it alone. Would allow forge and develop enough, self initiative within me. To feel what'd already turned into. A form of, "Non-physical" research to, possess these answers!

Ones in which, were still "quite obviously" not at, my disposal. But right on the verge of becoming. Like, a required "must have" access to, in my world.

Heck, I was even willing to, resort to. Giving a certain amount of consideration to, the idea of, writing things down on paper. As a way of allowing myself to, sort these things out.

But, that theory immediately "went south". As soon as, I'd caught some "nosey nurse". Giving herself the liberty of, going through my stuff. When she'd thought I was asleep!

Besides, as I've stated previously. For at least, the first week. These details had almost seemed as though, they were "too complicated." For even me to, follow. Let alone, decode!

That is, until the bulk of, my own "personal footnotes." Started coming together and allowing me access to, the beginning stages. Of what I'd considered to be, a "useable" fall back plan. That'd actually work!

Which is basically, what'd inspired me to, found my plans. On discovering an adequate way. To influence a type of, "Silent Comparison". Between the two definitions made available.

Which is why, I wasn't in the least bit surprised. When out of the several visitors I'd received that week. Not one so much as suggested or, even hinted. That they'd had the privilege of, seeing anything portraying itself as being, close. To my own personal observations of, these events.

But even though, I can't pretend that, it didn't all strike me as being, just a little bit strange. Like I've said, I'm not a fool! So, even though I wasn't willing to reveal. What I'd already classified as, my "Well guarded secret." To a bunch of, "Ya-hoo's that, I'd never even met.

Thanks to, my unknown ability to, compare their observations to mine. In a "less chaotic" atmosphere. I'd easily come to the conclusion that, the only similarities they'd seem to hold. Would have to do with the fact that, even if they were different. At least, they were there!

Besides, since the act of being, "Shallow minded." Doesn't actually qualify as, a crime. I couldn't just start demanding answer to wants either!

Yea, I've known that, this so called, "Newly acquired challenge." Would just end up turning into, another one within itself. When I'd first witnessed it taking place from the middle of, "Washington Street." On the afternoon that, it'd happened!

In fact, until my body was at least, feeling a little more on, the mobile side. I'd just have to for, "discreetly searching" out the "missing" rational answers. To a certain subject that'd instantly became, a very "inconvenient problem". In my world.

Heck, if I wouldn't've even mentioned this part. It probably wouldn't have so much as, qualified as being, possible!

Which is why, I'd felt the need to use my spare time. To try to, get inside "their" heads in, such a way. That'd give me the liberty of, stepping past their "mentally" delusional obstacles. Without the danger of alerting them. to what they'd clearly "didn't know!

Something in which, according to the behavior they'd insisted upon exhibiting. Every time they'd walked either, in or out of, the room. They didn't have the insight to acknowledge!

So, since the only thing I'd had to keep me "mentally motivated. By this point. Lied within my need to find the true significance. Behind the things I'd knew but, couldn't interpret.

In other words, no matter how badly they'd stacked themselves against me. Taking the rush of, telling anyone else. What I already did. Wouldn't become, an option!

But, because all of the input I'd receive. About, what they thought they'd witnessed. Only appeared to, humor two specific breeds of people.

1.) The kind that, due to "whatever" circumstances. Were willing to let their own personal fears seize control. By preventing them from slipping up to deal with "their" problems...themselves!

2.) The kind that's "Not afraid" to do, whatever it takes. To seek out and uncover their "Need to know" answers. Allow me to explain in, further detail...

Heck, one night. I'd actually found myself being, awakened by a nurse. Whom'd claimed that, she was there to, check out a noise. Of which, I'd apparently made in, my sleep!

But instead of, jut leaving me alone. After I'd reassured her that, I was O.K. She decided that it'd be much more fun to grace me with some lengthy explanation. Concerning a subject o and how having to relive something like, "repetitious flashbacks of, a traumatic event." Could only be done during what she'd referred to as, "The REM stage of sleep."

I mean, yea sure. She may've tried to claim that she'd held the intellectual capacity. To understand exactly what I was going through.

Which is why I'd decided to, return the favor. By giving her my input as to, what I'd thought her goofy theory. Was really worth in, my world!

While, all and all. I can't deny that, her being, a "medical professional". May've given her a certain amount of leverage over mine. Then again, the last time I'd checked. "Having a nursing degree doesn't "allow" you access to, the required amount of insight. To understand the full impact of, a patient's trauma! Just what you need to know to, fix it and even then...it's questionable!"

"Mame!" I continued before, she'd had time to interrupt. "I don't mean to sound disrespectful by saying this. But, the only insight you capable of, giving me in, this particular subject, is one that of, a medical level!"

"Whereas, I, for example. Am speaking from a perspective that, can only be molded through...personal experience!"

"I mean, don't get me wrong. Because, that's not my intension and I'm sure. That the method you've taken time to acquire. Works just fine on, a "medical basis?" But hey, your a scientist so, your supposed to think that way!"

"However, on the other hand. Well, I'm just a seven and a half year old kid. So, from my perspective. Not one of you are as intelligent. As you're attempting to give yourself credit for!

"In other words" I continued impatiently. "I neither asking for or, giving this information. From a "medical professionals" point of view! So, I'd really appreciate it. If you'd try to answer me in, the same fashion!"

"Now, here's my question. Are you ready?" asked curiously. "Yes," she replied confidently. "Have you were actually been hit by, a car?"

The only problem was, that her "return answer!" Never went any further than for her to look at me like, my mere request. Had went straight over "her" freaking head!"

Therefore, in interest of salvaging our "brief conversation. For whatever it still may've been worth. I attempted to break the "sudden silence that, my mere question. Had obviously provoked! By giving her my point of view. Towards this "specific subject."

"Mame, whether you care. Or even better yet, aware of it. Is irrelevant! Because, your making it pretty obvious through. Your choice in tell signs. Is that, you really don't have an answers to, give me!" So, just for fun. I'm going to go ahead and take the liberty of, filling your in...on mine!"

"Heck, everybody knows that until someone has actually had the opportunity. To experience a "traumatic event like this. On, a first hand basis and I don't care, what their line of, background training is! Because my ability to understand what's really going on. Is a fact not, an option! So, just consider yourself blessed that, you don't..."Next question please!"

As I've already explained. I wasn't trying to appear rude to her. In fact, I was doing my best not to! But, there's no way I was willing to just sit there listen to her. Preach at me about something that, she'd obviously. Had no way of, comprehending!

However, since the only thing that'd appeared to, capture her attention. Seemed to focus itself towards my pointing out that, unlike her. I'd had the advantage of, "Personal Experience." Working on, my side!

Which is, probably why our brief exchanging of words. Ended when I'd reminded her that, she'd still hadn't bothered. To answer my small assortment of questions.

Then again, what I'd thought or felt really, didn't matter. Because, what'd started out as, just a small five minute long lecture. Suddenly finished with the words, "No, I've never been hit by, a car! But, if you need anything. I'll be at my station!"

A theory that would've most generally, worked just fine! Especially with me not being, is what most people would consider. To be, "a socializing type of mood."

Besides, whether she'd liked it or not. Mine was a fair question and it didn't take the talents of, a "professional poker player. To recognize the tell signs from, having a loss of words.

I mean, I may've only been in, the second grade. But, I didn't need her to tell me as to, why I was there! Let alone, how it felt! Just common sense!

In fact, since my dreams had been "practically infested." By several unprovable events from the afternoon of 3/12/74. In which, no one else had given me any reason to suspect. That they'd known "diddly squat" about!

Going to sleep was like, volunteering to spend all night. With it's flashbacks jumping up and down on, my forehead. As though it was trying to, haunt my dreams after I'd fall asleep each night. As a form of, "personal amusement."

So, with my body not being, in any type of emotional, mental or, physical condition. To except any new challenges. I'd have to rely on, trying to keep myself busy. By inventing methods of, amusement. Such as, drawing, watching T.V., and counting the dot's on the ceiling. With everyday insisting upon, crawling by!

Then one day after a nurse walked in and handed me a, "manilla envelope". That'd clearly been past marked with the return address of, "Jefferson Elementary School." The whole aura within, the room itself. Just, temporarily changed!

At first, I think I'd even felt a little leasy about, what I might find. When I'd opened it!

But, instead of, just opening it up and finding something. Like a lunch of, missed homework assignments from, Mrs. Fetly, for example. I sat there and watched as, all of there "get well" cards. From, my fellow classmates...fell out.

I mean, sure. This may've been meant as, just a small gesture. On their part. One that'd consisted of nothing more than a little crayon wax, some construction paper and a little creativity. On their part! But, just the fact that, they'd cared enough to send them. Meant everything to me!

So, all and all. I guess it'd took "not being," able to freely socialize. With my fellow classmates everyday. To show me as to, exactly "how much" I'd actually missed. Having the ordinary, everyday, "dismissal bell" choices for entertainment.

But key, my butt wasn't going anywhere. Until my body'd at least, reached a point. Where it was once again able to, move under it's own power. The real question would be..."how far?"

Not to mention, giving me no other options. But, to put certain "unresolved issues on, the back burner. Until, "further notice!"

Although learning the key factors to solving it's mysteries. Would only allow me to unlock a "temporary" mental distraction. Belonging to, what I'd apparently missed. But, was, right in front of my face...All along!

Since I'd usually, be so freaking tired that, if I was lucky. I'd regretfully fall into, a deep slumber so deep. That, even "my mother" couldn't interrupt it!

Not unlike, when I was bought into, the emergency room after getting hit. My ability to both, hear and comprehend the voices. Belonging to the people who'd drop by to visit. Waked juts fine!

Which, reminds me of how the doctor in, the E.R. just wrongfully assumed that being, unconscious. Automatically meant that, I couldn't hear what they were saying.

But, then again, the wrath of, their flaws. Weren't amongst my issues "to, resolve either!

Plus, according to what info I'd managed to, "conveniently" overhear. As I'd pretended to be, locked deeply locked in, an, asleep mode. Allowed me to easily recognize most of, the voices. I'd meet during my stay.

However, since most of these peoples comments. Had never "verbally" so much as, struck me as being, capable of seeing past. The boundaries created by, "Modern Medicine" and reality. For such things as, references concerning, what they'd thought they'd knew. About, my secret quest for, it's answers, ect. I've never thought of them as being, a potential problem!

Then, there were also those opinions from people. A theory that always succeeds at arousing other areas of suspicion. Opening up room for "potentially unfounded" probabilities. That never stray'd "too far" beyond the boundaries restraining. At least, one the two "following factors."

1.) How lucky I was to be alive.

Or,

2.) The amount of pain I must be in.

So, just between us. Them "not being" willing to, speak to me on a "Medical professionals level. Made my point of view, unlike theirs, strictly of, a "personal nature".

In fact, if having to ride out this specific "Chapter of, my life on, a first hand basis. Was what it take to enlighten me to, anything other. Than the true definition of the word "pain."

It would be that, their always "a lot more" to everything. Than first meets, ones sexes. Some in which, I'd learned from recent events. We're "not" supposed to, witness or understand!

Although I must admit that at, first glance. It'd just seemed as though, I was in a, "temporary dilemma." That I was more than determined to, remedy.

That is, as soon as, my body. Decided it was in good enough, shape. To extent my "secret quest" for answers. Beyond my mattress without it hurting. Every tine I'd attempt to, inhale.

But finally, after spending these "very long" weeks of barely keeping myself. From dying of, "major boredom." With a bull game I like to refer to as. "94 billion reasons to hate the color of, hospital white."

My pediatrician, Dr. Fisher, decided that, he'd felt both, confident and comfortable enough. To approve the discharge papers. Releasing me from, my "hospital imprisonment!" So I could begin what was about to, become. "Stage two" of a "very long" healing process at, home.

Leaving the plan itself with a few minute glitches. That'd require a certain amount of, "ironing out." Before, we could actually, "Make it happen!"

1.) With my bod "still being, in a "very much of, the fragile condition. I had to wait to be, transported back home. By way of, ambulance.

2.) Well, up until discharge day. I'd actually believed the hardest part about, my hospital stay. To be trying to control my impatience with, their administrative department.

All yea, then there's the other part. Where just the process of, waiting on them. To get off of their "two-bit" butch to, push the paperwork through. Took hours! For to be more precise...lucky me!

But even though, I wasn't able to place them to, the from where part. Whenever they'd first showed up. There was just something about, the EMT's uniforms. Not to mention, their vehicles markings. That'd immediately caught my attention as being, "uncomfortably familiar."

Which, for as crazy as, this may also sound. Never fails to, bring a few fun facts to mind. Involving, the impact of the as to, where. On my brief transport "back home." Such as...

1.) My curiosity as to, what'd made it's "short amount of, necessary travel time." Seem like, it was taking "so long."

2.) How my level of impatience. Would have absolutely, nothing to do. With the amount of time it'd took to get, from here to there. But, what'd taken place, during it!

Heck, I'd known the second those dudes entered my room. That I'd seen them before! I just couldn't place the how or why part.

So, as a last resort I'd end up spending every last face second I'd had. Between, them showing up at, my room. To us leaving the hospital parking lot. Clear to the traffic light located about, ¾ the way across the "Newell Bridges"

Literally racking my brains to figure out. Why my not knowing that, particular answer. From night off the freaking top of, my head. Bothered me, so much!

But, after that. It was like, all of the details. That'd apparently created my "lapse in time" memory loss. Just started pausing right back at, me. A little faster than I was, "mentally prepared" to, grasp ahold of!

Which, interestingly enough. Brings me to, the "paramedic". Who'd close to, ride in the back of the ambulance with, me and mom. During our return trip home.

And

Ended up being, the "very same". Who's shoulder I'd watched my hand passing straight through. Only "three weeks" earlier!

With the good news being, that. Even though, I did manage to restrain myself from, readily sharing this info with them. After I'd made the connection.

The act of me gritting my teeth. All the way back home. Probably wasn't what I'd consider to be, the best method. For aiding this process out. Especially with both, my jaw and every tooth in, my mouth. Feeling like, they were barely dangling there!

Plus, with the view from the back of, the ambulance. Was on, the rather limited side. I was lucky if I'd even had one window to, myself. That'd even offered me the "smallest glimpse" of, the outside world. I'd missed "so much!"

Which, would've worked just fine for me! If the goofy "EMT" who'd insisted upon, riding in the back with, me and mom. Wouldn't've kept on, obstructing my view. Every time I'd almost get on actual chance to see. What I'd both craved and missed. During my "three week long" hospital imprisonment.

Heck, I suppose for most people. Just knowing that, the "so called" hardest part about, making it officially "over with". Would've probably been able to, form a "suitable aura of, contentment. In "their" minds.

But, there are also exceptions week long "time stretch. By inventing reasons to, "hate" the color of, "Hospital white." Just to keep myself amused.

The definition of the word, "Patience." Seemed to've lost it's standing in, my vocabulary. Not to mention, it's statis on all levels of, My things to do list!

Bringing me to my explanation of, all the "Still unknown" fun facts. Involving, what and whom I'd find myself having to deal with. "After" I'd got back home.

Things like, how my little brother", Walt' and sister "Hanna". Along with, my aunt, "Melenda Karen Wilard and three cousins. "Rebecca Karen, James Samuel, and Michael Jacob." Had gathered in our living room only, a few hours prior to my getting home. so, they could scare the happy "Bagusus" out of me. As soon as, the EMT's. Brought me through the front door.

Which, just for the record. Isn't what most people'd theorize as, the proper protocol. For making it happen! Especially, when it's being thrown for someone. Who's just been hit by, a car!

However, since trying to do things that, you'd usually, take advantage of. Such as, walking up and down steps by myself, moving, ect. Wouldn't become an option working in, my favor. For awhile yet.

I'd end up spend; the next six to seven months "plus." Trying to live out my life on, a day to day basis. From a near cot or, a roll away bed as, some people call it. That they'd set up in, our living room. So, I could have a good view of the television as, I awaited. For my bodies "very long" period of, recooperation. To finally be, over and done with!

Plus, since my mom and second grade teacher, Mrs. Fitly. Had already made the necessary arrangements. So, I could stay at the same grade level as, my fellow classmates. By having my homework assignments. To be sent back and forth to school. Courtesy of, my cousin, "James." Instead of, having to repeat the entire year, over again. Did make things at least, a little but easier. For the most recent reaches of, my mind to swallow.

After being forced to "impatiently tolerate." Their very long weeks worth of, "unwelcomed flashbacks" from the day that, "All Hell broke loose on, the streets of, Newell, W.Va.

I honestly thought I'd never hear the words. "Now that all of, the welcoming home surprise party hoo-ha has finally, wound down." Leaving my mother's lips.

"Heather Lynn". Mom began nervously. "To tell the truth, I was giving serious consideration to, just throwing this away. But then, I started to think about it a little closer. I decided to salvage your "Candy bar of choice." So you could enjoy it later. You know, like, when you actually able to, chew it?"

Heck, just judging from the amount of, sarcasm. I could hear in mom's voice, when, she'd suppressed her opinion towards this matter. I wasn't entirely sure if I was being, scolded for my mistake. Or, rewarded for surviving it!

But, I do know when I'd looked down at, the coffee table. To see what she was handing me. And realized. That she was, talking about, the very same "candy bar of choice". I'd been so anxious to purchase, try and almost ate. Before, I'd even leave, "Harts parking lot. And according to, my mother. Still had clutched in my fingers "after" I'd been hit by, a car: I've learned how to "fake" An odd since of, fabricated appreciation. For her "misguided" theory as to, it actually being worthy of keeping.

However, other than my jaw still feeling so sore. That I wasn't even sure I'd even have the strength to, consume it. I did manage to figure out a little trick. To make the "chewing it" part. Seem a "tid bit" easier!

But, as I'm sure you've already "quite aware." Where there's a will, there's also a way!"

I mean, yea! Even though, I'd thought the gesture itself was, pretty cool! When my mom decided to, salvage it and all.

Just between us. I'd lost my enthusiasm for "tasting it." Somewhere in between, the time I'd purchased it and point a. of the viewing of, the only made visible to me. Repetitiously haunting, slow motion, details that'd came with it. In order to supposedly" mark it's test "as, it fell into play...Go figure!

Well, at least, that's how things went. Until, Walt, Hanna and I'd began making our, "long awaited" preparations to, sit down. Or perhaps, I should say. When they'd sat down. So, we could watch our "first" T.V. show together. In..."three weeks!"

Just to learn that, the T.V. station we were about to, watch. Was being, briefly interrupted by, "The National Broadcast System." So, they could run one of their, "infamous tests."

Although, it'd definitely struck me as, seeming "A lot louder". When it came to me in, "A deafening ring." I'd recognized the frequency of, it's "High Pitched tone"...Almost immediately!

It shouldn't be "too hard" for you to, figure out, "Exactly what" would make the next six to seven months of, "going. "No-where fast." Seem like, it was impossible!

But hey, what do you expect? I was injured, not "dead!"

Besides, I may've been assured of being, just a "tool bit" hyperactive as, a child. But having to, co-exist in a horizontal position". For long periods of, time. Has a tendency to, get old...quite fast!"

Then, just as, I was about to, give up. All hope of, even getting any better. The moment I'd spent only "Lords how many months of, my life. Waiting on to, show up..."Suddenly Arrived!"

So, even though I'd never been given the "Slightest opportunity". To actually disgusts my bodies "health statis" with, Dr Fisher, directly. Where as, my mother, for example. Seemed to have the luxury of doing so. About, every other day!

Which basically, made my own personal evaluations of, it's acuteness in, general. Seem alot more like, mere guess work.

The afternoon she'd finally, walked into our living room. To announce that, according to Dr. Fisher. My pelvis along with, various other bones in my body. Had healed enough, to begin making preparations. For what I'd considered to be, "Stage three". Of, an "Extremely long" recovery process.

One that'd actually allow me to feel like, 30 thousand pounds of weight. Had been "instantaneously" lifted from my, "Horizontally positioned" shoulders.

With a task that, even after I'd spent several days practicing. What my mother'd referred to as being, "mandatory" sitting up" exercises. Between the hours of, 12 and 2:00 PM. Had the tendency to, pinch a bit "here and there". But, definitely necessary to build up the amount of, strength I'd need. To pull it off! Allow me to, secrete the image for you...

Everyday at, the same time. Mom would enter the living room. So, we could begin working on, "further preparations." For something that'd already proven itself to be, a "Non-easy" task. With what'd at first glance. Would appear to be, an "optimistic attitude."

But, from there. The procedure that, I'd been led to believe. Had been "originally designed" on the theory of, me. Being able to practice my "Sitting up" exercises." Would never fail to, stray off subject. Into, what'd seemed a lot more like, "a saddle interrogation." To make me feel guilty forb being "Stupid enough." To create this level of, an "inconvenience" for her!

In hopes that, her throwing around of, shallow minded, seemed hand input. Would actually give her the "Ultimate Wisdom". To figure out what I'd known..."Month Ago!"

Which is, just one of the "many reasons". I'd thought it'd be, a lot safer. To keep my "unknown assortment" of, personal comments. About, all of the details I'd witnessed taking place. On the afternoon of, 3/12/74. Strictly to..."Myself!"

In interest of, accurately quoting mom on both, the words and actions. That she'd insisted upon, using. When expressing it. I am willing to try.

Well, since the first words out of my mom's mouth. Whenever she'd enter the "living room" so we could practice "Sitting up exercises. Was at least, in my mind. Information from the completely pathetic and unnecessary on, her part. I've decided to, let you. Draw your own conclusions on what it took. For me to keep my patience with her.

"Heather Lynn?" Mom would confidently announce like, she'd actually been made aware. As to everything it'd involved.

"Before, we start working on, these "Sitting up" exercises. I should probably remind you that, certain bones in your body. Such as, the pelvis, collar bone, ect. Still haven't properly healed themselves yet."

"Which means, that it really be in your "best interest." To avoid trying to put "too much" of, your body weight. On one side as, we're doing them. Your left one to be, more precise!"

"That is, unless you want to spend. The next, six to seven months of, your life. Lying on, that cat!"

Then, once mom'd decided that she'd finished torturing me. With her, "trying to throw "invalidated", facts in my face "routine. Of which, unknowingly to, her and everyone else. Held the key to, "relevant, inside details". That'd only been made visible"..."to me!"

She'd never fail to, close her "Clueless lecture" off. By portraying me as, being. "Solely responsible" for forcing her to suffer. From what she'd referred to as, my "Supposed inability "to grasp." The entirely of, it's outcome." With what's better known as, the infamous "How dare you Glare." Like it was, "the happening thing to do!"

While I can't pretend that, both mom's emotional or, physical reactions. Wouldn't be good enough, to create strong doubts. Towards her "overly flowed" methods to, pull it off.

Now that, I've had the time to step back and rethink it's terms. "From her perspective." I suppose, it's possible that mom's comments could've been meant. As a form of, "abstract reasoning" to. Assist me during, "My Stroll through Hell!"

Which leaves me with the "other times." When what'd "originally" seemed like, nothing more or less. Than just another one of, "Mom's" prearranged speech's". Would turn out to be, "A whole different problem". Rolled within..."itself!"

Especially, when it came to listening to mom's constantly reminding me. About, something life had given me no other choice but to, feel. Every time I'd either, move or breath.

Which is why, when I tell you that "more" than just a "little bit" of consideration. Had been given to the idea of, "me" telling her. To just, "Shut the freak up..." I'm not kidding!

But, thanks to my "Not having" A "much better" comparison to, fall back on. I have to claim the hardest part about, the chain of pretending I'd even "Slightly cared." What comments mom'd attempt to, send my way during, "Setting up" exerciser.

This "event," so to speak. Would just end up reminding me of, exactly what it'd taken to endure. The "Atmospheric vibe" I'd picked up on. In the back of, "the Ambulance" on, my way back home.

Because, just like, I did then. I'd find myself lingering. Right smack dab in the middle of, a "Situation." Where the company itself "Seriously Sucked" and the pain I'd felt. From gritting my teeth until I'd arrived. Would be the only thing standing between me and literally, voicing my opinions.

Although, this time. It just didn't seem to, hurt as much. When it came down to, trying to antilize the base "What's and whys." That'd inspired me to, officially designate. This stage of my recovery as being, number four.

Well, in all due fairness to, myself. I'd say I had several reasons to, close from. With my "absolute favorite" being that, it'd at least, bought me "one step" closer. To overcoming the only thing holding me in, my "bedridden" state of "imprisonment." But, it wouldn't remain that way forever.

Since, just the simplest luxurious such as, walking up and down stairs. You know, things one would usually, just "take for granted. Wouldn't become, an option working in, "my favor" for awhile. I ended up having to bunk and co-exist on the cot in, our living room. Until, what my mother'd to as..."further notice!"

So, other than my being, forced to overlook "the extreme "lack of," privacy. Which was, "Constantly compromised" by anyone with a set of, working eyeballs to watch.

The non-stop embarrassment the situation itself created.

And,

Watching what'd started out as seeming like, zero to none odds. To whether or not I'd ever be able to, escape it.

Things were finally, beginning to show a little hope of ceasing!

As for, my reaction when, "Dr. Fisher", first gave my mom the OK. To send me back to school?

Well, just between you and me. I wasn't even sure if I could still remember what the inside of, "Jefferson Elementary School" looked like!

Besides, it's benefits may've definitely been of, the "far and few" between. But, being forced to bunk on, that not. Did hold it's fair show of, "Top Secret" but, "very much" appreciated advantages. One's that, no-one use had even so much as, "Hinted or Suggested. They'd known existed. Like...

1.) How the "pre chosen" location of, my cot. Came with an "extraordinarily view" of, our "dining room" table. AKA, Mom's favorite place to go when she was feeling the need. To create one of her, "infamous" do's and don'ts lists.

Although, I'm positive that,

2.) She wouldn't've hesitated to, change her, "location of choice." If she would've known how easily the window. Allowed me to "discretely" read them.

It was pretty obvious

3.) by, merely watching her behaviors. As she'd become, literally engulfed "in the process of, writing up, what mom'd believed to be, of solid grounds.

Which, in her mind. Both described and supported her so called, "Mother knows best best" theory. Concerning, what she'd understood to be, the state of, my bodies "Mental and physical" condition.

Where as, the "good doctors" I'd dealt with. Based their on, their "medical experience".

4.) All yea, then there's also the other part. Where my pollution of details. Clearly triumphed kees...any day!

Therefore, before I proceed to take my version of, this chapter from my life. To completion!

In all due fairness, I should probably point out. That it'd be the details that'd go down. "Before, I'd even leave the house for, my first day back at school. Which, I'd personally found to be of, the most amusing. Or, perhaps I should say..."The most ridiculous!"

Heck, with all of the pain I'd been forced to endure. During the act of performing "Sitting up" exercises. Putting up with my mother's know it all lectures and...so forth!

You'd think she would've found a way. To refrain from making "Sarcastic remarks" that, "Strongly Suggested." My not being intelligent enough, to wrap my head around. The "extent of, my physical condition. Without her "Ultimate Words" of, "Non-wisdomed" theories to, assist me.

Which brings me to her idea of, what rule number 1. On my list of, things "Not" to do while..."I was there!"

1.) No jumping up and down a, making loud noises!

I mean, maybe she thought she'd got away with it. But, I knew better! Because, as soon as she'd attempted to, "blindly compare". What'd clearly proven itself to be, an "Extremely limited" amount of knowledge. As being, far more superior to, mine.

Her input would just make the rules. To what my mother'd claimed to be, "the Main Concern". Sound even lames than, they already did!

So much, that it'd literally up and change. What'd only months ago, started out to be, nothing more. Than just a "very unwelcomed" but, "ignorable" bout of sarcasm on her part. Into, what'd came off as sounding like, a complete insult. Towards my level of, intelligence.

But, after that the "Topic of Conversation. Had somehow managed to, immediately shift. From what was, just her quoting every rule on her, "infamous" do's and dont's lists.

To her not shutting up about it. Until, I'd suspend her need to, hear me. Quoting everyone of then back to, her at least..."four times!"

It was a relentous choice. In which, I did succeed at, pulling off. Before the hands on the dining room clock. Had even struck 8:00 am.

With myself being, the only person. Whom knew both, my mom's opinion and the real circumstances as, a result. But, other than that. My 8:00 am. briefing, went pretty smoothly.

That is, until I'd made it to school. Because no matter how much I'd hated. The idea of, "Not-being" able to participate. In the usual daily "extra-curricular" activities. With, the rest of, my fellow classmates. There really wasn't anything I could do. To change how impatient it'd make me. Let alone, the consequences as, a result of, my own actions!

One's in which, I'd for some reason or, another. Had been granted the privilege of, telling about!

That is, if I could ever "muster up" enough guts. To actually, go there!

So, in interest of, distracting my now "overly active" mind. Away from the ever frustrating levels it'd created. That, I'd had no other option but to, deal with!

I decided to use it to, my advantage. By devising my own plan of action to, counter it!

Which, just as I'd suspected it would. Happened to hold the hidden key to, decoding. It's still "unresolved" mystery.

The only difference is, that this time. Instead of, traffic. I'd be stepping well beyond the "having to put everything in my life" on hold. Until, further notice" routine.

Which also explains, how. I'd come to find myself. Becoming even more acquainted with, my own "personal emotions" that, I'd some how overlooked. During all of the "bedridden" hoo-ha.

It was the beginning of, stage six in, my recovery process. AKA. The moment that, I'd been waiting on. Since, all this "bull crappola" first started!

I can't deny the several hours I'd spent, "Reluctantly" searching for it's answers!

But even though, I'd never suspected it's "hidden to everyone else insights. As being the key to, "what would allow me access to them."

Until then, they were just a tool that'd inspire me to, discreetly inspect and evaluate. It's numerous "unspoken" details that, still died "hidden" beneath the surface.

I mean, sure! I may've been made "quite aware" as to, what I'd witnessed happening.

The only problem was, I couldn't take the risk of, exposing them. Without creating an extreme probability of, leaving myself completely vulnerable.

Drawing "unwanted" attention towards myself.

Which, would either, leave me wearing the "I'm Crazy" brand for life.

Or, leaving an entirely different area of, prospective. To onlookers that'd driven myself "half bankers". Trying to make sure remained in, the dark. Until, I was done serving my time in, captivity!

You know, questions like, how or even why. All of the "Significant" details pertaining to it. Didn't actually begin "falling into play." Until, after I'd got home from school that day!

In fact, since in the flash backs I didn't ask for. But, found myself relieving every night in, my dreams.

Had never failed to begin. With me. Picking up on, the "strange vibe." That I could neither, place or shake. Not long after I'd kicked my shoes over by, the front door.

Ignoring how easily, the minutes would "Slowly" progress forwards. As they'd force me to, distinctly retrace the "Exact Same" path I'd taken. On my way to "Harts Market to, retrieve my "Candy bar of choice."

Would only last until, I'd hear the incredibly loud "Thud" part. After that, I'd once again find myself "Witnessing" my "Entire World." Turning upside down right in front of, my eyes and...So on!

For some reason or, another. Everything around me would just "immediately" shift into, a "Slow Motions" made.

It was almost as though, everything I'd either, accidentally or, on purpose. Witnessed during "round one." Had went on a mission to, haunt me. Until, I'd be made "fully aware" as to, the depth. Of the miscellaneous details involving it. So, I be able to sense and recognize the "True meaning."

Behind my being, forced to, endure. A very long and painful comeback. From the moment of my life that would be "branded." Into my mind as, "The day that, All Hell broke loose" on the streets of, Newell W.VA.

You'd think by this time. I would've had "more" than enough to reach the "undeniable conclusion." That whatever'd decided to seek refuge in my body. Had absolutely "No-intensions" of, going anywhere!"

But, because the actual process of, learning there answers. Had already evolved into, what I'd considered to be, a race against time. It was really just a matter of..."how much?"

Although, in my gut. I've always known I'd 'eventually" find myself, crossing paths. With my "Temporarily dormant" companion..."again."

Until the moment of truth actually arrival. I'd just have to, try and keep my curiosity level surfaced. By sifting through it's "dormantary state." As it'd supposedly, layed low inside me.

It was almost as though, it'd had to wait on something significant to take place. Before, it could acquire the amount of, "Strength it'd needed. To step up and reveal the secrets to, it's mystery. AKA/it's "true colors!

CHAPTER TWO

Then suddenly, the dreaded curse of the go between days...came true!"

Two years later...

Since, I'd still not in, anyway, shape or form. Made any type of, "formal entry" pertaining to this particular matter. I've decided that, now. Is as good of a time...as any!

But, trust me. A lot of things in, my world. Had "drastically changed" during, the past few years!

However, once I've had the chance to finish discussing the complexity of, it's details. You'll be given every opportunity, to, learn even more!

Such as, how come the things I'd witnessed and attempted to touch on, 3/12/74, which, just so happened to be, taking place. Right in front of, my eyes. Had appeared to be, from "Another persons body?"

Why no one else but, me. Had so much as, "acknowledged" it's presence?

Or, even better yet.

Why it'd left me trying to, "co-exist." In a world that'd only humored a very "touch and go" lifestyle. Which'd required the use of, "extreme cautionary" measures. Before, performing a sequence of, "Top Secret" investigations?

Well, as I've already painted out. When my companion and I'd last met up. I'd just been hit by, a car. Which, resulted in my having to, ride out. A full year's worth of, recovery.

While trying to, prevent it's beyond "far fetched" visual. From straying any further than, the boundaries that'd allowed me to perform. My "Top Secret" sequence of investigations...in privacy.

In hopes that, just it alone. Would allow me to, solve the "Big mystery." Behind what'd already proven itself to be of, the "mind boggling!"

Where as, now. Due to the path life'd given me to travel. I'd spent a little over "two years" worth of, my companion's dormancy period. The act of being, repetitiously jerked between, two "completely alienate factors". Which, were about to become. An even more "mentally complexed" journey!

Heck, I'd even go as far as to, salvage, guard and protect. Some kind of stability within, everyone else's "inability." To acknowledge what'd went on right in front of, their eyes. But, they didn't see.

By "virtually wrestling" my way through a form of "brief consideration". That'd activity revealed insights from, my side of the fence and I'd veto almost immediately...if not sooner!

That is, until it'd finally reached the point of, exposing it's "untold secrets. To a woman whom tried to claim. That she could actually be, trusted with them!

In fact, I believe my mom's "Exact Words", were, "Heather Lynn." She tried to bring up "non-chalantly." "You do realize that, everything we discuss during our, "Casual Conversation' exercises. Will remain strictly bet us...Right?"

It was the statement. That as soon as, the shock from it being, asked... Wore off! Would rapidly "dissipate" and become, all the motivation I'd needed. To counter even faster than, it'd taken her to make it!

It's called, "The art of throwing my mother a "Stray bone" to, nibble on. So, I wouldn't get another, "migraine headache". From tolerating her "daily lectures" concerning, "How important" she'd felt it was." For us to have a "Casual Conversation".

However, since I'd grown rich and tired of, just ignoring her. Like, I usually did. I guess, I'd just felt the need to be, different..."go figure!"

In other words, I'd not only, grown "Sick and tired of, listening to her. Spout off about, her "Shallow minded" bull crop. I was bound and determined. Not to be, the only one regretting. What she'd felt was, "her "God Given" right!

It was a task that'd just get easier and easier by, the second! Especially, when mom finally figured out. That the real brunt of her foolish joke. Was...on her!

No, I can't deny feeling more than just, a little bit lazy. About, the shortly workmanship my insisted upon, using. To pull her scam off with.

But, she'd finally succeeded at, pushing me. To my absolute limitations with her "Stupid" two bit lectures. Only now, they'd reached the point. When they would've been too much. For anyone to just, sit there and tolerate!

As far, my weapon of choice, well, that part still hadn't been determined. But, it is where this particular chapter from my life. Started to get "a lot more" intense and I don't mean..."In a good way!"

However, because this situation would practically resolve itself. When I revealed the things I'd witnessed on, 3/12/74. But, no one else but, me saw! Such as, personal insights, experiences...ect.

My version as to, what'd really taken place that afternoon. As I'd stood there and watched the top secret "for my eyes only" files being, learn. From what'd appeared to be "inside" Another person's body! WOULD make it sound like, a bad "Sci-Fi" flick! Allow me to set the mood...

Well even though, I myself. Could've devised a more suitable plan. In which, would've easily given me free access of both.

1.) Successfully pulling it off

2.) The luxury of, "not having" to worry about, being caught. By arousing "unwanted suspicion towards, what I was really doing.

Although apparently, my mother's efforts to try to, "Phyco-Antilize" me. From the other end of, our dining room. Seemed to be the best plan she could come up with on, "such short notice." Here's my version of, how. It all started!

Since, I've always had an, "intuitive sense" for knowing. "Exactly" when mom was, setting me up. So, she could what I call. One of her, "Well, below my "mental capacity' attempts. To randomly, pick my brain.

I've learned to rely on, The many flaws. Lying deeply within the non-stop" flouting of mom's "Never ending." "I'm trying to be sly about it attitude." To reveal her "True Intensions."

Then again, after two solid years of, silently studying them. I've learned to read all of the signs. That she'd thought she was, "So good" at, hiding them from me. Like...

1.) The off vibe I'd immediately "picked up" on. As a result of. "What I'd took as, a mere side effect." From my "sudden" lacking in, "Self-esteem."

But, since my mother had a weird and "very distinctive" habit of sitting. Clear at the other end of, what I've came to recognize. As her "infamous" do's and dont's lists table. Picking up on the "extremely off" vibe that, always came with it, was never a problem!

Yea, I may've found a way to ignore it. Or perhaps I should say, pretend to. When it was, really just a mere after effect, instilled by, my sudden lacking in, the "self-esteem" department.

Where as, my mother's previous success rots is, this specific area of expertise. Pretty much like, everyone else's. Spoke for itself! It wouldn't be enough, to prevent her. From investigating more inventive ways. To interpret them!

Besides, thanks to my mother's "Non-escalating" talents. They'd already been recorded in, my mind for future reference. So, I've never felt any purring need. To wonder about, the potential of its outcome. When it made it's "repeat performance."

The still unknown details that, personal experience itself. Had revealed for "My eyes only." Repetitiously proved that, the actual privilege of avoiding. This type of, conversation episodes with mom. Would never be mine to, bark in. As a form of leverage!

But, by giving them the space they'd needed to fully expose themselves. I could easily coax mom's "unspoken suspicions out into, the open. When I'd pretended not to, even not to even notice. Her presence within the room.

I mean, sure! While this specific technique I'd devised to, counter her's. Would have a small tendency to ruffle mom's feathers a bit. It was one that'd never fail to reveal. The true depth of her supposedly, "cloaked intensions."

Whereas, the concept of my figuring out. How to buy myself a few extra seconds on, the side. Always paid off!

While, I'd had "no-proof" that'd allow me to confirm the false illusion. My mothered created to interpret. What she'd felt hers was worth...either way!

Just judging by, the attitude she'd insisted upon sliding my way. I'd have to say that, to her. Creating it's "highly unnecessary" existence. Was more along the lines of being, like...a sport!

Which, she'd created for the sole purpose of, finding a way. To perform what she'd obviously felt wise," inconspicuous attempts". To obtain closer studies of, my behavioral pattern!

But, once we'd finally, reach a point. Where making any form of, verbal exchange. Would become like, an issue beyond resolution.

It'd leave me with no other options but to, conclude. That we'd clearly held two "completely different" theories as to, what. The true definition of the word, "mother" was! For example...

Although, according to the Webster's Collegiate dictionary, the true definition of, the word "mother." Is either, a parent of the "female" gender. Or someone in whom, exhibits a "mothering" instinct.

My mother's "seemed to fall. Somewhere along the time's of being." A false position of, authority. That'd automatically gave her the power and an excuse. To make random attempts to, trick her oldest sibling.

Into, unconsciously revealing my inner most and private "None of her freaking business thoughts" to her. Like, I wasn't intelligent enough. To see right through her pathetic illusion.

So, now that you've been briefed as to, what the terms. Pertaining to this specific chapter of, my life. Were forged from.

Let's, get back to reviewing the basics of it...Shall we?

Sure mom may've felt that her procedure of choice. Added a glimmer of promise to, her overly persistent drive. To read my personal thoughts like, a diary.

When she'd pretend to be, engulfed in an article from, the "Cosmopolitan Magazine. But, I knew it was really just her way of, trying to disguise. The sudden and discreetly made glances she'd send my way..."Rookie!"

Yea, I suppose she may've foresaw. Her, "All that and a box of chicken game plan as being, the most to say...the least! Where as I, for example. Failed to share in, the enthusiasm.

So, as long as this particular thought. Is still "fresh in mind. We should probably get back to, "Cross examining." All of the nitty gritty details we'd end up disguising. During our first and only "vocalized" interrogation session.

Because, even after I'd spent. At heart, ten minutes worth of "wasted time." Trying to just play along with what I was willing to let my mother believe. Qualified as being...suddenly done.

I guess the wrath from my mother's "serious inability to reap any return benefits. Finally caught up with her in, the "Psycho Analysis" department. Which was, obviously what'd triggered her "unexplainable urge". To kick the stakes up a few notches!

"Heather Lynn." Mom sturdily asked. In a tone of voice that'd definitely suggested. I'd held the necessary words to pass itself off as being, a mere "Casual Conversation" exercise. Stomped all over it. "Is there something you'd care to share with me?"

Well, even though, I'd never held access to either, the guts or on opportunity. To actually step up and vocalize my own personal opinion. Concerning, her "So called" technique of choice" before then.

Thus was absolutely "No way" I was willing to, let just it alone. Be enough to mark the aura of, it's co-existence. Which'd never failed to be, looming nearby.

Although, the trick to maneuvering it's "Abstract" obstacle course. Would sent solely on, mom's ambition to, complete it.

The key to decoding it's disturbing mysteries. Would end up remaining in, the form of both, an unanswered question and reply. That my mother had never been willing to ask.

Therefore, with no where else to turn for rational theories in, this matter. I decided to spare myself a little excess travel time. Between then and wherever this, "going no-where fast" conversation was leading me.

By using what's known as, "The jumping in with, both feet" mode. While maneuvering and bluffing my way through. What'd prevented itself as being, "The makings of," potentially hazardous "waters.

"No, mom." I replied in a very distinctive "I'm not saying any attention to you" tone of voice. "I don't! Why do you ask?"

Which is, when my mothers "false came front." For what she'd only seconds ago. Would've sworn up and down to be, "the most to say the least." Literally went..."Krisplot!"

So, of course. When my mother of whom, has always been the type. To step up and readily volunteer her input. At, the mere drop of, a hat..."didn't!"

I couldn't help but to, find myself wondering "exactly" what I'd said. To carb her appetite for..."doing it anyway!"

Well even though, the expression my mother'd had smeared all over her face. When I'd glanced up to get a visual of it's circumstances. Practically screamed that it'd forged from her "temporary" loss of words. Or perhaps, I should say. "Whatever'd triggered it!"

You can rest assured. That before this particular days form of, "Casual Conversation." Would actually, come to a close. I'd "not only" find myself having to seek out but, stretch the nerve. That'd apparently, awakened it! But, leave her holding the ticket for a "double whammy" effect.

Although mom would make a quick recovery. A soon as, she'd found a way to, counter. Her "so called" loss for saying words. It felt like, she couldn't run out of comments to make about, the situation…fast enough!

"Oh, no reason, Heather Lynn! I was just curious in all!" Mom continued suggestively. After what'd seemed like, two full minutes. Worth of what I think was, a "Well earned" state of silence on, my behalf.

"I just thought that, since we're both sitting here at, the table. You know, doing nothing. That you might be interested in, having a "Casual Conversation" with me. No Biggy! Why do you ask, Heather Lynn?"

"Well, mom. If you remember correctly." I answered respectfully. "I didn't! So, the way I see it. The only person here who's interested in pursuing amusement of this kind. Is you! Or, did you already forget that part?"

"No, Heather Lynn!" Mom replied in, what'd clearly changed. To a mildly impatient tone of voice. Which, was already beginning to produce vivid signs of frustration within it. "I haven't forgotten about, that part. But, you're right. Because, it was my idea to, bring it up! So why don't you just cooperate with me by explaining. What makes you so sure that, your not interested "in, having one?"

Yea, mom was definitely trying to play. The "I'm attempting to" inconspicuously pick your brain. Without having to worry about, drawing "unwanted suspicions" towards her intensions card alright.

The only difference was, that this time. She'd chosen to deliver her lame presentation of it. In a much more recognizable form.

"Well, mom." I replied with a serious lack of enthusiasm for "playing along." "It's like this." I explained hoping that, just it alone. Would be enough to, dowse mom's flame of, "false" inspiration. "Call me crazy and if I answer your question. Trust me, you will before, this conversations over with!"

"But, even with that, thought in mind. If if shuts you up then, it's worth it!

Although, I'm definitely "not" comfortable with the idea. I'm going to go out on a limb here and say. That the reasoning behind my choice "not" to get into this conversation with you. Has a lot more to do with me refusing to be, stupid enough. To waist my time pondering a theory of, that magnitude. With you or, anyone else...for that matter!

Which, brings me to the details mentioned in, our discussion. That'll explain "exactly" how I'd chose to deal. With my mother's refusal to fold. When it came to, her persistence to provoke it forwards.

But, before I actually go as far as to, describe. What it was like to dial with the complexity's that'd most concern me. I just have to brief you. On what I'd suspected to be, driving the "True Motivation. Behind what I'd prefer to recognize. As the rules to mom's "Double C word" exercise.

Because most of, what I'd witnessed about, mom's behavior patterns. Involved, her ineffective procedure to, make me talk. Still seemed to fall under the category of, the highly inaccurate.

The several flows and glitter that, her non-profitable "psycho-analyses' session" revealed. Would end up being more than enough evidence. To make me a firm believer in the probability. That a certain amount of thought and energy. Had been inverted into the planning of, it's "so called" "Fool proof" design.

For the sole purpose of, discreetly gathering hidden insights and miscellaneous facts pertaining to it. all in which I would felt perfectly content. About using to, leave hers. Completely in, the dark!

Besides, it wasn't my fault she'd hadn't properly earned her "sea legs" yet!

Then again, something in life. Do seem to take a little longer to get the hang of...than others!

Like, as to why I wasn't in, the heart bit interested. In letting her to so much as, come close to learning. What I've came to interpret quite well.

Mom's lame expose to confront me. About, what she'd felt the need to. But, didn't know.

Or,

How uncomfortable it'd make me. When she'd attempt to, surface her serious need to perfect her, blowing unwanted attention off of, herself routine. Instead of, using it. to salvage. Whatever she may've felt had been left of, her "Cover performance" act.

Which is why, I used to hate it so much. Whenever mom'd get one of, her sudden urges. To bring the "Double C Word" into, any conversation! Especially since they never failed to end. With her trying to squeeze the hint of, blandly rational probabilities. Onto, the badgering table for revaluation.

Besides even then I wouldn't have to worry. Until, the conversation had "officially", kicked in. But, after that. All I could really do was to, wait and wonder. Where it'd lead me.

Then, just as I'd already knew it would. Mom's sudden loss for saying words. Would be over and she'd attempt to declare our conversation. To be "officially"...back on!

"Heather Lynn." Mom continued impatiently. "I'm very much aware as to, whom brought it up!" But, we've already covered that, part...right?"

"Yes, mother". I replied reluctantly. We did! We've also covered the as to, why. I don't feel any desires to, participate in one."

"However, since we've apparently, reached the part of, this conversation. Where your refusal to, refrain yourself. From trying to, drive me on the subject even more. Has become, no longer an option. Let's just get it over with...Shall we?"

"Yes, Heather Lynn," Mom replied as though, she'd actually tricked me. Into handing her a few access pass. To all of the information I'd managed to, keep locked up inside me. Until the day they could no longer be avoided Had finally, arrived.

"So," mom continued as though, she felt she'd figured out. How to trick me into, handing her a free pass. To all the information I'd managed to keep trapped in my mind. For safe keeping. Until, the day it could no longer be avoided. Had finally, arrived.

"Heather," mom continued like, she'd actually knew. What she was about to, voluntarily become, part of. "Why don't you just stop trying to stall the inevitable? By telling me the "real reason." Your so dead set on, us "not" discussing it?"

"Mom!" I replied defensively. "In case you" haven't been" paying any attention. To what's been going on during, these past few years. You "not" the only person sitting at this table. Of whom, has had more than just a little bit of experience in this area. Especially, when it come to mastering the "Secret" art of, "Reverse Psychology!" But, I am the only one who's learned the trick. To making it work to, my advantage!"

"In other words, mother! I may not have a plausible theory. Or to exactly "Where." You think this conversation is headed. But, sinks it's already been brought up. Yea, I do have a few questions I "still haven't figured out!"

"Therefore, if it's going to take "us" having this conversation. To get you to just, "Shut up about it. Then please, feel free to, ask away!"

"Besides, like you said. As long as we're both, just sitting here at, the table. You know, doing nothing. I suppose, having a fresh pair of eyes. To help me "mull" things over. Could be, a good thing! But, I seriously doubt you'll like, my answer! So, are you like, in a what?"

"Yes, Heather Lynn" mom replied. As she'd grew more and more impatient by, the second. "I am." Now, let's just cut the bull crop and do it already...Shall we?"

"Well, mother." I began. Even though, I've never mentioned this before now. But, I'm just curious as to, why the thought of giving me my personal space. In this particular matter...Bothers you "So Much!"

"Well unless of course. Your feeling like, this expectation. Is just way "too" much for you to handle."

"OK, Heather Lynn," mom remarked insistently. Like, she'd found some sense of satisfaction. Within a techniques that'd already proven itself to be. A very limited resource for answers. "You've made your point."

"But, before we begin this discussion. I need you to give me your word. That you'll be answering my questions..."Straight up!"

Which is when, my mother. Started laying down the rules to her, "So Called," casual conversation exercise.

"Hey, mom!" I interrupted insultingly. "In case you haven't noticed. I'm always straight up with you! Or, anyone else for that matter! So, I really don't see any reasons as to why. That fact should change now...yourself?"

"No, Heather. I don't!" mom replied agreeingly.

"However, just between us. I remarked suggestively. "Sometimes I just can't help but to, get this feeling. That your not willing to do, the same for me."

"All yea and by the way, when I choose "Not" to, answer your question. It's usually, because I personally. Just don't see any worth in waiting either, the time, effort or breath. That it takes to, do so!"

"Plus," I continued even more impatiently than, I already was. As I'm sure you're aware. Or at least, I am anyway! When I choose to ignore your questions for...Whatever reasons!

It doesn't automatically make my statement. Or, in this case. I suppose, my lack of, "having one". Would be, a more "accurate" comparison. Qualify as being, a lie!

"Oh, yea? Mom remarked doubtingly as though, she'd caught me in the process of, trying to pull one off. "Then, tell me, Heather Lynn." She continued. "What do you think it means?"

"Well, mom." I beg an frustratingly." It's like this. According to my definition of this process. Not mention, the "Webster's Collegiated dictionary's. It means that, "It's none of your freaking business!"

"However," I sarcastically replied, "Since I'm such a nice lady and all! I'm willing to go as far as, to warn you. That if you so much as, think you're feeling a little bet leasy. About, learning what you would've obviously "not known" otherwise. Then do us both a favor and...don't ask!"

So, mother, with that thought in mind. It's time to either speak now. Or, forever hold your piece! Because, since I've already stated mine. I should probably ask you. If there's anything you'd like to add to, our current "Do's and don't's" list. Before, we start!

"No, Heather Lynn!" mom remarked impatiently. "There's Not!"
"Well, then by all means mother...Let's play!" "Yes, Heather Lynn! mom replied insistently. "Let's!"

But, since mom'd always led me to believe that, a deals a deal. I guess, I'd just assumed that, mom would've been more willing to, devote a little more enthusiasm. Towards the idea of, learning how to, uphold hers!

While I've "never" doubted for a second that, this specific moment. Would eventually, reach a point. Where the subject itself. Could no longer be, avoided.

Where as, now. The hardest part about, having this "Secret Acknowledgement of, it's presence. Would appears, to have to do with, "how fast." I could locate and suppress mom's trigger switch. To set it into, motion.

"Yes, Heather Lynn!" mom insisted like, she'd actually believed. That the secret to, regaining complete and total control over this situation. Lied solely within, her hands alone. "I think I'm more than capable of handling whatever you're feeling the need to, tell me!"

"In fact," she continued reassuringly. "Even if this conversation is, only long enough. For you to open up about it. I'm just happy that, you've finally decided. To come to, your senses!"

It's just too bad that, the disguise she'd attempted to portray. In order to, masquerade the room's atmosphere..."Didn't work!"

Especially, when it ended up being, from a statement. That'd easily, reveal and threaten. The major flaws that were responsible for her missions success rate!

"Just look at the bright side, Heather Lynn" mom continued supportively. "As soon as, we're done having this conversation. Who knows! We might've even figured out, what's been bothering you "so much!"

Well, other than there being, the exact words I'd used. To determine how far in the dark my mother actually was. About, what I'd been going through.

Only unlike, my mother. I'd already been made "quite aware" of, the "For my eyes only" files existence.

So, of course. When I'd still refused to just play along. With her misguided theory of, a "Casual Conversation" exercise. Mom decided to use her "OCD" like, form of persistence. To push the conversation forwards even further!

By diving into some seriously dangerous and uncharted waters. That'd make her wish like heck. She hadn't been foolish enough, to leveher life jacket in...her underwear drawer!

Besides, it wasn't my fault that, mom couldn't refrain herself. From looking for ways to badger herself. Into my, "None of her freaking business" personal thoughts. But opportunity, this sound. Was just destined to be, different!

Although, just between you and me. I don't think it really mattered "How" one would choose to classify it. Because, this next sequence of random events. Would all come down to, the same theory!

First, there's what's known as, the infamous "Snow Ball" effect.

Which clearly suggests the complexity of a problem's source. Is measured by the amount of "flakes" it accumulates. As it rolls down hill.

Therefore, making each went leading up to, it's final circumference. Just one of, the many!

Second, there's what's known as being, "The Claim link" effect."

Which basically, allows you to evaluate the weakest one. As their linked together!

That is, until it revealed how dead set my mother was. About, learning the truth. When she attempted to trick me into humoring. Her overly annoying to get inside my head..."casually."

So, doing my best "not to" because what were already "unwanted suspicions" towards myself. I decided to "cautiously" play along. Until I was able to, draw a more accurate conclusion as to, the situation.

OK, Mom!" I remarked sarcastically. "Have it your way! Because, we both know that your not going to, just shut up and let it go. Until, you do!"

"No Heather Lynn! mom insisted angrily." I'm not going to just, drop the subject altogether! I've never done that before and won't do it now either!"

"Well, mom" I interrupted defensively. "Now that we've both been brought up to date. On your argument as to, how this conversation "should go." I believe it's now "My turn" to give you the opportunity to, evaluate and compare. The difference between your insight of, what you think you'd witnessed. On the afternoon of, 3/12/74...and mine!"

"I mean, kick look at the bright side, mom! Yea, the conversation said may seem a little on, the brief side! But, like you said, It does involve both of, us...right?"

Plus, after listening to mom's. "How far she'd went out of her way to help me" speak. I guess, I'd hind of expected, Mom's response to've been a tool more "verbal."

So, when she sat there and just looked at me. Like, she didn't have one to contribute in return. I immediately found myself trying to, "Single handedly", keep up "both" ends!

"But, before we begin. I'd just like to, take a few extra minutes. To remind you of, how many times. I've "very politely" asked you "Not" to go there!"

"However, since you keep insisting upon, "readily" doing so anyway! Then who knows! Perhaps my next statement. Will keep make the idea of, "going there." A little easier for you to ignore!

"Mom!" I continued. "Out of the many hours you've spent. Trying to execute your habit of doing so anyway. I've "not once" found anything about, there "casual conversation exercises. That's even come close to, capturing my attention. As being, worthy of mine!"

"Yea!" I continued frustratingly "I'll answer your lame questions! But, the little "habit you've developed. For the soul purpose of being, able to stick your more. Into, my inner most and personal thoughts! . . Stop now!"

"OK, mother." I continued frustrated. "Now that we've both, "clearly stated," our opinions about having it! I think we need to, settle on it's terms!"

"Well, mom! It's your case woman! . . Make it!"

"Heather Lynn!" mom replied assumingly. "I can understand the terms perfectly, and yes! We do have a deal!"

"Mom." I interrupted. "But, since I'd still felt "more" than, a little baby. About the idea of, just laying my cards on the table for, further evaluation. I couldn't help but to, wander. Where our conversation was, leading me.

"I'm not going to just sit here and pretend. That I'm in any way, shape or form. Interested in learning the logic behind your "persistent" request!"

"Or, even better yet! I insisted frustratingly." What's driving you to have one now!

"Besides, mother!" I added defensively. "You and I have never even so much as, came close to replicating. What'd I'd consider to be, a conversation of, the casual nature. I seriously doubt" there's any probability of, us having one now!

"However, if you really interested in hearing. My opinions towards, this matter mom," I'd hinted with a "small hint" of, sarcasm lingering in, my voice.

"I think it'd really be best for everyone involved. Or, at least, for those whom, think they are anyway! To take the little exercise you've devised to pick my brain and hopefully learn. What's clearly, none of their freaking business. So, you can stick it. Where the sun "doesn't" shine!"

Yea, it may've taken my mom a total of, 2 years. To push me to the point, where she'd finally, succeed at rattling my chain. Until I could "no longer" resist my "ever-growing temptation." To return the favor with something a little more "substantial." Than her flimsy, bull crap "fall back" line.

So, hoping to, blow a little bit of, the "unwanted faces" off of both, the subject and myself. I tried to, "suddly" enlighten my mother. To the actually depth of, her, "unacknowledged" shallow mindedness.

With a "very vivid and detailed explanation of, what I'd witnessed and experienced. Right after I'd seen the "flash of white and heard the incredibly loud "thud" and "deafening ringing" sound.

All in which, judging by whatever'd triggered mom's "big malfunction/spay out "session", I'm more than positive there wasn't any way of, confirming it" visually.

All I could really do was to, sit there and watch. As my mother "poor excuse" for, a "casual conversation" exercise. Immediately elevated itself into, a "mildly intense" argument. Between, mom and I!

By measuring how frequently she'd attempt to, rephrase her questions. To make them sound like, they were meant innocently.

But, after that, any judgements or conclusions I'd make. Towards how my mother'd react to, the answer. Concerning, what were still "unknown" facts. I could neither verify or prove.

Well, they'd just have to be, drawn. From the tone in, her voice. Upon, reply!

Forcing any and all effects she'd attempted to, put fourth. To support her "so called" poor excuse for a "casual conversation" exercise. To basically, just go "Kusplat" right there!

As for what'd caused mom's "big freaking" problem. With my trying to, tell her the truth, about, "What I'd really witnessed and experienced on, 3/12/74?

Well, that part was, hard to determine! But, I'm pretty sure it could be, very easily filed. Under at least, one of the two following categories!

1.) How rapidly the truth that, I'd "silently predicted" two years earlier. Would become, just that! "All over again!"

2.) How rapidly mom'd attempt to pull her little "back peddling" maneuver. Once she'd been confronted and "properly introduced." To what'd originally, created my little attitude problem. With her "Because, I'm the mom!" theory.

Or even better yet...

3.) What'd made her just readily assume. That her being, one. Automatically, gave her this "God Given" right. To randomly try to, sick my brain for "disclosed" details. That she'd clearly needed for leverage against me. But I, wasn't willing to share!

Just to have them practically, "slammed" right back in "her face." When she heard the words. "Mother, contrary to what I'm sure you'd "prefer" to believe. My inner most and personal thoughts. Are none of, your freaking business!" Deal with it already...I did!"

In other words, once you combined my mom's chosen approach. For learning answers. With my serious lack to enthusiastically humor her stupid request. For about, the one hundredth time and counting!

Something in which, I've always done. When it came to being, forced to tolerate. One of mom's attempts to violate my privacy. With her, "casual conversation" exercises.

My rain of patience. With mom's repetitiously "frivolous and completely in the dark lectures. About, how to handle this particular situation. Had surpassed their limitations quota and the act of just ignoring it, was no longer an option!

Making it "verbally on"...between us.

"Heather Lynn!" mom insisted offensively as though, my choice "Not" to humor. What I'd considered to be, her completely "out of line request. Had been a "direct insult". Made towards the level of "her" intelligence.

"Mom" I insisted impatiently. "If answering your pathetic questions, will get you to shut up about, it! Then, yea! I'll play along with your little exercise!"

"But, just to make sure we're both, made perfectly clear. As to exactly where each one of us stands. On such things as, the rules pertaining to it, how it will work...ect.

"I'd first like to, point out. How useless I believe your little attempts to, pick my brain. Really are! Then, just for fun. I'm even willing to go as you. As to explain "why" I feel this way!

"So, tell me something more!" I asked intimidatively. "Are you like, in or what?"

"Yes, Heather Lynn!" mom replied eagerly like, she thought she'd already won this round. "As a matter of fact, I am!" Mom persisted over confidently. "Now, let's get down to business...Shall we?"

"Yes, mother. Let's! I agreed impatiently. "Well, mom. It's like this! I began. "If my body'd been in any shape to do so at, the time. I would've just got up and walked away. From the curse of, having to listen to, your "Bull Crap" theories related to, this specific topic...Two years ago!"

"But, in case you still haven't been made aware of, the circumstances. That your so called, "casual conversation" exercise holds. Which, just judging by your current reaction to, what I'm trying to explain...you haven't!"

"Then, here's a little unexpected "News flash" for you. I'm not the one here who's trying to warm their way into, a conversation. That's none of their freaking business...you are!"

"Therefore," I continued defensively. "I really don't care as to, how much. You'd prefer I'd believed otherwise. Because, my inner most and personal thoughts are not now. Nor, will they ever be any of your freaking business! Not to mention, within your realm of, "rational plausibility's!"

So, when my mother, of whom, for the first time ever in her life. Didn't have some form of verbal reply to, offer me in return.

Strictly out of, respect for her. I did what I'd could to keep, whatever I could about, our "one sided" conversation. Flowing in a direction: That I'd at least, grown "vaguely" familiar with. During the past two years I'd spent. Doing my best to ignore it!

"Mom," I continued frustratingly. "Honestly, you can sit there and persist your foolish efforts to, spout off. About, how "you alone" feel this conversation should be handled. As long as, you remember to leave me and your feed back of, "verbal expectation. The heck out of it...dig?"

"Then again" I added calmly but, frustratedly. "Since I've officially stated "my piece" in this matter. Or at least, as much as I'm going to, get away with."

"If you feel as though, your actually willing to, refrain yourself. From falling under the "self made" assumption. That anything that you either, say or do during it, will mildly hold some form of, significance in, my world."

"Then I'm willing to, "Not go" upstairs to my bedroom. Where I can attempt to pretend to forget that, your efforts. To bring this specific topic up for discussion...even happened!"

"Young lady!" mom insisted demandingly as though, she'd had, some kind of I'm putting my thing down" attitude happening for her.

"In case," you "haven't noticed, Heather Lynn!" Mom insisted accusing by. "You lost all rights to just blow this conversation off like, it'd never even taken place. The second you decided to start treating me. Like some kind of, immature child!"

"No mom! I haven't!" I insisted defensively. "You're the one who's wrong! Where as I, for example. Am the person who's "trying" to, walk away from it!"

"Which, basically means. That the concept of, me pretending this conversation has, never even taken place. Doesn't bother me in the least!"

"While you, for example," I continued sarcastically. "Look like, you head is about to, self-distrust. Right off your shoulders!"

"Heather Lynn!" mom interrupted demandingly. In what'd "very rapidly" began shifting from an ora of, the extremely irritating. To what'd quickly end up being, like. An even "more" intolerable method of, the same fashion, "I demand an apology and I want it...Right now!"

"No, mom! I interrupted angrily. I refuse to except the blame or responsibility. For things I haven't done!"

"In other words, mom! That's just "not" going to happen! So, deal with it already...I did!"

"Young lady!" mom insistently as though, she'd been the one. Whom just had the level of intelligence purposely insulted and undermined.

"Since you seem to think that, this little conversation we're having," she continued insistently, "Is such a big joke." "Well, mother!" I interrupted even more defensively than before. "It looks like you're wrong again! Because, if what you're saying. Were in any way, shape or form true and this particular conversation. Even held the slightest bit of, an amusing quality to it. I'd be laughing in your face...right now!"

"But, since I'm not! Well, you get the idea!"

"Heather Lynn!" mom demanded like, she'd still held the upper hand, in the leverage department. "If that's how you really feel. About participating in a mere "casual conversation" exercise with me!"

"Then I guess, I'll just have to exercise. My authority as, your mother! By relinquishing any rights you may've thought you'd held. Towards determining it's outcome! How do you like, that idea missy?"

"Well, mom!" I answered impatiently." Although, I've never so much as, "once" assumed. That neither, me, myself and I'd actually held any form of control over this specific conversation, your attitude alone, does allow me to confirm that, this theory. Is pretty much of, the mutual between us! Next accusation, please!"

"Young Lady!" mom remarked offensively. "How dare you speak to me. In either, that tone of voice or fashion! I'm your mother and I insist upon, being treated. With a little bit of respect. In fact, I'm demanding it!"

"Therefore," she continued sternly. "The only thing your little butt better be doing right now. Involves it sitting itself back down in that chair and apologizing. For it's ignorant behavior towards me. Like immediately if not sooner! Do we understand each other young lady?"

"Yes, mother." I replied irrelatively. "Both myself and my little butt as, you put it. Can hear you just fine!"

"But," I continued, "unlike yourself, for example. I refuse to allow myself to be, intimidated. Into, apologizing you saying something that, I'd clearly meant!"

"What's the matter, Heather Lynn?" mom implied tauntingly. "Are you too proud to, just admit when you're wrong?"

"No, mother! I'm not!" I replied defensively. "In fact, contrary to what I'm sure that, you'd prefer I'd believed. I refuse to go around asking for any kind of forgiveness. For making a decision. In which, I'm perfectly comfortable with. Before it even leaves my mouth!"

Well even though, I couldn't resist the urge to, give it a good whirl. The act of relying on my usual "Nod of reassurance" maneuver. After quoting a statement like that. Just didn't seem to be, enough. To surface the fully self-made, image crazed, authoritative figure routine.

In which, mom'd clearly needed at her disposal. Before she would hold the "final say." When it came to, how she'd seen it destined to end!

Then suddenly, from what'd seemed like, out of no where. What had at first, only felt as though, it, was just another replay of, mom's scolding routine. Turned into more of, an immediate attempt. To pass the blame from "how badly" our "casual conversation" exercise was going. Off on me!

With mom trying to, twist my words around. Like she was proceeding to expose them as being, not of the "straight up" truth.

Which is basically, when the infamous "For my eyes only" files. Became, part of the conversation.

So, just as, I'd silently predicted two years earlier. After I'd finished enlightening her to, the details. That I'd alone, held the capability of witnessing. The next words out of, mom's mouth were.

"Heather Lynn!" she exclaimed angrily. "Do you even have any idea as to exactly how ridiculous, you're sounding right now?"

"Hey, mom!" I replied defensively. "In case, you haven't been paying any attention. I don't really care as to, how ridiculous you may think it sounds! Because, just like, everyone else on this planet. You also have the right to your own opinions!"

"Besides," I continued suggestively. "When it comes down to it mom. It really doesn't matter if you're fond of it's terms or not! Because, what you'd prefer I'd believed. Won't come close to either, trumping or making. Anything I'm about to, tell you. Any less true!"

"However," I continued impatiently. "If you may find yourself in, any way, shape or form. Feeling as though, learning the truth from my perspective. Is becoming a little "too much" for you to handle."

"Then perhaps, you should start looking into investigating. New approaches for acquiring answers, such as, the "I'm minding my own freaking business" method...for example!"

"Heather Lynn!" mom interrupted offensively, "I was there the day you got hit and what you're claiming to have witnessed...Never Happened!"

"Yes, mother! I replied defensively. "I know you were there!" I continued hintingly. "But, if you remember correctly. So were a lot "of, other people and accosting to, my perspective."

"Which was apparently, a lot better than yours! Unlike, yourself and everyone else's concerning it. These details ran a lot deeper than what was visible at, face value!"

"OK, Heather Lynn!" mom interrupted with this, "I'm trying to jerk you around" tone of voice. Which, in my case. Was a pitch I'd only hear. When mom was trying to make me feel either, foolish or at fault.

"Heather Lynn," she began scolding. "If what you've claimed to have witnessed was real. Then how come you're the only person. Whom has so much as hinted towards the idea of, seeing it?" Mom asked as though, she'd actually thought. I'd made the "whole story "up" all along.

"Mom!" I explained frustratedly. "No, I may not've found the secret mystery it holds yet! But, trust me I will and I have absolutely no intensions of halting. Any investigations towards learning this answer. Until, I do!"

"Heather" mom insisted reluctantly. "If you're really feeling that, determined to learn. The details about, what'd happened on the afternoon of, 3/12/74. Then fine, I'll tell you!"

"Young lady," she began hesitantly. "You were in shock from being, hit by a car! So, there's absolutely no way what-so-ever" that, you could've seen. Any of those things! It was just your mind playing tricks on you!"

"I mean, for Good Lords sake, Heather Lynn!" She continued disapprovingly. "Why is that "so difficult" for you to comprehend?"

But even though, as I've already stated previously. It'd eventually, end up changing my entire objective as to, "how" I'd felt. I should try to regain control over a dwindling conversation.

While being, "forcibly" trapped inside a world. That was rapidly becoming, one without the foundation of any!

After I'd attempted to, heavily humor my mother's request. By politely introducing her to, the actual depth of, her "shallow minded" misconceptions. With a sharp "virtual" slap in the face "reality check.

Which, according to my observations of mom's reactions to it. She was neither, prepared for or cared to here. Not to mention, managed to cause. Quite an extensive amount of "emotional stress." In a "very short" time.

When mom attempted to, twist my words around like, she was on a quest. To expose the "hidden secrets" lurking within me. As some kind of, fabricated lie I'd made up.

For the sole purpose of, trying to make her. Look like, some woman whom, couldn't control her child. It didn't take me long to realize that, my assistance… wasn't required!

"Young lady!" mom exclaimed disapprovingly as though, she was positive. That any thing she had to say. Would be enough to, sway the odds back into, her favor!

"Heather Lynn!" mom exclaimed insistently. "Don't you so much as think that, I'm going to be willing! To just, let this subject drop! Especially, after what you've told me!"

"Well, mother," I interrupted frustratedly. "I was hoping! But rest assured. I can both, hear and understand your choice of, words so vividly. That I'm actually starting to, get a "migraine headache" from, listening to them!"

Besides, even if I wasn't "completely sure" as to, how I should react. When mom first started trying to grill me. With her lame interrogation tactics. Before, our so called "casual conversation" exercise was over. I really "wouldn't care" either!

So in hopes that, I wouldn't. Just end up revealing something else. That'd only get me in even "more trouble. Than I apparently…already was!

I decided to take a slightly different route. By describing exactly what kind of, "big impression." Her lame, completely out of line request and behavior as, a result. Had portrayed for itself from, my perspective.

To tell the truth. It was like trying to repair, an average every day care of, "a seriously bruised" ego on, her part. With nothing more than a band aid that…didn't fit!

"OK, Heather Lynn." mom continued like, "she'd" held the only "ace" in the desk. "I want you to explain to me. Exactly what "you" think the sole purpose of, us having this conversation is, "based on. Then, in return. I'll tell you what "I" think but, can't prove!"

So, while being careful "not to," arouse any unwanted suspicions. That mom could either, hold or try to, use against me. I attempted to, inconspicuously shift the room's atmosphere. Back into, what she'd tried to portray as being, a "casual" type of mode.

By saying the words, "Mom, I have absolutely "no idea" as to, what your problem with me is. But, please!" I mentioned optimistically, "Feel free to correct me if I'm wrong!"

Something in which, I already know that, I'm not! Then again, since you're the woman who's always steering the importance of, telling the truth. Yea,! I suppose, I can make an exception!"

"Yes, Heather Lynn!" mom replied anxiously. "But, I'm failing to recognize the connection. Between, how what you're saying, relates to it!"

"Well," I continued with an ever-growing hint of sarcasm in my voice. "Mom, I really hate to be, the one. Whom, puts the damper on your, "supposed victory" for you."

"But at least, in this case, whether you care to believe it or not. May seem like, it's completely of, the irrelevant! Irrelevant! Not to mention nothing to do with what you're insisting upon, us disgusting!"

"Is that right?" mom remarked curiously as though, somewhere in the back of her mind. She'd somehow managed to, construct a "self-fantasized" image of it's circumstances. That'd practically handed her the ability. To comprehend "whatever answer" I'd come up with. From within a level of intelligence. That didn't require any form of consideration to mine.

"However," I persisted in interest of portraying it's full illusion. As politely and within her range of grasp as possible.

"Now that, I've taken the liberty of removing. The burden of it's suppressed wright from my shoulders. I think we should take a few seconds to reveal and review. The depth of the "hidden terms" lieing deeply within our so called, "casual conversation" exercise."

"But since my own suspicions of your allowance for it's limitations. Has just been pushed beyond your concept of rational plausabilities."

"Then perhaps, we should start off with something a "little less" of the complicated. Such as, why you keep insisting upon, making me out to be, nothing more or less. Than, just a liar...for example!"

"Therefore," I continued irritatedly, "Since, other than the fact that, your version of it's terms, sounds like, it's of the "incredibly stupid and lame from my perspective. I can't help butts, wonder. What's wrong with this picture mom? Go ahead...I'm listening!"

So, of course, when my mother refused to, offer up. Her usual supply of "unwanted" input for" conversational purposes. Something in which, as I've already explained. Was a definite rarity with her.

I decided to try and start the conversation off. With a "very distinct" description consisting of, exactly what I'd witnessed taking place. Between the timeline of 3:30 and 3:35 pm on, 3/12/74. From "my side of, the fence!

Heck, maybe I should've slung mom along for, a few more minutes. Before, trying to submit her to, the wrath of, it's "straight up" honesty. Or, even better yet as to, it's extent! But, I didn't!

"OK, mother!" I began sarcastically. "In case, your haven't been paying any attention. Your "seriously" poor excuse for a "casual conversation" exercise. Keeps tipping all the odds of, success in this matter. Back into, my favor!"

While, I may've just been judging from, my own personal fantasies. As they were in, "The actual seasons of, coming together. An insight of which, no one else apparently held access to.

The only thing I'd actually, manage to achieve. By choosing to humor moms overly annoying request to add her "creative criticism" into, the picture.

Would involve, a sudden amplification within it's, "Non-visible" ora. Which, belonged to something, I'd already "socially designated" to be, from another "highly uncomfortable" situation.

But, even with everything I'd had, going down around me. Whatever amount of, stray leverage and odds that, it may've managed to acquire. During it's "temporarily dormant" state.

It would immediately, if not sooner. Take a turn for, the worst. When it's so called collection of, intolerable intenseness. Took the liberty of, doing the same.

By upgrading it's state's to, what's better known as, a "formal interrogations" mode. Making everything I'd either, "accidentally learned" or "previously treasured" as, "vital inside" information. About, what were still "very much unknown standards.

Which would not only, require assistance from those. Of whom could properly evaluate exactly, "how well and in what condition. The miscellaneous secrets it'd held locked within it. Could be retrieved and decoded.

Not to mention, finding whatever proof of, it's existence. That it'd purposely left behind. Without arousing any suspicions of it's presence. For my mom or anyone else to investigate.

Yea. I suppose, the theory itself. May've sounded a little "too" difficult and complicated to, pull off. When, it was really, a lot more like, performing a "last minute" task.

That I would've sworn only required following. A few "relatively simple" rules to, make work!

All in, which. I'd find myself "Not being" either, qualified or prepared. To deal with! Such as...

1.) Having to reveal the secrets. I'd "mistakenly" learned about. On the afternoon that, all of it's "Bull Crap," was actually in the process of, going down!

2.) Trying to get my mother to, take me seriously. After I'd told her the "straight up truth" or to, what I'd witnessed on 3/12/74. That, "no one" else...did!

3.) Enduring the repetition of "stress endured, panic attacks. That ironically enough, only emphasized the reasons as to, how and why. My mother'd felt if, it were to ever become, exposed. This information, would absolutely and totally destroy her social statis. With the "communities" eyes!

And of, course...

4.) Making sure I'd kept very close tabs. An what'd by, everyone else's standards. Suring by been dismissed as, insignificant, stray or non-verbal gestures. That'd never even takes place.

With nothing more than, "unprovable, step by step" observations I'd made. On the afternoon we'd "accidentally," crossed each others paths. As, back up!

Such as, the kind you might encounter and I've only noticed to, come in handy. When you find yourself in, a position. Where there are no other options but to, deal with.

What'd recently became more like, a newly acquired talent for "unpredictedly" picking up on. Something as slight as, the changes people'd "unknowingly" portray. With nothing more than, this "tell signs" or "behavioral patterns"...for example!

But even though, this had been something that, they've never failed to, act upon. Either, before the conversation itself had even started. Or, even better yet. Been declared to be, "officially" over with.

I'd noticed as soon as, my mother'd stepped up. To actually, pup herself and perform. Her usual "poor excuse" for an, "I'm miss completely and "totally is, control of everything" routine.

That anything she may've so much as, tried to proclaim. To be what'd "originally," awarded her the right. Not to mention, the required amount of, power and authority. To manipulate my mind at random. Until, she was convinced that, I'd no longer cared or believed. The "Hard Cold" facts about, a subject. That I'd learned through, good old fashioned "personal experience"...does exist!

Would "almost" immediately, if...Not Sooner!

Make it's attempt to, shift the dining rooms "over all" dike. From one that'd so far. Only been able to, project. The ora of it's presence to me. Though a realm of, repetitious "bad dreams." That'd managed to, get away with "inconsprinlously" haunting and following me around. For the past two years of, my life!

To another that, even if it was only done in, "complete secrecy." Wouldn't require the IQ of, a "freaking genus." To walk down the exact same "way too familiar" but, "Non-Visible" path.

I'd accidentally, stumbled across and learned to except. As a "permanently irresolvable" issue in, my world. Ones it'd been "officially," set into motion.

But even though, my mother just didn't strike me as being, as gifted. I myself have never failed to rely on, the "simplest privileges." It'd neglectfully, left behind you "further investigational" purposes. When searching for a sense of, refuge or satisfaction.

Such as, my recently acquired talent for either, ignoring or temporarily blowing off. Mom's usual assortment of, the "overly annoying, But of, the completely worthless efforts. To trick my nine year old berth.

Into, foolishly giving up "highly classified" information. Concerning a sequence of, recent events. That I'd taken extra care to, hide deeply within. The darkest cavities of, my mind.

I mean, yea! I may've only been in, the "single digits." But, I wasn't blind!

Plus, judging by my own personal observations of, it's circumstances. Especially, after being forced to watch my mother's "overly dramatic" exhibition of, tell signs and trust me! They were definitely of, those being made. Within..."snatching distance!"

It'd still only leave me with, just enough room. To investigate the one "plausible comparison." That even comes close to, offering a "slight," form of simulation. As to "What it was like to, ride out, on a "first hand" basis for...the "second time!"

You know, for the sake of, "literary purposes!"

"Therefore, other than the annoying distinctions being, the "biggest problem." I'll never be able to, get over. Exactly, "how fast" it's rate of probability. Would permit me to predict as to, "whether or not." My mother'd even be qualified enough to, "fully comprehend," what the resurrection of, it's hidden details..."really meant!"

Let alone, juggle the up coming magnificence of, the consequences. That'd await its unrevealed statistics. Until they'd finally come off as, sounding. A lot more like, a "ruff interpretation. On...her part!

Which, she'd kept insisting upon, focusing towards me. Or, the how's and why's that'd seemed to, fuel her disturbing effort to, "Not stop." What she'd already taken the time to, start!

By trying to intimidate the likes of, me. Into believing that, she was the "only person" on, the "planet Earth." Of whom, held any power or authority. To decide if, "What she'd attempted to portray as, our little "casual conversation" exercise. Was worthy of, pursuing "further investigations."

Or, even better yet. Being forced to sit there and listen. As my mother gave herself the liberty of, "blurting out." A more advanced version as to, exactly "why and how much." My mother "almost" despised to, the point of fearing. The whole idea of, having her "self-fantasized "social statis.

Completely overrun with people. Who'd have absolutely no problem "What-So-Ever." Either, treating, gawking at or, talking about. "The woman with, the "incompetently crazed" daughter. Just to, mess with..."her head!"

And

Why I'd regret it. If so much as, one spree of, "what we'd discussed. Where to accidentally, reach someone else's ears!

But hey, don't get me wrong! Because her "childish" inhibition of, "clumsy flaws." Would end up working to, my advantage. Before, it was over!

Which is when, I decided to, give myself the "unrequested" liberty of, nudging. The conversation that, she'd alone. Insisted upon, us having.

Even one step closer to, "where I didn't want." But, clearly needed to be.

Before, I could begin enlightening my mother's "shallow minded" potential. For obtaining and submitting a rational thought. Beyond the capacity of, "what taken place in, "plain right." But, had only been made visible. For my eyes only...to view!

With a few of my own personal insights. As these so called, "unexpected events." Fell into, play around me. From within a realm of, perspective. That'd struck me as being, within "another person's body."

Which is when, my mother decided to, break the "5 minute long" silence.

But since, I "didn't" quite know how to respond. Especially, when her already "absurd attitude" towards this "specific subject." Got even more intense. With the question as to, "whom I'd thought I was...I didn't!

"Heather Lynn Jensen!" she'd out right demanded offensively. "How dare you try to, belittle my "level of intelligence. With a screwed up, fabricated lie!"

"Personally," she continued angrily. "I've always had you pegged as being, a lot smarter than that! I mean, how stupid do you think I am any way?"

Although, there is a "pretty good" rate of, probability. That only a "Sci-Fi" author them self. Would've considered this as, holding any kind of potential.

The action itself, had "already" started and with their "Not-being, an alternative in handy! I decided to, make an exception!

"Mom!" I interrupted defensively. "I really don't care as to, how your seeing this. Because, when it comes down to, how I feel. About, us having this conversation? I'm good!

"In fact," I continued impatiently. "As you as, I'm concerned? Well, you can "believe" whatever you want!"

"Just remember that unlike, yourself and apparently. Everyone else who was there but, didn't see anything! I actually, know the truth. About, what'd really happened on the afternoon of, 3/12/74.

"Then again!" I remarked sarcastically. "If knowing the truth, I just "too much" for you to handle. I guess I'm left with no other choice but to except. Your "intellectual limitations...As is."

"Look, Heather Lynn!" Mom explained defensively. While preparing to step in and salvage. Whatever she'd felt may've been left of, her "Improperly Executed technic." For "Routine interrogations!"

"Heather Lynn!" mom remarked angrily. "I don't know what you're "freaking problem" is! But, whether or not you're willing to except. What I'm telling you as being, true? Well, that's your case...Not Mine!"

"However, just so you know. There are always "two sides" to, everything!"

"So, with that thought in mind." My mom continued blamingly. "Once alls been said and done. Well, I guess it's outcome. Really depends on, how you'd prefer this set of, problems. To resolve them self. Don't you think?"

"But, now that you've been made aware of, the "Basic Circumstances." That'll surround this "so called" disturbed theory of, yours. Let's just go ahead and take a few minutes. To review the their consequences...Shall we?"

In fact, I can't even remember the exact combination of words. She'd used to, end my refusal to, break under pressure. But, I think the interesting part about, them. Lied within how easily." I'd immediately, if...Not Sooner!

Recognize them as sounding like, she'd actually knew. What the heck, she was talking about. But, the expression on her face and in, her voice. Clearly said otherwise! Allow me to explain...

1.) She continued annoyingly. "There's the fabrication of, what've you've claimed to have witnessed. On the afternoon of, 3/12/74."

"In which, according to your statement. Is when you'd supposedly, stood right there. In the middle of, "Washington Street." Watching as, all of these events. Proceeded to, fall into, play around you."

From, and here's the most ridiculous part. Within the realm of, "Another persons" body!"

"Now, tell me something, Heather Lynn." Mom remarked concededly. "If what you're trying to claim, was in any way, shape or form. Even close to, being true. Then why hasn't anyone else in town. So much as, hinted towards the idea of, seeing it?"

"All yea," she continued determinedly. "Then there's also, my and apparently, everyone else's opinion!"

"Which, by the way," Heather Lynn! "Mom insisted as though, she'd alone. Held the upper hand to, it's outcome." Is 100%...for real!

"In other words, and I'm not going to say this again, Heather Lynn!" Mom remarked disapprovingly. "What you're claiming to have witnessed. Is not now and never was. Anything more or less than, a mere "figment of, your imagination!"

"I mean, for "Good Lord's" sake, Heather Lynn! Why can't you just admit it. When you're wrong?"

Well even though, I eventually, did manage to, somehow find a way. To establish a certain "Ironic" form of, amusement Locked within my mother's, "Non-challant," Ironic, type of attitude.

This particular procedure alone. Would also create, a "settle and inconspicuously" developed to mask. My insights and knowledge as to, her "true intensions. It'd only hold out for, a little while. Especially, when she'd tried to end. My "so called," refusal to break under it's pressure!"

"Now," Mom continued by lecturing me as though, she'd "actually," been there. To experience or, view the impact it'd left behind. On the afternoon that, "all Hell broke loose. Amongst the streets of, "Nuvell, Wiva!"

"Since, I've already made the effort to discuss. Whatever's been bothering you in, a mature, adult fashion. Without success, I must add!"

"An idea in which, by the way. I believe would've worked just fine. If you could've at least, managed to find it within yourself...to cooperate!"

"However," she insisted in her usual, "I'm the judge, jury and executioner" tone of voice. Because, you'd much rather treat me like, I'm a complete idiot! Instead of, your mother! I'm going to go ahead and get straight to, the point!

I mean, yea! I suppose this may've been my mother's way of trying. To pass off her "non-validated" words of wisdom. As something that'd been done in..."An authoritive manner.

But, unlike her...I knew better!

So, the hard she'd push me to, confess to, telling a lie. The easier it'd get to, coax out. Her "true" inner fears" as to, how our little conversation. Would turn out to, reveal them!

"Young Lady! Whom do you think you're talking to?" Mom demanded as though, the act of my humming. Her persistence to, "Not mind" her own "freaking business. When it came to learning the "Straight up" truth. About a subject I'd managed to, keep to myself. For the past "two" years!

The only difference was that, this time. What she'd "previously claimed" would stay "strictly" between us. Would turn out to be, nothing more than a "mere lie." On...her part.

When mom tried to, assure me of, fabricating. From right off the top of, my head! So, I could insult her "level of, intelligence...For fun!

"Well, Heather Lynn!" Mom continued in, what'd now. Elevated itself to, a "more demanding" tone of voice." Since, you're "clearly not" intelligent enough, to care. Exactly where your "poor excuse" for a "seriously bad" joke is leading."

"Not to mention, how big of hole you're digging for yourself! Let alone, the rest of, the family! It doesn't mean that, I don't!"

"In fact, Heather Lynn!" she continued. As she'd attempted to, sway. The purpose for us, having this conversation. Back towards her own needs. With the words, "How you even so much as, considered. How badly this line of, "Bull Crappolla," would effect my standing, within the eyes of, the community? Or, don't you care about that, either?"

"But, hey!" mom added degradingly, "If you're really that, anxious. To have a bunch of, strange people. Whom, are all wearing "white cants. Come and lash your phyco butt up for being, "Mentally incompetent."

"Well, Heather Lynn! That's your case!" she remarked snidely. Just don't expect me to, stop them from doing, their jobs! Go ahead...I dare you!"

Which brings me to, the second time. In a matter of, ten minutes. That I'd actually thought that, my mother's head. Was about to, hit...a "self-destruction" mode.

Besides, even with my holding an, "unlimited access." To whatever personal observations. I'd gathered along the way to, "draw my conclusions" from.

I'll never get over how deeply mom's "sick sense of priorities." In other words, what she'd referred to as being, her "are in the hole" card. Ran!

When in, reality. It was just her way of, trying to unforce. Whatever may've been left of, her useless efforts. By trying to, make me feel, ashamed of myself. For bringing details to, the table. That were just "Too Big" for, her smug little butt. To grasp, ahold of!

So, when I just, downright refused to, contribute anymore "verbal input. To what'd already turned into, quite the "colorful conversation" piece.

Mom attempted to, give my "unspoken" words. Another nudge to, the surface. With a sudden performance of, what had to have been. The worst preaching session of, lies that, I've ever heard. In, my life! About, how my carelessness to, obey the rules. To what I like to, call. "My mother's poor excuse for owning an "intimidation" band wagon!

But, since it'd "already" grown. "Way too" late. For either, the likes of, my mother's "half-wit" theories. Or, anyone else's for, that, matter, of whom, seemed cursed with a less than imaginative. Range of, mental boundaries.

To step up and claim responsibility for performing a, last minute rave "maneuver. Something in which, at the time. I was "barely," dangling from!

A lot of things that, I'd noticed it to, "previously involve." Would beg in to, change!

While, even if I was, the only person. To, acknowledge it's area of, perspective. There will "always" be, a big difference. Between the idea of, just having to tolerate. The self-made guess work. That'd leave mom slinging "False Accusations" as to, what was "really" going on. In, the wrong direction....fast!

The concept of, "Not being" able to politely share. This little "tid bit" of, information. With...society!

What it'd took to, protect the "unrevealed answers. I'd unexpectedly acquired on, the afternoon of, 3/12/74. By way of, the "For my eyes only" files. As they'd literally, fell into play..."around me!"

Trying to keep what I'd knew, about the "doctored" information amongst, their contuse. To mom wouldn't get the "Not-So-Brilliant" idea.

To submerge her "unwelcomed" level of, curiosity. Any deeper into what would've surely put. "The antics of, "Mr. Wyle E. Cajote" himself... to shame!

As she'd attempted to, swallow of, the "abstract" details. Pertaining to a subject that, I'd. Had absolutely, "No intension" in, sharing, with either, her or anyone use! But, she'd felt the need to, know..."Anyway!"

Tolerating what she was now. Attempting to, portray as being, done. In the form of, a "casual exercise."

Keeping a "very class" tales on, how far. My mother was, willing to go. To make things happen.

Her efforts to make my agreement to, cooperate. With mom's "blind request" for answers. Sound like, a "foolish conspiracy. Designed by, "yours truly."

My referral to so much as, suggest. The existence of, my suspicions. Towards mom's "reckless actions" as, a result.

The theory of, my being forced to participate in one. Practically coming to a scratching halt. In the matter of, twenty minutes...tops!

If I would've in, anyway known. What was destined to, happen next. I would've let my mom provoke it from it's lair..."Alot sooner!"

Here's my recollection as to, how. It worked itself out!

"Heather Lynn Jensen!" Mom exclaimed. As though, she'd had me in, a partition. Where I'd actually, needed. The assistance of her "so called" wisdom, input and opinion. Before, I could even begin to, form my own!

Or even better yet! To decide how much I'd absolutely, despised. The idea of, having to either, listen to or tolerate. Mom's less than of, the "accurate" lectures. About, performing an oversize that, I'd been reassured. Was to be conducted in, a "casual styled nature."

"What the heck is your problem anyway?" Mom asked frustratedly. "Or, "do you just "Natchear." How "incredibly" stupid you're making yourself sound right now? Because...I can!"

"I mean, hasn't your being, hit by a car? Already caused enough problems for "everyone else." To have to deal with?" Or, maybe your odd choice in, behavioral patterns." Is really just your way of, surfacing your craving for more...I get it."

Which, beings me to the challenge of, trying to decipher. How mom'd felt "Mother Daughter" bonding rituals. Were supposed to be, conducted.

I mean, yea! There may've been "two ways of, interpreting them..."hers and mine."

"But, with myself "Not being" in, any position or mood. To just blindly drop all of the insights. I'd acquired during round one. Into, someone else's lap for...further investigational purposes.

It wouldn't take me "very long." To reach the conclusion that, everything I'd originally grasped. As something that'd been made "conveniently" invisible. To everyone else but, me. Had finally, reached it's "kicking point!"

Leaving me with no other options but to, reschedule. A "semi-virtual" performance of, it's..."True Colors!"

No! I may've never had luck at either, "randomly or, otherwise. Salvaging even the tiniest flicker of, rationality. That'd so much as, came close to, fulfilling. My basic needs in, this case.

Being able to, spontaneously, bring up. The "invalidated insights I'd witnessed on the afternoon of, 3/12/74. At the infamous table of, "Do's and don'ts" lists.

Or,

Finding a plausible form of, reasoning. To support my own suspicions as to, what I'd "strongly" believed. Deserved a formal introduction. To my mom's "highly inaccurate" concept of, what is and isn't...first!

By reminding her of, all the details that'd concerned. Our "whatever was said between us. Stays between us"...type of, deal. Like...

1.) As to, why. No matter how of, the abstract or absurd. My words either, may or may not've came off as, sounding. She could in no way, shape or, form use then. As an excuse to, cheat me out of, my "God Given" right. To speak my piece...in full!

   Without being, "rudely" interrupted by, her flawed sense of, input. In either, mid-sentence or otherwise.

2.) My "one-sided" evaluation as to, how fast and far. Mom was willing to let her "inner fears" grow.

3.) How they'd end up "consuming" her. Before, she'd even have the chance. To introduce them back into, our discreetly made discussion. As being, something else!

4.) The fine print to, our "previously made" mental agreement. That been added to, protest it!

As for, what it was like. To have every second of, a conversation. That I'd been led to, believe. Was nothing nothing more than, an innocent "casual conversation" exercise.

Immediately, ripped from your grasp. By one's own mother's inability to, control her "foolish" obsession. With putting the "precious" standing of, her "ego-infested" minds "social statis."...above mine! From my side of, the infamous "Do's and Don'ts" lists table?

Well, interestingly enough. This just so happens to be, one more. Amongst, the "never ending" pile of, the several. Still yet to, come!

But, hey! As long as, you're willing to, ask them. Not only am I the perfect person to, verify their answers.

I'll be doing it. Using exact same sequence of, events. This "non-revealed, straight up "and non-vocalized" version. That'd only been made visible through, "My eyes." On the afternoon of, 3/12/74.

All in which, I'd. Thanks to a rather "small" portion of, "solitude" on, the side. Still hold "free access" both, "to and from!" Every time I was forced to relive it's "emotional and physical" trauma. By way of, my dreams!

Now, just for fun. Let's get back to, antilizing our discussion. About, whatever was left of, our "casual conversation" exercise. Such as, the little argument I'd used. To close it...for example!

"Hey, Mom!" I blurted out angrily. "Please "feel free" to, correct me if, I'm wrong! Something in which. I've already learned through, "Good old fashioned" personal experience. That..."I'm Not!"

If it hadn't been for your "less than of, the brilliant" idea to, have one. We wouldn't even be having this "pathic" conversation. In the first place! No, mom! The blame for that, one. Lies solely on, your head...enjoy!"

"Yes, Heather Lynn!" Mom insisted scoldingly. "It does! But, if you didn't want us to, have this conversation. Then why did you agree to, go along with it?"

"Well, mom." I continued frustratingly. "Maybe it's because, you wouldn't shut up about, it. Until, I did!

But, now that we've confirmed the as to, why it'd started. I was just wondering if you'd care to, explain. What'd inspired it?"

Or, even bitter yet. Why I've just spent the past "25 minutes" of, my life. Listening to you "rant and rave." Because, you can't handle the idea of, how an "imaginary" problem. From our supposed, "discreetly made" conversation. Might make you look! Within the eyes of, the community... for nothing!"

"NO, Heather Lynn!" mom interrupted concededly. "I don't! But, as far as, I'm concerned. You definitely owe me one!"

"OK, mom! Have it your way! I'm sorry that, no matter how many times, you may attempt to, accuse me of being, one. I'm neither, a fool or, a narcissistic liar! So, don't expect my "straight up" answers...To change!

Heather Lynn Jensen! mom interrupted in, a "tone of voice". That'd definitely, struck me as being, an undeniably fake. "How dare you question the level of, my intelligence" pitch.

But, hey! Even though, I did find myself being, stunned. When she'd settled down enough, to acknowledge. How rapidly her lame two - bet act had changed. When the amount of, incompetence it clearly, gave off. Would reveal her "True intensions. Every time she'd attempt to, portray them. As us having a "casual" discussion.

"Heather Lynn!" mom began with a somewhat "calmer", tone of voice. "I'm just merely trying to, point out. That we're talking about, a time. When your mind wasn't exactly, at the top of, it's game."

"Which is why, I'm having such, a problem. With the idea of, believing. That anything you're saying during it. As actually, holding some kind of, "substantial tenth" to it!"

"I mean," she continued with a certain amount of, "sarcastic doubt in, her voice. "Why can't you just admit that, the only reason you're fabricating this huge lie. Is to, get attention towards yourself and to, be...done with it!"

"Well, mother!" I remarked defensively. "Maybe it has something to, do. With the fact that, I'm "not" living!"

"Besides!" I insisted angrily. "What in the heck, gives you the authority to interrogate me? About a subject that neither, you or anyone else. Was even capable of, seeing?"

"However," I continued sarcastically. "If you feel that, I may've revealed something. During, our "so called" discussion that, may seem like. It's just a little "too much for you to, wrap your head around.""

"Then perhaps, you should consider the idea of, investigating new approaches. For gathering "inside information on, your own!""

"You know, through little things. Like minding your own freaking business. Instead of, consistently invading mine…for example!"

"Hey, Heather Lynn!" mom insisted as, she'd struggled to, again control. Over her "less than incompetent." Because, I'm the mom" line.

"Hey, mom!" I came back defensively. "Unlike, yourself, for example! I've always been "quite aware" of, the validity. Behind my findings!"

"In other words, mom." I remarked frustratingly. "I'll answer your "pathetically lame" questions. But, after that! I don't want to, ever find my self having to deal. With your poor excuse for, a "casual conversation exercise…again!""

"I mean, that's how you explained the likes of, this stupid conversation. To me…right?"

But, when my mother failed to, show. Any symptoms of, having so much as, one imidient comment. To send my way.

I decided to, salvage. What few seconds I could. By finishing my final statement to, mom. With…

"Hey, Mom! Whether you care to, except it is, your business! But, unlike yourself. I was actually, there to witness, a "full viewing of, these events. In more ways than, one!"

"While in, your case. There statements may sound a bit on, the rude side. It's basically, just a nice way of, saying. That while you were watching me "lie motionless" on, the pavement. Right in front of, you. I might add!"

"I was preparing myself to, endure. What you're trying to, insert. Was nothing more or, less. Than a merely fabricated, unworthy of, your attention lie. On, my part!"

"With a statement that, wouldn't've even taken place. If I'd hadn't stood right there and witnessed my hand. Passing right through the "EMT's" shoulder and out his chest!"

"Or, even better yet!" I replied even more angrily. "Why the whole thing had struck me as being, from within. The ora of, another persons body?"

"Now, tell me something mother. Can you say that?" I added intimidatively. "Because, I can!"

"Hey, Mom!" I added in, what was now. More than just an, "overly sarcastic tone of, voice." Up until, today! I wouldn't've so much as, considered telling you, or, any one else for that, mother! About, this on, my best day!"

"But since, we're already standing on, this "particular subjects doorstep. I'd just like to, remind you. That us, having this pathetic "casual conversation" exercise. Was your of, the "less than brilliant" idea!"

"Plus, with this being, an activity. That I've personally, never held, any "previous" interests. In, playing along with! I've grown quite sick of listening to you. Try to, sling your "Bull Crappola" lines. Like you actually know. What in, the heck. You're talking about!"

"Which is why, I believe that, it's now my turn. To phyco-anlilize whatever "behavior patterns." That you've unconsciously unveiled to, me. Along, the way!

"In other words, mother!" I continued impatiently. "I may not have any idea as to, what kind of, problem. My answers will create in, your world. But, it's portraying itself as, a freaking "spaytard attack"...in mine!"

"Besides, I'm sick of, getting in trouble. Because, you can't digest. The straight up, no holds barred, truth. About, my answers!"

I mean, just deal with it already! I did! Then again, unlike, yourself. I really wasn't given much of, a choice either! Now, was I?"

But, my mother refused to, offer up. What I've learned to consider as being, a verbal or otherwise reply.

I knew I'd had "no other" option but to, start my "closing argument. Before, Mrs. "caught dead in her teacher. Could sway the current terms of, the "Do's and Don'ts" list table. Back in, her own favor!

"Mom, if your as smart as, you think you are. You'll take my advice, while, it's still a workable option! Because, trust me, This conversation is one mistake! That'll never happen again!

"Heather Lynn!" mom interrupted as though, she was making preparations, to run with an of, the abstract poker bluff. If you have something worthy of, saying. Then, do it now! Because, I'm extremely sick of, listening, to your "bull crap" lies!" "Hey, mother! If you remember correctly, I already did!"

"Then, tell me something, Heather Lynn!" Mom came back intimidatively. "If what your telling me is true! Then why hasn't "anyone else" mentioned witnessing it?"

"Because even though, I can only speak for myself!" She continued frustratingly. I'm pretty sure if someone else had seen anything! That'd so much as, came close to being, similar. They would've said something… yourself?"

"Hey, Mom!" I shouted defensively. In case you haven't noticed! I really don't give a happy "doodily flick" as to, what you think! Because, your self infatuated theories. Aren't worth two "died flies," to a "starving spider" in, my world!"

"No! I may not've been given an actual excuse. To explain my choice of, behavior…during it!"

"Plus, even though just the idea of, keeping, whatever's been said between us on, the download! I've been packing this big secret deeply inside me. Since, age seven and a half!

I've been forced to relieve the magnificence of, it's pain every day. By way of, my dreams! In other words, mother! Right now, I'm more concerned with it's outcome! Or perhaps, I should say, How it's just as much of, a mystery to, me. As it is you!

In other words, every time you insist upon, stealing. The unwelcomed privilege of, sticking your nose! Into, what's clearly, none of your freaking business to, start with…conversation over!"

But even though, the act of, revealing it's "top secret details to, my mother. Did turn out to be, a little busier than, what I'd had it pegged for.

Apparently, it's to be, expected. When you chose to, reveal. This magnitude of, it's hidden details...Go figure!

PART I

CHAPTER THREE

"The day that, Time...Stood Still"

Two years later...

Although, it wouldn't stay that, way. For..."very long!"

Not unlike, our first very much "unexpected," crossing of paths. The morning of, 5/5/78. Would also seem as though it'd been destined to, become. "Just like, any other ordinary, day. In the life of, me.

Thanks to, the extremely, "rude awakening" I'd receive. From something I've come to recognize as being, my dormant companions. "Self-resurrection" ceremony.

My usual, "before school" routine. Would almost immediately, find itself being, disrupted and consumed. By certain "unresolved" issues that, my mother. Had clearly, "forbade" me to, talk about. Only, "two years" earlier.

I mean, yea! I suppose my mother's "one sided, grasping at straws routine. May've been enough to, give her piece of, mind. But, deep inside. I've always known that, it'd be back.

Just so it could have the privilege of, flaunting and revealing. What it'd evolved into. During it's state of, dormancy." By presenting me which, a second sequence of, events. That'd just like, our first encounter. Had the tendency to, exhibit symptoms of, "frequently" varying. As the sting from it's wrath. Once again, took the liberty of, playing itself out..."around me!"

Which is why, you might want to take a few seconds to, prepare yourself before, taking a "blind" stroll through, this line of terrain with me.

Because, whether you care to, believe it or not. As you're about to learn. There's a rather "big" difference between, the type of, occurrences.

In which, most people. Would just naturally, assume to be of, the "non-tramatical" enough for anyone. No matter, what age to, ride out alone.

And

The one I like to, refer to as being, my own personal interpretation of..."The Twilight Zone."

Which is why. I'd also like to, take a few seconds. To remind you of, exactly how easily. My last encounter with this type of, situation. Managed to "successfully," get away with executing. The simple feat of, passing itself off as being, nothing more or less.

Than any other screwed up, pain in the "butt" experience. That I'd for some reason or another. I'd still just couldn't seem to, forget.

But even though, from my

Had the tendency to, "frequently" vary. As the sting from it's wrath. Once again, took the liberty of, playing itself out..."around me."

Which is why, you might want to take a few seconds to, prepare yourself. Before, taking a stroll through, this line of terrain with me.

Because, whether you care to believe it or, not. There's a big difference between, the type of occurrences. That most people, would just naturally, assume. To be that of, the "non-tramatical enough, for anyone. No matter, what age to, ride out alone.

And

What I like to, refer to as being, my own personal interpretation of..."The twilight zone."

Which is why. I'd also like to, take a few seconds. To remind you of, exactly "how easily." This particular situation managed to, "successfully" get away. With executing the simple feat of, passing itself off as being, nothing more or less.

Than any other entirely screwed up, pain in the butt experience. That I'd for some reason or another, still just didn't seem to, forget.

But even though, from my perspective. Mom'd made it "quite obvious" as to, how she'd felt. About the worth of, her more than "flowed interpretation. Towards the statis

But even though, from my own of, perspective. I'd make all of, mom's "lame efforts" to, prove her little "temper tantrum" episode. More than "quite obvious" as to, where she'd stood.

When it came to, evaluating the between, now and then levels of doubt. That'd clearly, co-existed within mom's more than, flowed interpretation. Towards the standing of, our "brief" conversations "validity statis."

Just the idea of, having to ignore. All of the "snide remarks" she'd "readily" sent my way.

In hopes that, it alone, would be enough to, dismiss. Everything I'd told her during, our "so called" casual conversation exercise. As nothing more than merely, a "fabricated hallucination." That'd been conveniently prevailed. By the likes of, "my own" imagination.

Would be more than, enough to turn. Everything she'd attempted to, portray as being, a lie. Into, an excuse to watch "foolish" accusations. Back fire right in, her face. With...a vengeance!

Only, this time. Insisted of, having it's aftermath. Just leaving me hanging without answers. I'd practically, go out of, it's way and...then some!

To provide me with an, "even more" accessible "point of entry. To an officially, one sided and completely of, the disclosed insight. That no-one else held the capability of, acknowledging.

One that'd contrary to, popular belief. Came fully equip with an even more "pronounced" visual of where. I could at least, expect it's "unwelcomed" awakening ceremony to, lead me!

As for what kind of, reaction. This particular chapter would "provoke" from me. Once I'd realized as to, how many details. That "round two's" list of, events. Held the potential to provide me with as, a result?

Well, since everything I'd hesitantly" attempted to, discuss with "my mom. Had as, you're already aware. Ended with her trying to, make me out as being, "solely responsible. For provoking the "uncontained, self-induced" fear. That'd co-existed" within her but, she still wasn't willing to, admit to.

To the surface so it could send her self induced levels of paranoia straight through the freaking roof. During our first and last "casual conversation" exercise.

My mother's uncontrollable passion to "freely voice" her overall "foolish" opinions. Has never failed to give me an "unmistakable" vibe. That'd strongly suggested as to, exactly how much she'd despised. The thought of, dealing with might happen. If her social statis were to loose it's standing. Within the "communities eyes." Instead of, mine!

But even though, my mother'd voiced the strong level of, insistence she'd held. For me to, believe otherwise.

I wasn't responsible for failure. To account for the probability of, me not being, stupid or gullible enough. To buy into, the "art form" like, talent she'd developed.

To make herself sound as though, she'd held every right. To manipulate and intimidate me into, humoring. The more than, flawed and self-centered attitude she'd used. To portray it.

Heck, I'd hadn't so much as, been able to steal one full night's sleep. Without having my dreams being, literally overcome, infested, consumed and devoured. By the very same nightmare.

That'd not only come, go and display itself. With the exact same sequence and series of events. I'd witnessed happening on, 3/12/74. But, my footsteps leading up to them.

In hopes that, it'd be enough to, give her some form of, insight. That'd let her feel as though, she'd regained some kind of, control over something.

In which, most people would've just looked at. As "not being of, the unusual in, our case.

Now suddenly, after spending the past two years of, my life. Without having anyone so much as, ask me how I'd felt. About the idea of, having to endure. My mother's insistent preaching spirts. Just as, she could push her "irrational and inconclusive" theories. To the level of being, an unwritten law."

I'd find myself reassembling, decoding and possibly, resolving. The ever-growing maze of, mysteries. That'd "still" lied deeply within it's realm of, the "For my eyes only" secrets. Just to final myself coming up, "empty handed..."every time!"

From an angle of, perspective. That'd insisted upon, "consistently" presenting itself. As any other extremely relentless and frustrating existence. That'd only survived inside the realm of, "my own" "steel trap" mind.

Which, just made the previous "four years I'd spent. Trying to suddly shoo-off anyone". I'd so much as slightly, suspected as, showing. Any noticeable symptoms of, humoring my mothers "poor excuse. For a "what your "claiming" to have witnessed happening. On, the afternoon of, 3/12/74, was merely just a figment or fantasize hallucination." That'd been supplied by, a insult of, it's "traumatic event" line."

Although, it'd managed to, refrain from showing any visible signs of, coming close. To either, scrounging, finding or even accidentally, finding. Even a minutely, rational or logical theory. That'd either, give or explain to, me. Any reason to, doubt the significance and depth of, every detail, it'd reveal to, me. Let alone...everyone else?

Which made the act of, finding off my mother's "child like," urges. To risk relying on something as, stupid as, her unrefrainable desire. To silently gloat about, details. That she'd clearly, felt. Had given her complete and total control.

Over a blindly but, definitely willingly made assumption. That my mother attempted to, recreate as being, carried out, under the terms of, "strict disgression.

Become more than, just a "little bit" obvious. That the only thing my mom was, prepared to prove. With her, "I'm forbidding you to ever speak of, this again" lecture. Was her ability to, "seriously underestimate"...mine!

In fact, just judging from my own "personal evaluations" of, mom's. Roller coaster like, behavioral patterns. When she'd voiced her "overly insistent" requests. For us to have, a "casual conversation" exercise.

I couldn't help but, to get the "oddest vibe from her. "It's merely just, a "fabricated hallucination" theory.

Yea, it may've came off as, sounding. Like it'd actually, came off as seeming. To be of, the legit within, her mind.

But since, there's never been any such thing. As an advantage that doesn't come without flaws. Some more than, others.

There's a trick to, learning how to counteract. Those that give off their vibe as being of, the "less than positive nature.

Which is which, I'd like a few things "perfectly clear. Before, releasing anymore "censored" details that, directly pertains. To my version of, the events. I'd experienced. During this particular from "my life."

Plus since, all of, the following details. That I'm about to, describe will beyond the ones I'd witnessed. From within the realm of, my own suspective on, 5/5/78. Or, been attired by world of mouth and shallow minded onlookers...ect.

They never failed to end without me. Having to endure the over being wright it'd supply. With what'd seemed like, a one repition after another "sequence of events."

That'd seemed to, come "fully equip," with only "Lord knows" how many of, mom's failed attempts to, flaunt something. That she'd promised was founded on an agreement between us. Under terms of, strict disgression."

When "it was really just an excuse to, "silently gloat," over the what she'd believed to be, what'd given her "complete and total control," subject. That just, wasn't "fake."

"Yea, I've always known that it be back. To perform it's "grand entrance" ceremony. It was only, a matter of, when. I'd just never foreseen it going down. In one of, the "following ways."

1.) With me keeping both, all of the "inside details" I'd "witnessed" taking place. "After" I'd got hit "and my" current suspicion's" towards it as, a result. Out of, my mother's "earshot range.

Which, according to all the pain in the butt hassles mom'd aroused. To prevent what I'd knew about, the situation itself. Back to the surface for "further investigation."

2.) Waiting for it to, finish it's preparation to, "expose" "the sting of, it's wrath". To both, myself and the rest of, the world…in silence.

3.) Trying to interpret the purpose behind, what'd drove my mother's over being attitude. Towards the "straight up" answers that, I'd gave her "during it".

And

4.) The extensive chose of, figuring out "what I needed to know." In order to keep it comfortable and restrained, until mom's, "I'm so stuck on myself that, it's not funny" attitude problem. Came back to, bite her in, "the butt."

All of the events that, took place. On the morning of, 5/5/78. Or perhaps, I should say. The ones that, for some reason or, another. Had only felt the need to, reveal themselves to, me."

They should be able to, provide you, with "several different" reasons as to, why I'm convinced. That it's always a good idea to, "expect the unexpected." At, all times…"No exceptions!"

Which is why, you might want to; heed this warning "wisely." Because, as you are about to, learn. In, my world! People are only capable of, dealing with "so much" drama. At, any given time.

So, for those amongst you. In whom, haven't found themselves coming "face to face" with the impression that, anything and everything in yours, was on the verge of, turning into. An even weirder situation than, it'd already "proven" itself to be.

You might want to keep in mind. That there are also people. In whom, like my mother. Just don't seem to have, what it takes. To co-exist amongst society. Without pushing their "shallow minded" input off on, everyone else as though, the world itself, would cease to revolve if, they didn't!

However, since, I've already taken the time to, brief you. As much as, I possibly can on, this subject. Without creating a spoiler about as to, what would make, my mother's "casual conversation" input. Not worth "diddly-squat" in my world.

We should probably set aside a few seconds. To discuss as to why. I don't think even "I" could've predicted. The amount of impact it'd leave behind. For me to, "clean up."

Which is why, if you haven't already done so. You might want to consider, keeping a few of, there "fun facts" in, mind. When I walk you through the one's, "I'd witnessed" going down. From within the realm of, my perspective. On the morning of, 5/5/78. Such as...

1.) What it'd took to, "single-handedly" deal with. The "aftermath" from a "car accident that," I'd end up being, the "star attraction" in. Only, "four years" earlier.

2.) How everything pertaining to, this specific chapter of my life. Has been down to, every last detail. Based solely on, my conclusions of the events I witnessed taking place. On the morning of, 5/5/78.

3.) Why I couldn't put together any form of senceable logic. That could provide me with a "rational answer" as to, "how or why." I'd ended up being, the "only person. Out of, "Lord knows" how many other onlookers.

That'd been granted the insight to, observe. The "for my eyes only" files as, they'd fell into, play "around me."

I realize that, my version of, this chapter's details. Just like, they did in, one and two. May also come off as, sounding. More than just a little to, "far fetched and creepy" to, grasp.

But if, you've made it this far. Then you're obviously, interested in, it's outcome. By investigating the answers to, questions.

In which, I'm sure are already coming to mind. As we speak

1.) What'd inspired me to, play. A quick sound of, "connecting the dots." With the way "too" familiar for my taste vibe" it'd aroused inside me. Before, I'd even went downstairs for breakfast?

2.) What'd caused me to, stumble over the "unresolvable" pieces to, the puzzle. That'd soon again the similarities I'd noticed. Between, "then and now?"

3.) Why I'd be willing to, dismiss my second "unscheduled" encounter with it's ora. As a random case of, "Dā-jă-vac?"

4.) Why I'd fell the sudden urge to, pause. In front of, our bedroom mirror. Just long enough to do both, watch and hear myself saying, There exact words "out loud." Before, heading downstairs.

"Ok, basic instincts" I commented nervously. "I know you're here. I can feel the presence of, your ora around me!"

I may've been "too young" to, decide the true meaning. Behind the "various attempts" you made to warn me during, round one. But your having "unsuccessful efforts to, do so. Doesn't mean that, they weren't "greatly appreciated!"

"I mean, please don't take this wrong! Because, trust me! That's definitely "not" how it's meant!"

"But, straight up! Other than the presence of, the "way too familiar for my taste vibe." That only I can pick up on."

"When it comes to, deciphering the clues you've left behind to, figure it out. You've never really given me anything "substantial" to, work with!"

Therefore, since we've already stepped past the point in our relationship where just the idea of, calling it quits. Has officially, surpassed it's range of, available limitations.

I think it's safe to conclude that, this is just a nice way of, saying when it comes to, ignoring, what will "undoubtedly" end up becoming grounds. For another one of, mom's "single sided" conversations…I'm screwed!"

"In other words," basic instincts. Not only do I know "you're here." I remarked respectfully." I'm very much aware that, your temporary, "state of dormancy." Is on the very of, expiring."

"No! I've never had any luck. When it came to, figuring out as to, how or, even why…yet!"

"But, I do know that, I was the only person. In whom, witnessed it and if "personal experience" really is, the "best" teacher. If I've learned anything from watching it fall into, "play around" me. Not just once but, every night by way of, my dreams! It'd have to be that, whatever's meant to, happen next. Concerns both of, us!"

"So before, this becomes "even more complicated than, it already is. I'd like, to make one request. "Do you think you can find it within yourself? To leave the freaking cars out of, it…this time?"

But, hey! Other than that, I'm good…"thanks!"

Yea! The small sense of, "sibling rivalry" we used to, stimulate. The "childish routine" that, drove us. To meet up. Right in front of, the living room TV every-morning. At exactly, 8:00 AM…"sharp!"

So, of, course. When "Hanna," failed to live up to her "sisterly" duty. By choosing to preoccupy herself with "before school" primping. Instead of joining in on me and Walt's race downstairs. We decided to cut our losses before, it became one. By not "slacking off…" on ours!

Heck, other than it having a "very distinct" I'm walking through a tunnel effect. The staircase at, our house only had "22" steps from top to, bottom.

I couldn't help but to, notice how easily its ora shifted. During the brief amount of, time it'd took for Walt and I. To relocate our "gabonza beans" downstairs to, breakfast that, morning.

Although, I can't speak for "Hanna and Walt," I myself, have never so much as, once considered the idea of, learning. The exact measurements of, our living room. To be something worthy of, further investigation.

If I have to, take a "ruff guess." Then I'd have to say that, it couldn't've been any less. Than at least, "20 x 15" square feet in, diameter!

The "6 x 4" plate glass window in, it's front outer wall. Was not only installed in, the middle of, it's front outer wall. But, had always given me the oddest feeling, it'd been there. Since, the house was, "originally" built.

But even though, I'll have to refrain from telling you. The entirety of, it's details. Until, I finished describing my over all impression of, mom's tendency to favor. Those of the less than, "fairly different shades" from outside the "normal" color spectrum.

"I never fully understood as to, "how much". I'd literally, despised my mother's serious looking of, any taste. In..."home decors."

Until, she'd attempted to, add, a form of, personality to, the room. Where we'd converse every morning for a little "Mystery Machine" action.

By trying to, accent the "humble characteristics" of our "living room's" qualities. With a very tacky "melon" colored paint and "rust" shaded "wall to, wall" carpeting.

That'd made me feel as though, I'd been forced to, consume my breakfast. In..."a pumpkin!"

Allow me to recreate a "visual image" of what this was like. On the morning of, 5/5/78...

Although, eventually. It'd come down to, "how fast Walt and I, could figure out the trick to, tolerating them.

Once, my little sister, Hanna. Had finished the process of, performing. What I'd learned to except as being, her daily "before school" primping ritual.

Just like, any other ordinary day. In, the life of, me. About, "five minutes" after Walt and I. Hanna came downstairs and headed straight for the kitchen. To retrieve her "breakfast."

Before, she'd waltzing back into, the living room. Where she could begin "proudly" quoting. The exact same off the wall comment that, only her and my stepdad. Me," Walter Allen Jensen I" seemed to, understand.

"Eggs, yuck! I ain't eating this stuff! This stuff'll kill ya!"

Then as soon as, Hanna. Would finish executing her "morning entrance" routine. Just like, any other "ordinary day. In, the life of, me. She'd make this weird face. That I'm sure even, "Me fuck" himself. Would've been jealous of!

Then once, Hanna, was satisfied that, she'd made her presence "properly" known. We'd all from "our own" "self-assigned" seating arrangements. Begin surfiering our daily craving. For example...

With myself being, the oldest amongst, our little clan. I'd always preferred the idea of sitting down. In my mother's antique rocking chair. That'd according to, her. Had once belonged to my "great grandmother."

Where as, Walt. Always seemed to prefer to, sit on the floor. About, "three feet" in front of, me.

While, Hanna. Would just grab a nearby chair and sit off to..."my right!"

So, in other words. Everything had appeared to be, going "pretty much of, the "norm."

Since, my stepdad. Was in fact, the "rightful founder" of, Hanna's off the "wall quotes." Walter Allen Jesen I." Would usually, just meet up with us kids in, the "living room." After all of, the morning excitement would die back down.

Although, with his "work schedule," wouldn't "normally, coincide" with ours.

When it did. He'd most generally, meet up with us. Either, right before, or better yet. Sometime after we'd finished performing our, morning obligation. To wildly sing and dance along to, the lyrics of the "Scooby Doo" show. Like it was, the "happening thing" to, do!

Yea! You know the one I'm talking about!

♪ ♪ ♪ ♪ ???
"Scooby-Dooby doo.

???

Where are you?...and so forth!

Then again, what kind of, behavior did you expect? We were just kids!

Which, brings me to, what information. I'd managed to, acquire through. "The Websters Colegiated dictionary." When it came to, learning the meanings for unknown words.

The true definition of, "normal" clearly, reads. "When one tangent runs perpendicular to, another. During it's time of, tangency."

In other words, if you're not just another one of, those idiots. In whom, not unlike, my mother. Insists upon, living by, societies rules.

It probably be in your best interest to, remember. That "not only" will the details, I'm about to, reveal from this particular chapter of, my life. Have the tendancy to, vary from, person to, person. No matter how stupid their answers seem. They never stop at, a mere few.

Therefore, don't be surprised. If "not one" of, their self-fabricated theories and beliefs. Don't so much as, even come close. To making any form of, rational sense. Next to, mine!

As for, what would make our daily "Scooby-Doo" clan. Seem so significant in, this case?

Well, just between you and me. I may've only been 11 years old when this happened. But, as you are about to, learn.

Not only, had I already been made quite aware. That my still unknown to, everyone else, but me dormant companion's existence. Fail to remain that, way for...very long!

I can also distinctly remember as to, how easily, all the little details. That'd taken place on, the morning of, 5/5/78. Seem like they only happened yesterday.

Yea! I suppose, from their side of, the fence. My dormant companion's sudden urge to send me "indirect hints as to, it's presence." Could have struck "Walt and Hanna" as being, something else. But, not from mine!

Because, I couldn't've even had enough time. To sit back down in front of, the TV. So we could bash in a little "Mystery Machine" action. Before, I started feeling like, my equilibrium. Had been thrown completely, off balance.

Then, the next thing I'd knew. I found myself sitting in, my "self-assigned" seat. As my little brother Walt, asked me the big, "Are you OK". Question! Before, what'd takes place. Even had the chance to, register in, my mind!

Plus, just to give you a little heads up as to, what it was like. To grow up with "Walt as, a little brother?

Well, to sum it all up in a few words. I've never known Walt to shut up. About, any given subject that, might. So much as, "slightly" capture his attention for...whatever reasons.

Which, in, my mind. Did have the tendency to, get. Just a tad bit on, the tricky side from time to time. Especially, when it'd involved one of, these two things.

1.) Either, Walt would drive you half-bonkers. With his inability to, just drop-the subject altogether.

Or,

2.) You supplied him with an answer. That he'd at least, felt adequately explained his question.

But, now that we've reviewed Walt's level of, curiosity. Towards the world around him. Let's get back to, discussing. The details that, explain how. Our little "Scooby-Doo" clan. Fits into, the picture...shall we?

Heck just judging by, what I could tell from the sudden change in ora. Both, upstairs and down. I've never had any reasons to, doubt. That eventually, there those amongst our little, "Scooby-Doo" clan.

In whom'd, he incapable of, grasping "specific details". About the morning's upcoming events. That were right on the verge of, becoming. My dormant companion's "self-resurrection" ceremony.

It'd almost made having my "equilibrium" suddenly thrown off balance. Feel like, I'd found myself dealing with the same crowd of, people. That'd started accumulating around me. When my dormant companion and I'd first crossed paths.

Only this time. Everything my mother'd insisted upon, forbidding me. To ever speak about, again. Would no longer be like, just mere fragments of, "my own" imagination. That'd according to, my mother. Had been aroused as, the result of, an accident. From "four years" earlier.

So, with myself being, the only person. In whom'd actually witnessed the truth about, it's existence. I was pretty much left flying this gig "solo.

But, just to make sure that, we're both, still working. Off of, the same vibe.

I should probably point out as to, how easily. The following events may seem as though, their just too far fetched to, grasp ahold of! Let alone, wrap your head around!

In fact, since from this point on. Most of, the details belonging to, this event. Will basically, end up falling under. At least, one of the two following categories.

1.) As to, how I'd witness each even playing itself out. From within the realm of, my own perspective.

And.

2.) Everyone else's opinion

It'd really be in, your best interest. Not to expect my efforts to, walk you through the steps I'd took that, morning. To allow you to, establish a time line. To determine exactly, how long each event would take. To do it's thing!

Because, contrary to, popular belief. Or, at least, the one you're used to, following any way. Your guess won't be worth any more than, mine was! During, our first encounter!

So, of course, with myself not being, given. Any other choice but to, realize as to, how easily. Almost all of, the "unwanted vibes" that, I'd had no problem picking up on. During, round one.

Had allowed me to, select the unwanted kind." Off of, myself and back towards the TV. Or perhaps, I should say, whatever was supposed to be, on it.

Although, I still wasn't sure as to, what part. About, that particular morning. I'd end up hating the most!

1.) My being, the only person in, the room. Of whom'd, showed any signs of, knowing. That they could either, recognize or sense. The unusual ora of, my companions presents lurking "around them."

Or,

2.) My just knowing that, it's atmosphere. Was bound to, get even trickier! Before, it was over!

However, now that, this particular "can of, worms." Has been officially, opened. Let's go fishing...Shall we?

Heck, I'd already knew through personal experience that, in "Walt and Hanna's" mind. It was going to, take "alot more." Than just the process of, having, something as simple as, my "equilibrium" being, thrown off balance." To arouse a certain amount of, curiosity from... their perspectives.

So, in interest of, trying to play along. With our "usual" daily routine schedule. I'd even go as far as to, intercept and interpret. Any other question that, they'd try and shun my way. By trying to, "voluntarily answer" Walt's big "Are you ok" question.

With the "very first" reply that, came to mind. "Yea, bro! I'm good! It's just that, my brains. Not all the way awake yet..."No biggy!"

Plus even though, I'd strongly disagreed with how. Most people "sudden spirt" of, dizziness. As I was being, completely "off balance."

Especially, when it came to the act of, gaining "full control." Over my own attention span. Because apparently, it was going to, take a lot more. Than just, my acknowledgement alone. To convince my "basic instincts" that, they've actually, achieved their goal.

However, since we've already discussed the "newest glitches. I'd found in the timeline between then and now. Not to mention, my current inability to, accurately measure them.

All I can really say. About that, mornings "upcoming events." Is that, I know not much time could've passed. Between when I'd found myself being, able to detect other hints. From my "basic instincts" that, it was "lurking" a lot closer. Than I'd originally, perceived them capable of, pulling off. With the rocking chair incident.

You know, hints like myself feeling as though, I was "loosing my breath. For absolutely, no reason what-so-ever.

And

The loud stating noise that, comes over the airwaves. When you've got bad reception from your TV. or radio.

Then again, my picking up bad reception. Didn't end up being, the source of, my problem. Something which, I'd felt the need to, confirm. By glancing over at, the TV.

In fact, the picture itself. Was coming in, just fine! But, there was, this loud "staticy sound." In the place of, what should've been voices.

Which, only made life from "within the realm of, my perspective". Seem like it'd elevated to, an entirely, different level. That'd belonged to, the "extremely weird." Without creating any solid proof of, it's exisance. To anyone other than, myself!

But, even after I'd spend the past four years discreetly, searching for a "plausible answer. That'd at least, satisfactorily, explain. What I'd actually, witnessed taking place on the afternoon of, 3/12/74.

Amongst a series of, options. That'd so far, seem like, it was nothing more. Than just one more question. In a nerve ending pile of "several."

I've only been able to find two words. "That's even came "slightly" close to, "adequately" describe. The next encounter my life had chosen for me. It's called, a "zoning mode."

Its a sensation that, has always reminded me of, how I feel. When my teacher catches me day-dreaming in, class and…calls me on it!

Then before, I'd even had the chance to, realize that, anything happened. I'd found myself sitting in, mom's "antique" rocking chair. While, my little brother Walt, confronted me with, the big "Are you OK" question for...the second time!"

But, with my comprehensive and vocal skills already being, "out" of working order. All I really understood just, sounded like, nothing more or less. Than a bunch of, extremely, muffled and jumbled up words!

So much, in fact. That I actually, have to go. As far as, to try and read Walt's lips. Or at least, attempt to, anyway. Just to blow his suspicions off of myself. Long enough, to return his cold question. With a quick "yes or no" answer.

In hopes that, just the gesture alone, would help to resolve. What was "very rapidly," becoming a much bigger problem within itself!

But since, we've already reviewed. Our unique choice in seating arrangements

Let's discuss the purpose of, their significance in, my mind..."shall we?"

You see, I've always felt as though, the title of being, the oldest Gave me a certain share of, benefits. Some in which, were as I'd recently, learned. Much more important than, others.

By secretly, testing the "true extent of, my little brother and sisters persistence. To arouse the same topic of, conversation. That my mother'd clearly, categorized as being, a "lightly treaded" subject for discussion!

Which directly pertained to, reading the till signs created. By the presents of, other peoples "suspicious behavior.

Therefore in instead of, "inconspicuously" blowing off. What'd already seed like, a major amount of, "unwanted attention. Off of, myself and back towards the TV.

I ended up trying to, play out. My last minute "fall back plan to, Walt. "With my infamous" nod of, reassurance maneuver. After all, it'd worked on "my mother" and more than just a few times...too!

Which is probably, what'd led me to, "falsely assume. If I'd taken more time to, execute it properly. It would've had the same effect on, my little brother, Walt. But, it didn't!

Yea! I may only be speaking through, my own "personal experience. In, this particular moment in time.

Plus, once you proceed to, contemplate its "unknown probabilities". From a sequence of, events. Such as, this...for example!

It pretty much makes them all fall within, a pattern. That just so happened to, create a nicely size mud puddle. Full of, invalidated and normally, "insignificant" perceptions.

That'd created a last minute realization on, my part. Which, would end up the key. To what'd help me make the "full connection."

Between what'd still established an extremely, unplaceable case of, uneasiness. That'd struck me with an entirely, new list of, complications. That would portray themselves as being, somewhere along the lines of, a medium paranoia. In the makings!

Heck, to an extent! I can even understand as to, why. My "particular version" of, this story. May sound as though, it'd been conceived from one specific extent. Which, to a certain extent...it was!

But, once you've had the chance to, review the "unperceived" details. That I'd collected and am now "giving to, you. From "within the realm of," my own" perspective...more closely.

It'll become clearly, obvious. That they'd really been based. On how everyone else had conducted them self. On those whom, weren't yet familiar with the "completely different," which have never failed to, lead me. To the same conclusions..."every time."

1.) Looks can be, "very deceiving."

2.) Size means, "absolutely and totally," nothing!

3.) Where as, good old fashioned "personal experience. With a small order of, "intimidation" on, the side..."works well!"

Besides, I may've originally, directed my main point of, focus. Towards the act of, trying to, discretely learn. Where the key to, making the annoying "staticy sound." It'd apparently, brought alone for the side...prised.

Before, the mornings "only detectable to me "series of, events. Had the chance to, add one more "unresolved" problem. To those that, were already amongst the "Never ending" pile of, many.

Or,

Fell beyond what my 11 year old mind. Was prepared to, grasp!

Which, at the moment, were both subjects that, "still qualified" as being, quite young!

Besides, the sequence of, "mild distraction" it'd aroused. When it's unprovable vibe literally, refused to leave me alone. Since, I'd got up for school that, morning. Would end up being, the "very least" of, my worries. Before, it was over!

Heck, if it'd been just like, "Any other ordinary day. In the life of, me. Which, it clearly, wasn't!

I would've got in Walt's face. When I'd just noticed him trying to, execute. What he'd believed to be, suddly made glances in my direction.

Whenever he didn't think I was, paying any attention to, "What he was doing! You know, like my mother did. When she'd attempted to, use her so called, "Double C Word" exercise. That I didn't want to, have in the "first place."

When it came to, absorbing the details. To my next "spur of the moment discovery. I honesty believe that, the crispiest part about, it. Would have a lot more to, do with my gift.

To immediately if, not sooner. Connect the miscellaneous dots that, ajoined the afternoon of, 3/12/74. To the ones from 5/5/78.

If I have to, make an interpretation as to, the meaning. Behind what little information I'd managed to, retrieve. By studying Walt and Hanna's behaviors.

In which, I just couldn't help but to, notice. Myself "very rapidly," becoming the "star attraction" in.

Well, due to the terms of the circumstances them self. I'd say it was as, exceptable. As they were going to, get.

Especially, when you're dealing with. The "impressionable intellect" of, 8 and 5 year old kids like, them...For example!

Therefore, no matter how strange they may sound in, your book. In mine, anything would've been a heck of, a lot better. Than having to, deal with. A thirty one year old "woman."

Of whom'd, other than to interrogate her "nine year" old daughter. On a subject that, didn't even qualify as being, any of her freaking business. To start with!

It was all just another part of, the little "casual conversation" exercise. That my mother'd insisted upon, us having. Only, "two years" earlier!

Then again, for whatever it's worth. We are discussing the laws to, a conversation from the past.

So, just keep in mind. That a lot of, things have happened since then. Such as...

1.) My having more than just, a few chances. To evaluate the choices made available to, me. When my mother'd practically, went out of, her way. To call off what she'd considered to be, the act of, having one!

But, by that, point. It really didn't matter anyway!

Because, no matter how hard my mother'd tried. To convince me of, otherwise. Her poor excuse for a lame, two-bit theory didn't trump. What it'd took for me to, keep a close eye on "Walt, Hanna and everyone else's movements. From the corner of, mine!

Yea! My mom may've felt like, her idea of, an art form. Had "pretty much" evolved into, her benefit. But, she was wrong!

Because, whether my mother'd cared to believe it or, not. In no more than, just a few minutes. The self-fabricated line she'd attempted to, use to, explain. What'd "supposedly, happened on, 3/12/74.

Would proceed to, make a very significant change. That was only, visible, from within the realm of, three different worlds!

1.) One that'd started out as seeming like. Jut another random case of, DĀ-JĂ-VOE. As I'd proceeded to, get dressed for school that morning.

But, I'd never even so much as, mentioned!

2.) What may've at, first glance. Appeared to be, inside the usual AM. activity range atmosphere. Between Walt, Hanna and I.

3.) To one that'd almost made me feel as though, "My dormant companion." Was sitting right there and watching the "Scooby-Doo" show with us.

Until, it was confident that, it'd finished warming up. For the grand entrance of, "self-resurrection" ceremony.
NO! I may've not mentioned the existence of, the loud staticy noise. That'd kept insisting upon, drounding out the sound of, our TV. To, Walt...yet!
But, as you're about to "very rapidly" barn. There's an "awfully big" difference. Between, just having what it takes to, ride out. Every specific sequence of, events I'd witnessed. On the afternoon of, 3/12/74. By way of, ones dreams.
Or perhaps, in my case. I should say...nightmares!
My chance to, see the expression mom'd had smeared "all over" her face. When I flat out told her what I'd thought. About her "poor excuse" for a so called, "casual conversation" exercise.
As she'd attempted to, worm her way into, my personal business. With a load of, "freaking" bull crap" lies.

And

What' would actually, take place. On the morning of 5/5/78. After my dormant companion "decided to, reveal it's "True Colors." To the rest of, the world!

Or, at least, to those of, us. In whom, were present to, see it…anyway!

Heck, I can even understand as to, why. You may think that, this next part sounds. Just a little "too hard" to, grasp!

But since, we've already wasted enough, precious time. On my "unproven evaluations" of, certain "unresolved issues." That I'd already known from "point A," was currently, "co-existing" in…my body!

I'd like to think if my "spear of the moment desire. To make sure you've been brought up to date. On the circumstances of, it's flaws… does anything.

It would at least, give you the ability to, recreate. What I could only assume must've been going through, "Walt and Hanna's mind.

When they'd first realized. That instead of, just pledging our loyalties to, the "Scooby-Doo" Show. They'd found themselves witnessing my "dormant companions" self-resurrection ceremony. From within the realm of, "their own" susceptive!

As the "overly annoying," staticy sound. That'd conviently, piggy basked it's way downstairs. Incurred it's statis level to, the equivalence of, a diafning ring!

But, after that. Everything around me. Just…"went black!"

Although, in reality. I'm quite aware that, this entire process could've taken any longer. Than what it takes to, blink ones eyes.

Which, in my case. Would interestingly enough, also involve regaining my state of, consciousness on, "a pouch." That'd not so much as, "came close" to, resembling. The one I'd grown familiar with!

Which is why, I'm going to go ahead and start "my interpretation" of, the following events off. By drawing your attention to "how rapidly," my "imedient surroundings." Would literally, "change "their" entire outlook!

So, trust me! It didn't me "very long" to, begin noticing. The woes of, it's ways. Within it's "wide assortment" of, other inconveniences. Such as…

The sudden shifting of, it's terms. From, me doing my best to innocently, pretend. That I was, just watching the "Scooby-Doo" show with, "Walt and Hanna."

To finding myself being, trapped inside. A serious state of, disorientation and confusion. With a vibe that, I knew I'd experienced before. But, for the life of, me. Just couldn't place with, a memory.

To a world! That'd only seconds ago portrayed itself as being, in "full color." But, had left me with nothing more. Than one that now consisted of, just "black and white." To evaluate the inconsistencies between "color variations."

To discovering that, my "usual" supply of, "AM brainpower. Had been reduced down to, the equivalence of, a "scrambled egg! Without, invasion!

As for, what all kind of, picture. All of it's "nitty gritty" details." Would portray themselves as being, from "my side of, the fence?"

Well, let's just say that, they lasted. A heck of, a lot longer. Than any "glitch in time" that, I've ever encountered!

Which is why, I'd took the liberty of, filing "very neatly." Under the category to, those. That'd belonged to one of, a "entirely different" world! Or at least, from "within the realm of, one..."any way!"

But even though, it's not for the lack of, my trying! I've never managed to, find "my butt" landing. Right smack dab in, the middle of, "no-where." Without any idea as to, "whom" I was!

I just couldn't help but to, get the "oddest impression." That it's stupid rules had been officially, verified. Long before they'd even been "brought up" for discussion!

In fact, if it hadn't've been for the loud "staticy noise. Or, the "muffled and fumbled "voices" I'd had running through my mind. Like, there was," no tomorrow!

The next minute or, so. Would almost seem as though, it'd held. A type of, "issue calmness" about it.

So naturally, when I reacted by, turning around real quick. To see if either, "Walt or, Hanna." Was have any better luck at, locating it's source than, I did! When I tried to connect it's persistent "noise to, the TV.

I think I'd at least, expected to, find. My little brother, Walt. Just starring at, me like, before.

But instead of, finding him. I'd found myself facing. What'd appeared to be, nothing more than, two "adult sized" images. That were located no-further than, the other end of, "the couch." I'd just "regained consciousness" on.

Although, I can't deny. That it'd sounded like, it. Was being spoken in a tongue from an, "entirely, different" galaxy.

Especially, when I'd realized how "overly" occupied they'd seemed. With their need to, argue back and fourth!

Although, I must admit. That I was really hoping to, have "a lot better" luck at, redirecting my main incentive. Back towards learning the "inner workings, behind, my worlds sudden "loss of, color."

Before, it'd had the chance to turn into. Another "very intimidating" but "highly improvable" staticy noise and "visa versa", without detection... ect.

All in which, as you follow and consider the circumstances it held. Will learn what it was like, endure and ride out. What was still a "temporarily, closed" subject. That'd, "so far." Just consisted of, a "few brief" dizzy spells."

So, with this particular thought being, fresh in mind. I think its more than, safe to say that, I'd handled myself "quite well" for…"A beginner!"

Of whom, was on a mission. Into, the still "yet unknown"…thank you "very much!"

No! I wouldn't actually, be in. The necessary state of, mind to put all the "miscellaneous details" back together. Until, later on that, day.

But, I think the worst part about, waiting on its "fall back" after effects. Would have alot more to do. With how easily, each consequence it'd held. Immediately, reconnected themselves to, the car accident I'd been involved in. Only, "four years" earlier!

Or, even better yet! My trying to figure out why it'd chosen to, resurface itself. After playing out such, a long "state of, dormancy."

Well, I may've already knew that, answer! I just couldn't prove it! Until, it reached for the true extremities of, it's hidden potential.

All yea! Then there's also the part as to, what I'd find myself reliving. Once this very descriptive but, still "unresolved flashback. About, what had actually, taken place. Both, before and after our our "first" crossing of, paths!

But, rest assured! With the amount of, major extremities that, this "messed up" encounter held. Not so much as, "coming close" to being, over...yet!

When it finally, did! It wouldn't be ending with just a few muffled and jumbled up voices. Or, even in some loud staticy noise for...that matter!

Plus, since most of, my visionary talents. Had been at least, temporarily lost due to it's impact. When it came to my ability to either, differentiate or distinguish between. What should've been as simple as, everyday "shades and colors."

The concept of, studying objects movements. Would from my side of, the fence. Pretty much leave me stuck with drawing all of, my conclusions. On a "spur of, the moment basis!

Which, once translated basically, means. That as long as, whom or, whatever was definitely, lingering nearly...Didn't move! Then, I... couldn't see it!

Although, I must admit that, at first! This "so called" wide variety of, circumstances. Would seem a lot more like, trying to play. "Pin the tail on, the donkey"...blindfolded!

When in reality. It was just the never-ending chase of, my having to, fall back. On my still "unrecognized talent for locating. Anything that was actually, stupid enough, to consider moving. In, "my" presence!

Therefore, with myself being, "volunteered for a position. Where I'd be given no other choice but to, deal with. The circumstances and slight inconveniences that it's "one sided" sequence of, events. Had "already" provided.

All in which, I'd just for sake of, record. Had in the past for years lived through. Or, would "very shortly, become one. That'd turn out to be, a "teensy-weensy" bit harder to, master. Than what I'd originally, presumed. The likes of, my "dormant companions" suddenly made hints. To actually, be worth!

If not taking me "very long" to, conclude. That what'd from my "colorless" line of, perspective. Had appeared to be, nothing more or, less. Than a "mere" black and white" out line of, a register or heating vent. Below a "nearby" wall.

Whatever I either, "could or couldn't" resolve, about, the secrets that, only I'd knew lurked "freely." Within the "extremely strange" rooms "over all" vibe.

Which, be it by way of, "accidental or other wise." Had allowed me to, catch a "brief glimpses of, something else. That'd moved "too fast" for me to, identify.

All I had to, do. Was sit back and wait for the pieces to, fall together!

But even though, "deep down" inside, I've always at least, half-way expected it's unproven distraction. To end up being, some stupid bugs flight path.

Unlike, the "adult sized" images. In whom, still seemed to be, a bit overly occupied. With the idea of, arguing on a couch." That I'd just "regained consciousness "on."

When I'd found myself just staring at. What was now starting to look like. Just an image of, a face "without" a body!

The lone image it'd portrayed. Just struck me as being, "a lot younger" in age. Not to mention, intelligent enough to, remain quiet.

So, since it hadn't showed me any reason to, suspect. It'd held some form of, "physical threat" towards "yours truly." Or, anyone else, for that matter!

Which, now that, I've had the time to, review the circumstances..."more thoroughly." Is something that, I've always felt. Could've "very possibly," worked against me. Before, the morning's chain reaction of, events... Were even over!

We should probably, concentrate. On it's more "important facts."

Or, perhaps, I should say. The one's that I'd felt would hold the "most significance" to, me. Before, the morning's chain reaction of, events. Were even over.

Yea! Everything I'd managed to pick up. About, this vibe had so far seemed to be, a little bit on, the quiet side.

But, the louder the sound of, sirens got. The more I wanted to jump up off of, the couch..."and hide."

Although, this alone. Was a maneuver that, "yours truly." Still hadn't been "quick enough" to, master...yet.

It did give the "female image." In whom'd, been so "overly occupied" with the idea of, arguing. At the other end of, the couch. I'd regained consciousness on.

Permission to immediately if, not sooner. Attempt to interrupt my efforts. By laying her hand on me. Like just that alone. Would be enough to, calm me..."back down!"

Which, just for sake of, conversation. Did work! But, not for "very long!"

Besides, even though it is true. That once you've had the time. To give it, a little thought. My description as to, how this assortment of, events portrayed themselves. From my side of the fence.

It will leave you with a lot of, extra room for suggestions.

This brilliant idea pretty much come to, a scratching halt. When I'd started hearing, what'd sounded like, footsteps and voices. Coming onto, the "front porch."

Which is when, they immediately began positioning themselves. Between myself and the "front door. Like they were "purposely" trying to, both me in!

Personally, I couldn't see. What the source of, this big, fat, hairy deal was. I mean, I'd never wronged them. Or, at least, not that, I was aware.

In fact, if it hadn't been for their "not so well" thought out need. To try and box me in technique.

I may've even managed to, have stayed "half-way" calm. Long enough, for them to keep it's statis. Or even better yet. Understand their purpose for being, there!

But, then again. That'd soon be their issue to, resolve. Because, as soon as, I'd decided that, this situation. Had surpassed it's boundaries to, an entirely different level.

Which included, making me feel that need to question the possibility. That they'd just showed up to, scrap it out with me.

So, with myself being, such a nice lady and all. I'd had absolutely, no-problem "what-so-ever." With the idea of, humoring. Their "poorly made," requests.

The thing is that, even though this information. Still remained to be of, the unknown. To both, them and everybody else.

They were very sadly, mistaken. If they'd so much as, thought that, I wouldn't respond. As becoming a form of, physical threat.

No, I'd hadn't been able to, wrap me head around. All the how's and whys I'd found myself there to, investigate. But, it doesn't mean that, I didn't have every intension in finding out.

Heck, as far as, I was concerned. Since, those whimpazoids revealed themselves. With the order of, stepping into, a world. That'd only came with, "two workable options of, how. This particular chapter of, my life. Was destined to, play out.

1.) They could either, do the more intelligent like, and less humiliating thing. By politely standing down. While, it was still an option.

Or,

2.) Deal with me doing everything within, my "eleven year" old power. To make absolutely sure they'd lived to, regret. Their fascination of showing up. Just to, "rattle my chain"…No exceptions!

However, since they'd refused to, stand down and cooperate. I made it my own personal business to, show them. Exactly, how I'd felt. About, their "lame idea."

Personally, I'd had absolutely, no theories as to, whom. They'd presumed themselves to be. But, I'd had absolutely, no intension" what-so-ever." At missing out on a scrapping-session. That'd only required me to, slap around. A bunch of, "half-wit" morons.

In whom, didn't have either, the intelligence or class. To just mind their own freaking business.

So, once again. The rules to, this "messed up" game. had elevated themselves onto, the next level.

Besides, with myself being, the only one. Who's ever qualified as being, capable of, doing so.

I'd just like to, take a few seconds to, emphasize. That whatever words I was at, the time. Just starting to, comprehend.

Would within no longer than, the blink of, an eye. Become, a recreation of, a loud static noise.

When suddenly, my entire world started to, turn. Even more of, the "topsy-turvy." Than I'd already knew it was!

Besides, with the absolute creepiest part of, our little "scrapping session. Having nothing to do, with the choice of, facial expressions. That they'd slipped my way during, their lame attempt. To execute, this exercise.

Other than myself being, aborted to, the minor flow. That they'd clearly breed upon, arrival. Their "wimpy-wiener" butts didn't bother me in…the least!

Well, now that, we've covered all of, the glitches. That it's "so called" black and white would held. Let's move forward by discussing their lacking of, "inconveniences and individual skills."

Although, the good news is. That thanks to, it's choice of, unwelcomed morning events. I can honestly say that, now I know. What the please, for every action. There's a "complete and total reaction" means.

The bad news is that, mine "clearly wasn't." The one that, they were hoping for.

Heck, whether or not I would've had. The "if I couldn't see it version happening for me or, not, was irrelevant!

Because, as far as, I was concerned. There was no way that, I was willing. To let something as small as, that. Keep me from taking every one of, their lame "gabonza beans" down.

I honestly think the hardest part about, making this happen. Would basically, revolve around my trying to, establish. A rough idea as to, how much room I'd halve to, work with. From my "if it didn't move then, I couldn't see it" perspective.

Besides, unbeknowingly to them and trust me when I tell you. That I was extremely cautious, about, giving them any reasons to, believe otherwise.

So as, I'd surveyed the rooms limitations. I managed to, spot what I'd took to be, a "full sized" dinner plate. An a nearly coffee table off to, my right.

Which I didn't hesitate to snatch ahold of, and immediately introduce. To what should've been image "number ones" face.

Where as, number two chose to, run. With a "slightly different" approach.

Heck, I could tell just by, the way it'd kept focusing it's attention towards my hands. That it was, waiting on me to, make the first move.

So, I went ahead and hooked it's "butt up." By putting it's pants down around its ankles and delivering a "full impact" strike. Straight to, the grain area.

But even though, image number three did exhibit. A significant amount of, confidence in, its maneuver. It's extreme slacking in, the "creativity department. Would just make picking up on, it's vibe…even easier.

If you're really interested in, knowing my "honest opinion" towards, what was right on, the verge of, becoming. It's maneuver of, choice.

Then I can probably get away with "defending myself." With your basic, "block and counter" move.

Plus, I may've been accused of, a lot "growing up." But, trust me being, predictable. Has never been one of, them!

Besides, since I've always considered myself to be, the type of person. In whom, takes pride in themselves for doing, the exact and total opposite. From what everyone else would prefer.

I couldn't proved this to them. Until, I'd finished quenching my thirst for enlightening, "the faceless four and company. To a certain amount of, leverage. That they'd given themselves the liberty of, creating.

So naturally, as soon as, image number three decided. That it'd felt brave enough to, step up and try its luck. With the "ever-so-dangerous" "Bear hug" from behind.

I'd chosen to follow the wise words of, my "Kung fu" master! In which, where. "Dragon, if all else fails. Then bite them! They'll leave you alone!"

Well, as usual, my "Kung-Fu" master...was right!

Because, as soon as, image number "three" stepped up. To make it's move! I hooked it's "pathetic butt" up!

Yea, I knew I'd counted a total of, four in all. When they'd unexpectedly, "invited themselves." Into, the likes of, "my lair."

But, with myself "already" taking "thus" of them down. With literally, no problem. It only made sense that, somewhere hiding out. Amongst it's mere veil of, "black and white."

Was the likes of, image AKAI number four. So, when it'd finally, made it's leap.

I'd had at least, been lucky enough to, scrounge together. An even "slightly verge" idea of, "how." It's supposed. "If it didn't move." Then, "I couldn't see it. Sudden lacking for distinguishing color "bull crappola"..."really worked!"

So, since all and all. The most "difficult part" about, taking image "four" down. Would basically, instill the chase of, figuring out. Exactly, what it'd took to literally, provoke it." Into, revealing it's true "whereabouts." Within a room full of, shadows. That'd held it's mysteries "captive." Before, Id even had the opportunity. To, step up. To either, reveal or execute. My counter move!

As for, what would become. From my "spur of, the moment" defense plan?

Well, believe it or, not. If defending myself against it. Was as easy as, jerking a nearly curtain down from, it's rod!

Trying to throw it's remains over image number four "faceless head." While, running for. What'd "just recently" became, our "unguarded" front door.

But, now that, we've had the chance to discuss. All of, the details that, this particular chapter from my life..."more thoroughly." We should probably, "redirect our attention" towards. How I'd actually managed to, make my way. Outside to our, "front porch."

However, if you're really "that curious" as to, the how's and whys. That'd readily inspired, my "spur of, the moments" chase. Or, even better yet. What'd drove me to, use a "nearly wooded" area. As my "escape route?"

Well, in reality? I can't say for sure as to, what'd aroused it's attention..."to me!"

But, I'm more than, positive. That I can come up with a few "irrational plauseabilities." To humor it! You know, for the sake of, making..."Casual conversation!"

So of, course. With myself being, left behind. Without any other available options working in, my favor! I just stuck with the "main path." Until, I'd finally, reached a creek bed located. About, "180 yards from, our house!

We should probably, begin discussing. The several other forms of, "unforeseen complications." That'd came along with "my" having to, "deal with" it!

Yea, my "brain waves" may've "still been" a little "too" overly occupied." As it'd surprised me through this "first time" experience episode.

That'd to me felt like, it. Was derived from a "scrambled egg."

After I'd spent every day of, my life playing in, those woods. I grew "very familiar", with the "general layout" of, it's land."

Which, from my perspective at, the time. Only meant that, I wouldn't have to, worry. About making the "stupid mistake" of, getting lost. Within the realm of, "it's terrain"...first!

Besides even though, my purpose for taking down image number two. Would've "more than likely," had a lot more to do. With how my brains "sudden lacking" for the enthusiasm. To humor my "over-whelming" desire to, find an, immediate cover" for something.

That'd at, the time. Han only seemed to belong, to everyone else but, me!

So, once I'd realized. That the "spur of the moment techniques I'd devised. To aid me with executing my "plan of escape... "failed!"

It'd only took me a matter of seconds to replace them. With an entirely new set of rules called. What it'd take me to shake. Their "non-invited image prayer," butt. Back off of my tail!

Although, this was, a flat. That I'd just by, comparing their "behavioral habits." Be able to send their "lame buts." Off on, a "wild goose chase" with.

They'd inevitably, led me in their different. But, highly profitable directions!

I mean, sure! At the time. This may 'de been about something. That'd still just needed done! But, with any leech! They'd have no way of catching. What they couldn't see... either!

As for you the question of, "which image." I'd choose to tag along with. During this "poor excuse" for, a "freaking ride?"

Well, even though I was "clearly located" right smach dab. "In the middle of it all! It's my stay still remained hidden. But, not for "difficulty dong" long!

Because not unlike, everything else. That I'd interestingly enough, "found myself involuntarily" standing in. "Before," my life'd decided to turn. Into one of a "baby gorillas". During, these past "four years" of silence.

It didn't end up being, my call to, make!

No! Since the key to figuring out. What was about to become just one more unanswered question. Amongst a "never-ending pile" of, the many "still..." get to Rome!

That'd not only, possessed an "unscheduled time of arrival. But, solely controlled my" basic instincts.

In fact, for as wild as, this probably sounds, which, I'm pretty sure that, it will!

Even with myself still feeling, al the disorientation and confusion from it's aftereffects. Still swimming around in, my head like, "wildfire!"

This was the only instinct at my availability. That's actually, handed me access to both. The privilege of them being at my disposal. When "nothing else" clearly, was!

As making any farm of, since. Out of my "from within the realm perspective. I guess, it was, my job. To... "follow them!"

But now that we've taken the time, to "carefully review" the "miscellaneous highlights." That'd not only, led me up to the seriously abstract details. Which had already successfully escaped. The realm of "our house" that, morning.

Let's go ahead and take these details even... "one step further!"

By crossfamining the state of significance. That'd actually, lied behind the various repetition of Frisbees and flashes... this experience held.

Well even though, from my perspective. What things I can remember about it. May 'de stuck me as being, "too short" to connect. To any "plausible memoir."

Or even better, yet to exactly "how rapidly," this "particular exercise." Wouldn't "end up working" in "my favor!"

Which basically, means that just like, it'd did before. I felt it's position was spinning. At the minimum of "I different angles. At the "exact same," time!

Although, I still hold a guy distinct, flash back of, myself. Trying to run down the "main path" to... it's creek bed.

I can't deny that, things. Had to have, at least, blacked out on me. As I attempted to, escape the wrath of, it's clutches."

It'd really seemed as through, this had to, have happened. Somewhere in between then and arriving at my "cracked" destination. A lot of things had just seemed to... change!

In fact, since the next thing I'd knew, I was standing "ankle deep" in, "Creek Water." My so called "spur of the moment time. Would "very abruptly," end up becoming, all about. What my "Basic instincts" needed me to, do!

Plus, with myself already making you "entirely aware." As to "how easily," this small path of refuge. Has always had the tendency to, wind up. An the "soggier side" of things.

You shouldn't have any problem understanding as to why. The significance behind my mom's "overly inaccurate," theories that, drove them. Wouldn't actually, became, visible. Until, we've moved a little further along with this chapter.

But because, unlike, the almost "missed escape" I'd made from... our living room.

This rather "screwed up" maneuver wouldn't end up putting me. In the post that, automatically, required me to, run away from something. I couldn't even see "visually."

Once you consider how lead the images lack of morals actually, was. I don't think that, I could've looked at, this situation. In any other way if, my life would've depended on it!

So now that, we've covered. This part of, the morning's events... more thoroughly!

Let's go ahead and begin our "nitty gritty" discussion. About, how "each detail", flaw and disadvantage." Will influence my refuge of escape.

All of which, were "very capable" of, playing themselves out "as, follows." In this own distinct time and fashion!"

Although, according to, my observations. When it came to, the layout of, the land. Each one would be very capable of, taking. Both, me and it's "chain-link of, circumstances." That could either, "come or not," as a result of, each decision... ect.

The real question would be. Which, one should I pick and... why?

Well, after I'd taken a brief summary. That'd concerned, "The limitations each option provided me with. These were my final conclusions!

Heck, what'd seemed like, an "extremely plausible" route of escape. Would've required the use of, a "small bridge." That just judging by, my already managing to, "conveniently overlook." It's most "recently," past experiences in, this case.

I really wasn't even able to, figure out that, much..." yet!"

That is, until I'd heard. This loud splashing sound, felt the "cold water" literally running across my feet. Just so I'd look down long enough, to realize. That I was "not only standing. Within the mist of "ankle days" creek water. With absolutely, no recollection what so-ever as to, "how." I'd came to find myself... right there!

Although, the truth be told, I could've probably, got away from. The likes of, dealing with those "faceless images." By just playing out option "number one."

But, after I'd performed my "brief evaluation" survey. Even I being in, the seriously "discounted and confused" state.

Could've easily allowed anyone the amount of room they'd needed. To precisely play out their "undesirable quicks"... for example.

1.) Because there were houses located. Just right on the other side of, the creek beds align. It made the "probability rate" of, my choosing it as, a route of escape. "Rapidly divided. When I realized that, my expectations last their potential.

When they'd left me in, plain view of, anyone. Whom, just "so happened" to be, looking out their window. At the time, it'd taken place... 'Not cool!"

2.) While I must admit that, my curiosity towards option number two. May've also offered me a certain amount of, potential for escape.

It'd only allowed me to, travel downstream far enough. To reach the "Ohio Riverbank."

I mean, sure! I suppose that, this sound may 'de held. More than, just a few secrets. Which, may 'de been worthy of, "further investigation."

But, with everything else being, almost "immediately" triumphed out." Especially, after I'd noticed "how large", It's ever-growing pile of, abstract "bell crap"... was!

I decided to, access what line of, effect it possessed... as follows.

1.) Because, when it came to, executing this "particular plan. I suppose I could've just "followed" the creek bed... "downstream."

If I would've done it precisely enough. It would've more than likely, worked out... successfully!

But, not without having me. With the "new wrecking" question as to, how. I should go about, trying to, "back track." The area of, my steps carefully enough. To remain close from a "direct line" of, sight.

So of, course. With myself being, located only, 20 years away. When it came to, "building up the confident to, just "go for it." It did "absolutely, nothing" for me.

Therefore, when I first attempted to perform. My "brief evaluation" as to, what kind of, promises it'd exhibited. Towards, my achieving bath.

1.) The highest ratio of, my plausibility for pulling it off. Without having to, deal with. "The "devastating inconvenience." Included in the process of being, "buried alive!"

Although, not unlike, the several others I'd encountered. It'd a lot come with me more than it's shair of flaws.

Something in which, contrary to, "popular belief." Would have more than likely, held no significance to the "untrained life." I may as well as, be saying this.

Because this is what let me "move through. The terror that, lied within this creek bed... "liberally!"

It'd basically, given me a "temporary" free access pass. Not only, through it! But, allowed me the choice of, "not arousing" any "unnecessary suspicions." While trying to, hop from stone to stone.

Besides with just this within itself. Inspiring a disturbance in, the waters "over all" make up. It actually, gave me the piece of, mind I'd needed. To not worry about, the "stupid stuff."

It could've "very possibly" reveal the where. To my location of, hiding. You know, it was like, leaving a teach in the sand. For them to, follow!

Then again, once you consider the amount of, "unnecessary hoo-ha" after effects it'd caused. Which, wasn't even a problem. Until, the unwanted arrival of, the "overly annoying, no-faced," images.

Just the act of trying to ride. This "highly questionable," experience out.' Had so far, been like, nothing more or less. Then just a sudden rush provoked. Curtsy of, them!

But even though, I didn't actually experience the "Big yacht." Being around from it's wrath. Until, I was at least, 30 seconds and twenty yards further upstream.

When I finally did, It was like being, slapped across the face. With something that held the equivalence of, a "2x4."

Plus, with myself being, over come by. An uncontrollable form of, exhaustion. I immediately, started scraping the grounds for, a suitable place to, hide out.

Until, I'd had enough, time to, "interpret and fix. What'd all of, the sudden became. An even more unignorably "scrambled egg" like, problem. Going an inside... my head!

So, to those of, you. Who'd been blessed with the privilege of, "not" having to find themselves experiencing it.

Yes! My vision of, this story may sound pretty stupid. But, trust me... it's not!

Besides, as you'll soon learn. When you're in the middle of such a thing as, riding out. This type of "irregular circumstances." An, a "first hand" basis.

I'd just like, to, mention. That it's "not" a style of, "behavior". Which is, distinctly unheard of! Especially, when they'd "first arrived."

Just having to, hear the muffled "false assumptions that, they'd reached. As, at least, the ones that, I could understand. My depiction of "self-confidence." Just struck me as being, part of the package.

However, since, unlike, them... for example.

My inner strength had been stemmed from, a "previous personality." That'd obviously, possessed the ability to, grasp. What I'd as of, now considered. To be on the realm of, "my deal." That'd played with a "completely different" set "of rules."

Besides, you'd think after how easily. That I'd managed to, fend them off. They would've at least, acquired enough, common sense. To just, leave me... alone!

However, since they'd closer. To go out of, their way. To officially, embarrass the crap out of, themselves. By chasing me into, a nearly wooded area. Like, it was, the "happening thing" to do! Well, that was, their own "personal stupidity!

Plus, with my "No-longer longer" dormant companion" being, loose. It'd been made "quite clear" by, the careless images "blind actions." That trying to, keep the nature of, my escape. At a "ground level." Just wasn't in, "the cards" for me!

Heck, I could tell from my perches location of, choice. That everything had all "pretty much" ended. The second I'd started to, scape out. The local tree tops for a, better cover!

Yea! I may've always harbored. A certain kind of, regret. When it came to, dealing with the hardest part. About, feeling this wrath, while, I'd rode it out, for... answer!

But, they've never failed to, rest on. My abilities to, ignore the frail after effects it'd aroused! As, even better yet! My so called, "birds eye" point of, view.

Especially, when it came down to, whether or not. It'd held any hint of, significance. That'd help me acquire both, the gift of, receiving my comprehensive and vocal skills, so, I could create a world where it'd worked in... my favor!

And

Learn to acknowledge the simple theory of, tolerating the inside secrets it'd harbored.

But because, I'd unlike, everyone else, was the only person that, seemed innocent enough to spectate. When they'd attempted to, follow me upstream. This chase ended up becoming, quite the task to, achieve! Especially, when you're trying to do it. From within the atmosphere of, a "fifty feet" in, the "air" porch!

So, it was easy to, see. That, them bringing the "female image" with them. Instead of, just blowing her off as, a tag along!

Plus, with the circumstances that, guided. My seriously "messed up guest to, get away. Not hesitating to, change. They'd "very rapidly," turn into, a "much larger" breed.

Just Like, Any Other Day in, The Life of Me | 137

Besides, with the circumstances being of, the pretty freaking bad. That it actually, takes the total of, five images. To track my eleven year old butt... it was on!

In fact, since they acted as though, this was a "miscellaneous quest," for stray insights and answers to, tip them off. I know they were in reach of, something, to "fuel their fires" with!

Therefore, with not having anyway off hand. To investigate their intensions. It was like, trying to, evaluate their behavioral habits... "blindly!"

Yes, this side did end up becoming a bit more difficult. Then I'd first had it... "pegged for". But, it was also, doable!

In other words, if you're waiting on me to, give you. A fairly accurate comparison between my interpretation and what'd appeared to be, thieves.

Well, let's just say that, I. Curtsy of Einstein's in famous relatively theory. Didn't need their assistance to, interpret them!

In fact, their tone of, ignorance. Just made my romp through, the woods by, unknown intruders... sound dumb!

Especially, after I'd sat down to, watch the 'Scooby-Doo" show. Just so I could find myself, where I was now!

Besides, I'd grown extremely fatigued. By, just inspiring their "goofy butts" back into, reality. So the last thing I'd cared about. Was keeping track of, their stupid extent quota.

Plus, since I couldn't just ignore their foul comments drawing closer to, "my hide."

I'd no more than, seconds ago. Been suddenly, awakened and dragged to a world. That didn't involve any color!

I mean, yea! I may've been literally, forced to, participate, In what'd definitely, turned out to be, a "seriously messed up" ride. But, at least, it'd allowed me, to begin interpreting bits and pieces of, "what"... they 'were saying!"

Then again, this may seem like, it just comes from "nowhere." But, it was, as suspicion I'd had for a while. Not to mention, gave me a "very distinct interpretation. That'd directly concerned my need to, handle things. That'd been within on, a "gut instinct" states! When interpreting what'd set a spark "very interesting" questions. That I'd apparently, overlooked amongst my trying to step past. All of the 'ihoo-ha" typed atmospheric pressure... so, to speak!

As for how much that, my life changed? Between any other day of, watching. A little "Mystery Machine" action with... Walt and Hanna?

To finding myself standing "ankle deep" in, "creek water." About, 100 yards from... our house.

To a scream that'd been littered the remnants. That'd only held the vast potential of, flickers and flashes from a memory. In which, I couldn't place!

Although other than that. I have absolutely "no memory." About, how I came to, find myself there?

Well, since, I'd never personally, done anything to, implicate this. That is, other than, pride myself. On my gift for keeping all my ducks in, a row. Before, I tried to, take anything to, another level.

Especially, when it comes down to, little things. Such as, names and ages... ect.

Other than, my growing extremely curios, about, what was "really" going on. I couldn't help them "do" anything!

Which is why, I attempted to, "cleverly," shake them from my tail! But because I'd, knew I could hear something calling out "Heather!" In, the farm of, a question.

So, now, with myself being on, the wrong end of, becoming. A solid fixture of, the worst freaking case. That not only qualify as, what I'd call the "Herby Jubies." But, I've ever freaking encountered!

Especially, the "how Easily" it'd abruptly did both. My vocal and comprehensive skills. That I didn't hesitate to, leave me flying "solo."

Which, designated my lack of, inspiration qualities. Towards the words they were about to, say. As my "reason" number two"...

Yea, it's possible that, my jog through the woods for cover. May've had a lot to do with it. But, I wasn't willing to, give up... yet!

Then finally, there's infamous reason "number there"...

Heck, even though, they couldn't catch me on, a "good day." I couldn't have communicated with them. If my life... depended on it!

So, rest assured. The last thing I wanted to, do. Was to, witness a "visual of, them "circling back." Other than, annoying the "crap" out of, me!

Therefore as I hid and waited on the "female image" To finish imitating her "uncalled for" "spaz out" session.

This was just the beginning of, the first experience I'd encountered. With my now "Non-Dormant" companions existence.

The suddenly like, it'd slipped into, the mornings events. Without being noticed by, anyone other than... "me!" It was gone!

But because, just this realization alone. Wouldn't be enough to, enlighten the view of, the chase to, decoding. What'd mostly, still sounded like, a line of, jibberish.

The only thing worse than tolerating. What they'd "already" proven that, "tolerating it"... "didn't" cover! Would've been, a "repeat performance. So, I took my chances and... "Confronted them!"

Here's how it went...

For as "amazingly, ungraspable," as, this may sound. After finding myself being, the "star attraction" of, a "human" retrieval dull."

Which, had so far. Only been filled, with nothing more or, less than an, extreme bought with "disorientation and confusion."

Not to mention, a few muffled and jumped up voices. That'd been thrown in on, the side for "decorational" purposes.

I'd still found myself in a state of, extreme surprise. When I glanced down from "birds eye" accommodations. Just in time to, hear one of, the male images. Ask the female... "This!"

"Excuse me mame." He requested "politely." But, how old did you say that, your daughter was?" Which, she'd quickly replied with the words. "Eleven. My daughter is eleven!"

But even though, I was only capable of, judging their reactions. From what few bits and pieces of a brief conversation. That "I" couldn't interpret.

From my angle of, perspective. It was "pretty clear" that, the reply he'd gave and the one he'd expected, weren't even that of, the same origin.

Yea! I suppose his question. Isn't what most people'd consider to be one given in, a "serious" and 'more kosher" surroundings. But hey... that's life!

"Mami," the male image commented apologetically, "I feel sorry for you... I really do!" Then again, his "falsely made" gestures, be they verbal or, otherwise... spoke for... themselves!

Although judging by the she'd gave in return. She'd portrayed herself as being, at a "loss for words" I really didn't care!

So, because of, "the" reply. She didn't give back. Just didn't portray her as being, at a "loss for words". Her reply never dwindled past that of, "a mere "shoulder shrug." Which is why, I didn't "trust" either, of "them."

Especially, after everything got so messed up as, a result. Then again, after everything else that, they'd proven and I'd debt with reached this point. I felt like, I'd owed her some form of, "reassurance."

Although, she didn't see me rented, I'd started coming "towards' her. Once, she'd felt satisfied that, I was safe we started up to, our house."

But even though, I didn't have to, see or hear them. During, their quest do so. The images quest to, 'tag along." It'd even seemed a little "too." Farfetched. For me to, believe.

In fact, with myself, being apparently, acquired, to take on, an expedition. That'd fell outside "anyone's league." It'd actually, allowed "me." To feel and locate it's area of movement. Which, was "invisible" to, the "naked eye."

My basic instincts would have to, find a way to, intensify. What'd obviously found as being, an "immediate situation," That'd unknowingly to, "me" taken place. During the time that, I was stranded... "unconscious." In front of our TV set!

Since, my "new experience" with, this "talent," Just seemed to give me, a big case of the "Herby Jubies." That was now, even "worse than," before!

With the only difference being that, this time around, so, I could "hopefully catch them in their mist. If it hadn't been for the lady images persistence... I "wouldn't have!"

But since, my body felt like, it'd been drained of, all its energy so something could literally reach inside me and steal it!

Then again, with myself already proving to them that I'd had the ability to, defeat their "lame butts."

To whether or not they liked it ??? which, made a, was irrelevant!

Yea, I may've tried to, give him a dirty look in, return. But, if they so much as considered, the theory of, trying to, move "without suspicion... I knew about it!'

Especially since my extraordinary breed of personal experience. Kept telling me to, do otherwise!

Therefore, I guess inside. I'd learned better. But, part of, me. Just assumed it'd stop. Once we'd reached the house, so they could do, the gentlemen like, thing and letting me go!

Well, at least, that's what I was hoping anyway!

But instead of, just letting the details drop. The woman's image kept insisting that, ignoring it, wasn't the way to go about, "solving it."

So, when they started leading me to, the ambulance. Which, was conveniently parked at, the top of, our hill.

I admit that, if may've taken me a "few" seconds. To recognize it's markings fro, what they were. But, it didn't keep me from trying to escape... again!

However, with my body feeling like, it'd been drained of, all its engines. It was as though, something had reached inside me and... "Stoll it!"

Then again, with myself already proving how easily I could defeat their "lame butts." Whether they'd approved or, not was... "irrelevant!"

In other words. Since, my trying to, remind them. That creating a repeat performance. Wasn't a "great idea." It was "the least" of... my worries!

Besides, with the word "ruff" being my "new" middle name.

The female images newest set of, behavioral patterns. Not even "more interesting." As the day... "progressed itself.

But because, the female images next move required "me." To actually, "step in" the ambulance, "voluntarily."

By then, I was so seriously so that if what I'd did next "didn't slap them. It'd definitely, make them "wonder!"

Plus from what I could tell. I actually "think" they'd expected "me. To oblige their unspoken request. So, even though I'd thought their freaking "two bit" tap dance was, hilarious... go figure!

When I'd prepared myself to pounce like, a tiger. Just to, entertain my silent thoughts like... "Cowards!"

But, when it came to, figuring out, "what'd rattled my claim?

Well evidently, when they'd halted their "foolish" effects. I reluctantly, got in at, my own "free will." Just so we could make our way,. To "East Liverpool City" hospital. But trust me. If I would've known as to, "where we were going. I wouldn't've got in!

Therefore, since I'd finally reached the point in this demented exercise. That'd at least, allowed me to, vaguely grasp the connection. Between the female images face and my life. What it said and acted like. Almost sounded "ignorant!" So, like before, I handled them. The best I could due to, the circumstances that, came with them!

"Header Lynn!" The female image remarked angrily. "I have "absolutely" no idea as to, why. You've decided to embarrass me in front of, every one. But, trust me. I will and we're not having. Until, I do!

Although, almost everything she'd said, did and I'd heard after that. Had sounded alot more like, foolish jibberish remarks she'd made up. To protest her ideas. In front of, those whom mattered in her mind. I couldn't help but to, recognize the color of, "hospital white" forming around me.

But even though, in my mind. This was just stage two of, it's procedure happening "all over" again. The details that, protected the secrets. That'd happened four years earlier. Just didn't go away... go figure!

Yea, I may've held good suspicions as to, why. To me they'd seemed way too familiar! To "not" identify. With everything mom attempted to use. To foolishly prove as being, otherwise. I still "knew better!"

So, after spending the past 30 minutes. I'm what'd now, felt like hell! I may not've been able to, put an identification. On what'd appeared to be, the female images sower of, "rude reactions" to them.

When it came to, evaluating all of, those. In whom'd became, more than just a little flabbergasted by it's results, I clearly wasn't the only person involved!

No! I may've "not" put an identification range to them, but, from what I could tell. By that point. I clearly wasn't' the only person. In whom, ended up a little more than flabbergasted from it's results.

Especially, after the images. That'd referred to themselves as being, doctors & nurses started slowing their comments with mom.

In fact, I'm convinced if she'd hadn't verbally insisted upon ending. All of her "flaw infested" comments. With the please. "What the heck are you people anyway? Morons!" they may've even been willing accept it as holding. Some kind of, relevance.

Especially, after they got ahold of, this "Dr Fisher" character. This is what "I overheard...

"Mrs. Jensen," the ER doctor patiently came in and announced. Her pediatrician, Dr. Fisher. will be here to, evaluate it's circumstances "personally!" So he can establish his conclusions more "accurately." Within the "next hour!"

But, that's only because, I could hear. Their "discretely exchanged" words in the hallway. Before, this "caught my attention."

Although, until now! They so far, never held any significance or, meaning. Instead of my deciphering their empty words. I'd found a way to, focus my realm of, attention. On figuring out how to direct mine towards their reaction. Towards thoughts that, no-one else. Had even knew existed! Such as...

How the so called my story that, they "didn't know." Had allowed the doctor to, calm. The female images overall image attitude down.

The occurrences that, no one else even knew existed. Not to mention, the temporary fix it'd provided. As I attempted to, deal with it's "real meaning." The real question was, for "how long?"

While, I've never held any doubts that, it's answers. Had lied safely hidden, within the realm of, morning events.

The story flashes of, paranoia it'd produced. Had loomed closely behind afterwards. Which, left a whole different game for me to, piece together. Or, at least, that's what I'd thought anyway!

PART 2

CHAPTER THREE

Then again, what'd you expect? Because, the second I'd heard the word epilepsy being, so. Whatever it'd meant. I'd automatically, knew that, the best way. To avoid another estranged burst of, paranoia. Lied strictly within myself.

Thus since, from what I could tell. Just the act of, having to, witness it's overly imacutant size. It was like, everything except, my own piece of mind. Had been exhausted by it's wrath. Everything else basically, was the same.

Besides with the clock on the wall practically, swearing. That it'd taken a lot longer to, ride itself out. To stand still in time. Without any truth to, back it up.

It wasn't until, all of the hoo-ha and nausea stopped. The concept of, falling asleep. Just could no longer be avoided.

Because, no matter how many times I'd silently, reviewed. What I'd already knew through personal experience. After a few hours of, having to wake back up. Just so I recognize it's result. Just wasn't like, any other set of nightmares. That we've all been guilty of, having from time to time.

Although, in all due honestly. I'd came real close to wondering. If I'd done something so imacutantly, stupid. That it'd ironically, enough had pushed. My already shallow status of, good luck over. What was "very much" a given end point.

Judging from my perspective. It really didn't matter when it got there! Because, the nurses made a very distinct and overly, annoying remark.

That'd possessed an even bigger question. Or even better yet, sounded horribly wrong.

No! I may 'de not possessed "riding out" next. But, rest assured. After we're done reviewing the fine details from this chapter. You'll have no problem understanding why. It wasn't done on purpose! Allow me to explain...

Yea, I may 'de found. What most people would refer to as being, a stand still. But, according to, w hat I'd learn and rode out that morning. I don't think I really cared!

Plus, since according to, my mom's theory. I've never been "the easiest" child in the world "to raise," I knew I'd have to be the one. I'm whom'd brought up this issue"... first!

Besides, with nothing in my world being, "that easy". It made the act of investigating her theory. Not seem to, work so well. "For example"...

Although, until I'd acquired enough information. To push this detail or chore along faster. I'd just have to, play it's circumstances "as is."

If I had to describe my impression of, "them." I could swear that I'd sensed the vibe of, someone. Or perhaps, I should say that, "something." Had decided that, it was hungry enough. To munch on "my butt" to "surface" its craving!

Until it decided that, it. Just didn't care for "the taste" and "spit me"... "back out."

Which is why, other than, my reaching for the emotional support "I'd needed. Before, it's sting could "successfully" bush me. I've never listed "step one as," the most" important.

To put it mildly, "so to speak." That "pretty much" describes "the experience."

In other words, I'd "clearly," had "much better days! But, wasn't designed to be, one of them! Something that, it had "already proven,".. "lucky me."

I couldn't've been there "very long." But, every nurse that, came in "my room." Just couldn't turn around and leave. Without giving me this "weird" vibe" that, they were going out of their way. Which, explains why, I didn't trust any of them!

In fact, at first! My mother's "attitude made." Just stench me as being what most skunks would call. "Basic "text book" add "behavioral patterns." Even for... her!

But since, so far. All of, my "casually stirring up" details. Towards "what'd happened" had been "worthless." Since, I'd first arrived! Having to tolerate mom's "silent interrogation" techniques. Had finally pushed me to the point. Where I was now of, the "seriously pissed me off! I wasn't surprised when they "didn't get" any easier.

"Mom," I'd insisted. "Just for fun, you could try ding, "something useful!" like telling me "what I'd apparently, missed" when everything'd "went down." That's a "fair question... right?"

But instead of, listening to my words. My mother just started to, "come clean." With what "she'd "thought" she knew. When all I'd got in return during "our talks. Is what I like to, refer to, as her "disapproving" look.

You know, what I mean. It's the one "adults" attempt to, slide your way. To make you feel as though, you'd had "no right." To even ask!

Therefore, when I'd finally, got my mom to break. Her supposed, precious "Vow of silence." It made getting her to, answer my question... "even harder!"

"Heather Lynn." Mom replied "reluctantly." "Do you really want to, know. As to what really happened?"

Yes mother, I do! Because, if I didn't! I wouldn't've bothered to, even ask! Now, would I?" I replied frustrated.

"No Heather!" She "quickly" interrupted. "But, if you're really that, curious. Then please, "feel free" to ask away!"

"Well, mom!" I replied defensively. In case, you haven't been, paying any attention... I already did!

Although, I 'd "seriously doubted "the extent of, her investigation. I was even more determined to, not let, her "verbal distraction" wasn't "strong enough." To keep me from the answer to, my question. That I'd already knew.

But because, only a few minutes later, I'd find myself "once again, standing "dead center". In the middle of what stage two would look at.

As another "unrequested" swing of mom's "worthless interrogation tactics. It wasn't really that, bad.

"Mom," I remarked sarcastically. "I may been subjected to, riding this crap out. But, the last time I checked. There's only one reason that, you'd even consider answering my question with another.

But even though, I'd personally. Felt that, just watching her emotional impact from my remark. As "quite worthy" of, further investigation. When she'd refused to, "mutually compromise" with my request.

"Heather!" Mom remarked defensively. "Whatever happened this morning. Doesn't qualify as being, a game or joke"! so, just for the record. I have a seriously difficult problem with the idea of being, acclimated. Into, discussing this, with an, "eleven year old" kid!

Which, once translated. Is just another way of, phrasing. Exactly how much that, she'd felt. It wasn't any of, "my business."

Then again, unknowingly to her. I'd had plenty of, choice words prepared. To slide "back" her way.

"Header Lynn," mom interrupted frustratingly. "I'm quite aware as to, how far. This realm of events played themselves out. But, I'm interested in hearing, your version of, how it "played out."

Heck, once you consider as to, what my mother'd demanded. You'll even begin to understand "how" I'd knew. That they'd eventually, stir up. A "new assortment" of, "unresolved issues." That, only I'd knew co-existed!

Which I why, I'd decided to, respect her "insulting request" anyway.

"Yes Heather Lynn." I know you're curious. But, as far as, I'm concerned! My opinions towards it. Are none of, your "freaking business!"

"Mom." I remarked impatiently. "Personally, I don't really care "how" you think things through," But at first, I was just sitting down to breakfast with, "Walt and Hanna. The next thing I remember." Everything had already, just "went black!"

"You know," I continued. "Just the expression on Walts face. Had belonged to one. That he'd never witnessed before, it'd came to life inside me.

"Heather," mom replied disapprovingly. "Walt may just seem like, a little brother to you. But, he's "not stupid."

Which explains why, I'd found my mom's "next comment". To be mocking less than, insulting.

"Tell me something, mother." Has anyone in "your family" ever finished a conversation. "Without being, interrupted in "mid-sentence" first?

Although, in my mind. This remark itself "still stands" true. To sum it up mildly. I should compare it's worth. To the reality check I'd slid mom's way. As though it'd held some sort of, "stray reference from "my side" of, "the fence."

But because, once it's circumstances at hand. Had been "fully opened." They'd produce another air of questions. I'd gave me an excuse, to push my request level... even further!

"Mom," I continued frustratingly. "I have no-idea as to, what created, your problem with talking to, me "straight up." But, like it or, not. Your giving some form of "serious consideration." To just, dropping it altogether. Would probably work best."

"Heather," mom readily interrupted, "you just said that, you'd found yourself lying on, "our coach." "No, mother." I interrupted immediately. "I'd said, "a couch."

"Yea". Although, I myself have learned through "personal experience." Unlike, my mother's need to refer to, everything. In the singular form. I'd told her like, it was.

"Mom," I suggested impatiently, "Perhaps we should try reviewing it's details. Without the interruptions... shall we?"

Therefore. Instead of, just focusing your attention towards a subject. That's so far, held nothing in return. Just try not to, act so surprised."

"When I interrupt you in mid-sentence. To explain my theories authenticity more clearly."

Yea, my commitment may 'de only been made. As the result of, my mother's reaction towards it. But, it'd definitely, left a lot to be, desired.

"Mom." I interrupted rudely, "Contrary to, popular belief. You have absolutely, no idea as to, what it means. Now, do you?"

"Heather Lynn." Mom interrupted scolding. "Quit trying to, portray this conversation. Into something that, no one else but, you..." even believes."

No! My elite choices in words. May've not sounded right "out loud". But, it at least, gave me enough room. To arouse an, entirely new level of, questioning.

Which, on my mother's behalf. Didn't hesitate to, send her concept of reality "completely off balance." Before it was even over!

"Heather Lynn." Mom interrupted accusingly. If what you're claiming is really true. It still doesn't fall within the answers that, make sense!"

But, by that, point. It really didn't matter either! Because, no matter how hard my mom pushed me to, believe otherwise. Her misdirected minds states. Didn't hold a candle to, mine. Only now, I was actually being, condemned for it!

Yea, I'd still held a sense of loyalty. Towards the inside suspicions it'd portrayed my way. But, I wasn't about to, compromise everything I'd learned. To support my mother's suspicions that drove it!

Not to mention, how she'd felt they couldn't be, confirmed. Whereas, I for example. Didn't really care if she'd liked it or, not. Because, she'd clearly stepped past grasping it's... "true meaning!"

So, as I provoked the conversation forwards. In hopes of showing it's reality. Right back in, her face. Things got even "more interesting"... so to speak!

"Mother!" I insisted impatiently. "I've grown seriously exhausted with the idea of, arguing about this. A few year ago, in fact. But, just in case you're interested. I've found that, just avoiding the "denial room "details. Doesn't work well, for me... either!"

"In other words, yea, it's consequences and results may be unavoidable. But, not ignorable and if you're so "dead sit." On trying to make your method of handling it, sound like, it's the only way to go. Then, hey. Help yourself! Just leave me out of, it!"

But, just between you and me. I really didn't care for her "next statement" much, either.

"Heather Lynn," mom insisted. "How dare you try to, interrupt me. In that tone of voice! I demand an apology, right now. You should be ashamed of, yourself!"

"Well, mother." I insisted impatiently. "I bet you'd just have to, hear it. But, like it or, not! I don't really care either!"

"Besides," in case you haven't been paying any real attention. To the likes of, what's been going on, this morning. This subject officially, stopped being, about you. The exact "same second" it'd happened!"

"Now, just for fun." I continued impatiently. "Here's my next question. Since, I'm the only one, who'll be stuck dealing with this crap. I don't understand why you can't refrain. From spaying out about it... I did!"

"Just face it mom." I continued, "This round isn't about, how it makes you look! This sails about, how they concern me! Heck, even I can see that! What's your excuse?"

But, like I said. My mother may've seemed highly uncomfortable. With just ignoring the facts. Like, they'd held "no significance" what-so-ever. But, I had no intensions in "riding it out" alone.

In fact, if it weren't for my knowing better. I would've almost sworn that my mom. Had also fallen victim to, it's wrath. Her blinding enthusiasm to, repaint the truth to, her satisfaction. Getting her to, shut up about it. Just wasn't an option.

Although, I've personally never cared. About, how my mother felt that, I should except it. I'd grown extremely tired of, putting up "her" as, a result.

Besides, it always came down to, the same thing. Plus, in all due fairness. Since I'd refused to be, subjected to, any more torture. Not to mention, had more than enough of, my mom's lame excuses. To "not" be straight up with me about, it. To last me for an, "entire lifetime"

Almost every attempt I'd made. To have a half-way "civil conversation with mom about it. Had ended up resulting in a heated argument between us. Before, our clock had even struck "noon".

Maybe it would've went "a lot easier." If I would've just given that, line of questioning up... "altogether!"

Well, at least, it would've for a while anyway!

But since, all it ever did, was to recreate my world. Into, a much bigger problem than, it already was. Well, I'd definitely had my hands full. When I was trying to, fit it's "missing pieces" back together".

Then again, how complicated could my life get. As I got ready for school?

Although, personally. I've never cared for playing along. With my mother's spur of the moment "guessing games". It was only because, 98% of, the time. I'd never fail to, pick the "wrong answer

I think that, almost anything, would've been better than, having to, put up. With the dirty life had dealt up for me then.

Which is why, I really didn't find myself surprised. When I ended up standing right smash dab in another. That'd when it came to, my life. Just struck me as being, a lot more along the lines of, "inevitable."

Yea, it may've been enough to, strike my idea. As to the beginning of, "plan to." But, once you consider the circumstances themselves. I really didn't have a problem. With making a last minute exception.

Besides, my mother may' or flaunted the idea of, talking to her. About, what we knew. I really don't think she expected this to be, one of them.

No, I don't think she'd expected me, to create such a "valid point" with them, either! But why that made two of, us!

Which is also, what made an incredibly discuss concept of keeping. Plan his level of importance.

So, of course. Since all my cards. We're already at, the dialers table. I'd made my attempt to, play them out. For whatever they either, were as weren't worth. While it was, still a "workable" option!

Heck, even for as curious as, I'd been. About, my surroundings. During my trail through it's curious flows. I'd still wouldn't have considered using her key carol. To solve this riddle.

With all due respect intended. It'd reached the point. Where it'd already exposed itself. So, I'd had absolutely, no idea. What'd part made me feel the most nervous. About, even suggesting our discussion!

But, other than tolerating my mom's "silent stare" routine. Which, back then, did hold it's significance from day to day.

No! I don't know what 'my mom'd' thought it was worth. But, contrary to, her belief. I wasn't looking for the blunt answers. That I'd always knew, either! Just the truth!

Yea, she'd made me "quite aware" of, her shallow minded viewpoints. You know, like before. But, she couldn't tell me anything. That I didn't already know through, "personal experience."

I quickly interrupted it's silence. Like I was being, betrayed! "Mom," I began. "I don't know as to, whom. You may think you are. But, tap dancing around the facts. Like I was, out of, line. Isn't cutting it!

"In fact" I continued frustratingly. "Just for records sake. "I'd like to, comment. On how many times that, I've seen you. Try to pull off your. I don't know" what you're talking about, routine."

"Besides, mother." I commented impatiently. "Tell me something. In whom, do you think your fooling. With your lies anyway? You or me?"

Well, between you and I. I didn't expect to, hear "my mothers" comment in, return. To start making any form of, "rational sense. Until, I'd already reacted "Z-land." But, I guess, I "was wrong."

"Heather," mom replied calmly. "Are you in any pain?". "No mom," I answered decisively. "Just a little tired."

Yea, I'd thought I pleased it suddenly enough. To close our "one-sided" conversation. But apparently, not by her standards. Because my efforts to calmly, drift off to, "Z-land." Was quickly interrupted with another.

"A little tired? Are you serious?" "Yes, mom I am. Why, does that, create a problem for you?" "No Heather Lynn." She replied frustrated. "But, I would! Especially, after what you've been through!"

Heck, with myself already being, decorated with doubt. I just blew her off. Like, she was nothing! But, when I woke up a few hours later. Everything we'd either, "accidentally or otherwise" stated. Seemed as though, it'd belonged to, a "seriously demented" conversation. That we'd still not even began to, finish… yet!

It really didn't surprise me much. When I'd woke up "two hours" later. Just to see that my evolution. Towards a new technique for approach was definitely, in order.

In other words. To put it mildly. After playing along with mom's nausea minded interrogation routines. That "still" didn't work. I just couldn't hold the truth back anymore. Yea, I know... go figure!

"Mom" I openly insisted. Although you clearly believe otherwise. I've grown more than tired. With your refusal to answer my questions! Not to mention, what you claim as being, none of... "my business!"

"But, trust me! My telling you "the truth." Will never happen again!" I replied insistently. "Now, just for fun! You can begin getting me out of, this place. At any time now!"

No, it wasn't close to, the one. That I'd expected from her! But, surprisingly enough! My mother actually, attempted to describe! The irrational form the reasoning. That'd supposedly, supported her use of, interrogation.

"As for, why your technique of, choice. Has managed to, creep me out so much? Well, mom. I remarked doubtingly. Where shall "I begin?"

"Well, Heather Lynn." Mom insisted sarcastically. "How about, the beginning?"

So with all honesty. After my mother'd exhausted. Al, nineteen different unsuccessful techniques to arouse. A sense of, doubt into, the conversation. I was, just amazed. When she'd actually, agreed that, she'd grown fatigued. With the idea of, avoiding my request. Instead of, humoring it.

It was almost as though, she'd grown willing. To hear my perspective of, this "very real" experience. Or, even better yet. Perhaps curious as to, how, I'd pulled it off.

But, after I'd scrounged together four years' worth of, "unexpressed anger." A lot of, my mom's "less than, brilliant" theories sent me straight for "the juggler!"

"Hey, mom!" I remarked sarcastically. "Have you ever so much as, "slightly assumed." That other than us both, being female. Not to mention, have never shared the same opinion on, anything!"

"That you have absolutely, no idea "what-so-ever" As to, "what" you're talking about?"

"Well, Heather Lynn!" mom interrupted quickly. "Between us, that's never been what I'd call "a sweet. But, that's" yesterday's news." She' scolded.

"Mom!" I remarked frustratingly. "As far as, I'm concerned. I don't care how "reliable" you think it is. Because, this "hospitals status." Will never be anything more than, a building from my perspective."

"Heck mom." I continued frustratingly, "I can't even ask you for a legitimist answer to, any question. Without your lying to, end it as though, I'd had no right. To discuss "what's going on," with "my own body. Without being called a liar."

"But, either way! I really don't thing that, it matters anymore! Because, like it or not, your "less than considerate." Attitude towards me. Has already led me to the conclusion. That there's no such thing as, having, a "happy medium" with you!"

"But hey! As least, my version gives you a choice! In other words, mother! I don't really care if you choose to, ignore me or not! But do yourself a favor and quit acting like, a child!"

"Heather Lynn," she insisted scolding. "You have no right to, talk to me like, that!"

"Mother," I interrupted angrily. "Yes, I do and since you refuse to, understand it's rules... "your wrong!"

Besides, in case you haven't been paying attention mother. I stopped being, a child "four years" ago! So, until you decide to, stop treating me like one. It'd be in your best interest. To just leave "me" alone!"

"Personally, I finished angrily. "I don't know "whom" you "presume" yourself to be. But, I refuse to be, insulted. By your inability to speak to, me. In a "mature adult" "level.""

"Heather," mom insisted selfishly. "In case you" haven't noticed. I'm the only person who's even "in" the room."

"Mom," I commented angrily. "No, I can't speak for you! But, for me. Just having to, tolerate this morning's realm of, events. With you being, nearly to observe them. Has been like, riding out nothing more or, less. Than just another tortuous "stroll through "Hell" itself!

Yea, it may've stated four years "ago!" I continued. "But, trust me. My having to, put up with you "feel sorry for me" act. Hasn't exactly made this rides journey... any easier "for me!"

"I mean, just for fun." I insisted. Why can't you do something creative for me? You know, like not leaving me hanging without answers for once!"

But before, I could look out into the hallway and yell "Are all of, you idiots getting all this. Or, do I need to say it louder?"

Mom quickly, came back with "Heather Lynn!" she remarked embarrassingly. Your purposely, not being, reasonable about this!"

"No, mother!" I'm not! "But, at, the very least. You could try, answering me!" "All yea, Heather?" she remarked doubtingly. "Why should I?"

"Well, mom." I commented. "Since you're the only person. In whom, keeps insisting upon, not cooperating with me. It makes your number one on, my list of, names.

"No, Heather Lynn!" mom insisted debatively "I may not'de been straight up about it... blah, blah, blah!"

But, as usual. Instead of, her useless efforts being, nothing more. Than just another lame excuse to elevate. What I'd considered to be, "A worthless" venture. Or perhaps, I should say... tried to.

I attempted to expose her to, the facts, that I'd already listed as, ones I... "didn't" have!"

However, as soon as, we'd reached the part. That'd brought back my memories of, Walts need to send. Weird glances my way. My life "once again" got, "even more" interesting!"

"Mom," I asked curiously. Has your mind ever felt as though, it was "rebooting itself." Or, at least, trying to. Before, your teacher catches you daydreaming. So, it can step silently into, reality?"

Yea, she may've felt she'd answered my question correctly. Whereas, I'd... "disagreed!"

"Mom," I exclaimed insistently. "I'd felt like, my whole power over equilibrium itself. Had been literally, thrown" Completely off balance! Or perhaps, my lack of, any, would be a "much better" comparison?

Personally, I guess a part of, me. Was really hoping, mom'd have a little more compassion for this sound. But, instead of her giving me.

Then realm of support that, I was counting on. Mom just looked at me. Like I was a fool.

"Mom." I insisted angrily, "Just the idea of, my discussing this subject with you again. Might be bad enough, to induce. But since, the magnificence behind "your concept" of, it. Has "already proven" itself to, lie no deeper than, two inches taps. What's the point, in even bringing it up?"

"In fact," I added angrily. "Since just the idea of, us reviewing it. Seems to mean nothing more than, a waist of my time. What's the point in even asking about it?"

"Because, as far as, I'm concerned." I continued. "If you're really that, interested in hearing. The still unknown answers it "may hold." Or, even better yet. What they'd meant from "my side" of, the fence. Then stop looking at me. Like I was nothing more. Than a "stupid idiot!"

"What's that supposed to mean, Heather Lynn? Mom remarked debatively.

"Well, mom!" I continued sarcastically. "Since, I've already bind up to, my end of, this deal. I guess, it means that, it's "your turn!"

Although, just between you and me. I've never noticed this less than, dependable situation. To do "very much" for me. Personally, I'd at least, hoped. That it'd help mom step past her "obsession denial" stage. So, we could approach it's details. In a more" matured like, fashion.

So, before my mother could impound. What I'd said with her last minute "lame concept." That allowed her to, call the shots.

Not to mention, rule my right. To voice any of "my questions" towards it! The real facts it'd possessed. Decided to step itself up "another" match."

"Mother," I insisted impatiently." If you actually, think your ridiculous form of, impatience. Is enough to, surface my quest for "legitament answers" towards it. Then please, feel free to, "ignore them!" All that, you want! I don't mind!"

"But, rest assured that," either way." Your "One sided" aca of significance. Isn't what I'd call "any easier". Or, better yet, any more "worthless" to me!"

"Because, with your negativity towards trying to, believe "otherwise". Well, don't be surprised if you're "not asked" to, step up. To help me fill in, the "few voids" from it. Which, I'd apparently, somehow "overlooked!"

"You know," I added determinedly. "Like the ones you supposedly, witnessed my reactions to!"

"I mean, just face it mother". Inquiring minds "want to, know. Mine did! As perhaps. I should say... deserve to!"

"Plus," mom continued disapprovingly. "I might be interested in helping you. If you'd stop acting "so ignorant" towards me. Long enough to, let me turn your "lack of, cooperation around!"

"Mom," I interrupted angrily No, I can't speak for anyone else. But, whether you like this idea or, not. Is irrelative. Because, I'll be speaking "for myself."

"Heather Lynn! Mom insisted cautiously." I really don't think hat, saying this. Would be a "very good" idea!"

"No, mom!" I insisted. In your eyes it's probably not! But, I refuse to hide. Your uncontrollable fear to, find out this answer. Like, you're more scared of, what you may learn!"

"Besides," I continued. "If you haven't already noticed, mother.

Unlike yourself, for example. I refuse to, cower at, your accusations. Any more than, anyone else's!

However, I continued. Since, I've never cared how you look at it. That call is, strictly yours! All I want to do. Is to learn it's "real answers. Instead of, just trying to, make them up. As I go along... "dig?"

But, when I as usual. Found my paranoid shaking "invisible limbs" from "the forbidden tree" of mom, I decided to investigate its "still hidden" realm... "even deeper!"

"Mom," I blurted out insistently. "Personally, I really don't care what you may think. That the status level of, your "major malfunction is worth. But, hey! Who am I to bring, that up?"

"Then again," I continued persistently "Since, my "not buying" into, your little act. Has also allowed me to see your I'm "too young" to, understand. Exactly, "what's been going on with my own body" routine. For what it's really worth.

"Contrary to, what you'd care to believe. Your" I have all the free will in this discussion "Act." Just isn't doing you any favors!"

"Which basically means," continued. "That if God "thinks I'm" old enough to side this crap out. Then, figuring it out should be easy… dig?"

Besides, mother! I continued patiently. "I have no idea as to, what your problem is. But, it's definitely, "not" mine!"

Yea, my choice in words. May've been the best way to, send mom's "touch and go" techniques. Into, the "closest available" corner. So, I could review the "depth of, it's details"… in peace.

Plus, with my mom's flawed display of, hands. Not come close to, "trumping" mine. By that time, she was pretty much on… 'her own!"

Which, took me back to, the car accident. I'd been in only, "four years" earlier! "Mom," I began impatiently. "It may've only been. By way of, my nightmares below, now.

Although, I can't pretend. That I haven't been forced to, review "the sting" from its wrath. In my world," I added impatiently. "When someone finds themselves reliving the "same nightmare" every night. By way of, their dreams."

"It usually means that, their lives are confronting a major" turning point. Which will more than likely expose. It's "long overdue" answers!"

"Such as, the ones you getting" slapped across the face" with. Just so, I can get your "self-infatuated" attention… for example!"

"But, as you walk around in "your chosen" realm of a world. You know, so you can protect "your own" butt.

It's not yet, encrypted codes. Makes the corrupt of, "Grimm's fairytales" look like, real stories. Which, my brain is creating as, we speak."

"So, if you're really "that, interested." In hearing about, this sound of, my "little playmates" actions." It was like, the wrath of the dragon was being lived from, it's "trusty lair!"

"Which," exposed a hidden. door." I continued. "To an" unknown crossroad. "But, rest assured. Because my recognition of it's presence. Didn't just, stop there… not even place!"

"Mom!" I angrily blurted out. "I don't know as to, "whom". Or, even "how" many times I'd wondered this about you! But, maybe you should try wrapping your head around. What you "do" understand. Instead of, hiding it in "the dark".

Heck, even though I must say. That "when she did attempt to do, so. Even I'd had more than, I could "wrap my head" around. With my own personal knowledge of what I'd seen. I'd decided to, go for it... anyway!

"Besides, mother!" I continued accusingly. "In case you haven't been paying any attention! I'd just spent the past "four years" of, my life. Being my absolute best to, "sing-handedly" reassemble the pieces."

"To what has been like, a "nerve ending" pile of, "bull pecky." So, I could hopefully figure out my next move. Before, it could show it's "face" again!"

Although, I'm positive my "step-dad" wouldn't've agreed. I've never doubted how real it's, toxic area of, significance was.

Since, in all due fairness. I can't claim how close that, my mom. Has ran a very close second place. Just so she could pick up the left over stray pieces. With a few of, her own personal remarks to, back them up!

But, since according to my mother's so called, "performed" words of wisdom. I'd been the only one who was responsible for my actions.

I looked at mom as being, the person who'd been responsible for putting the letter "s" in the word "stubborn."

Plus. Since it'd already proven it's worth in, my mind. I'd had absolutely, no intention in trying to, just blow it off. It put me in the mood to, prove her interpretation as being, wrong.

I mean, yes! I may've ended up having to wait. Until, mom'd get the idea. To push my patience level. Well past their normal expectations limit.

Before, I could get mom to, redirect her attitude. Back towards our "going nowhere fast conversation. Just by the way she'd casually, released it's words. But, contrary to her beliefs. I knew better!

"Heather Lynn!" mom insisted scolding. "Coming from me, this may sound a little ridiculous. But, after everything that's already happened today."

"Well, until I can get better idea of, what we're dealing with, you can't expect me to be, able to draw. Any form of, rational conclusions as to, its worth!"

"Because," she added intimadatively. "In case you haven't noticed. Apparently, I'm just along for the ride!"

"Mom!" I insisted defensively. "I really don't care as to, how many times you ask this question. Because, the answer itself, won't change! Can you understand that, mom?"

But before, this gets any more complicated. Then it already has. "I continue insistently. "you need to reconsider. Your colds of coming to, terms. With the fact that, I'm not the one."

"In whom's afraid of, us having this conversation... you are!"

"However," I continued persistently. "As long as, you don't attempt to, make it. Into, another "foolish disagreement" that, you "can't" handle... "will good!"

"But, other than that. As long as, you remember to keep. You foolish comments to, yourself. Who knows? Maybe we can avoid this stupid problem... altogether!"

"Heather!" mom readily interrupted. "Let's just review the "so called" images. That you claimed to, have witnessed... instead!"

"Mother," I insisted impatiently. "We already had that, discussion. A few times in fact! But since, I'm tired of being, looked at. Like I'm some kind of, an idea as, a result."

"I was just wondering if, you could find it within yourself. To answer me! Instead of, feeding me your selfish lies!"

"Personally, mother!" I continued impatiently. I've been more than, quite aware of, how. This particular conversation is supposed to, end. Since, point a!"

"So, tell me something mother. Why should I car? About, how "you feel" your "within the communities eyes" theory. Is supposed to, work?"

"Besides," I remarked impatiently. "I've grown a little more than, tired of being, blown off. Like I'm unworthy of, hearing the truth it concerns!"

"But since, I don't appear to, visually, grasped it's purpose. I'm actually, willing to ask you this. At least, one more freaking time. Before, I make my next move!"

"So tell me something mother!" I asked intimidatively. "Why should I be willing to, believe you?"

Heck, just between us. I'll never understand how my mother. Couldn't've seen! The amount of, "anger and doubt" I'd had. In just my eyes alone!

"Heather Lynn!" mom gasped innocently. "I'm not trying to make you feel like, an idiot! I just want to know what happened!"

"Mom," I insisted calmly. "News flash!" I'd already told you. What I know about it! Or perhaps, I should say. "What you'll let me know!"

So, if you don't want to, cooperate. Just leave me alone! Instead of, making less than useless attempts. To get me to, say more.

"But, mother." I insisted sarcastically," If you're really interested in learning. About, what I think it means. Then perhaps, you should try, investigating my words. Without interrupting me in, mid-sentence?"

"In other words, mother." The images I've claimed to, have witnessed. "No matter how much you'd prefer I believed otherwise. Aren't just "mere figments" of, my imagination! Deal with it woman... I did!"

"Heather Lynn!" mom replied impatiently. "I'm only asking you to, humor me! Just tell me what you can remember. About, this morning's sequence of, events."

"Mom," I interrupted. "No, I don't expect you to, care. But, I've heard the loud noise that, comes with this sound before!"

"Which is why, when I'd heard it coming onto, the front porch. I knew that, something really weird was up!"

Then suddenly, I continued hesitantly. These mere figments of, my "so called, imagination, just started to, box me in!

"Heather," mom interrupted doubtingly. "Did you see what these images faces look like?"

"Mom!" I insisted disruptively, "I tried to evaluate. What their faces looked like.

"Well, Heather" mom remarked sarcastically. "You can say allot you want about them!"

"No, mom!" I remarked angrily. "I didn't recognize them! Because, every time I attempted to, look at their faces. It's like, they didn't have a face to, supply!"

"So, you didn't see their faces?" mom commented curiously. "Heather, what's wrong with you anyway? Do you even understand as to, how ridiculous you sound right now?"

"Heather!" she continued disapprovingly. Everyone has a face! That's stupid! So, since "nobody," "not even myself. Is going to be willing to, believe anything you're saying. It should be interesting. When you try to tell them that, they didn't have one to, see!" she gloated.

"Well, mother!" I debated angrily. "It's like, this. It's a good thing that, I don't expect them to, believe! But, just as having this conversation. Tells me what you think "you know!"

"So, if you're either, having some sort of, problem. Or better yet, just don't care how this conversation ends. Then, tough crappola! Because I'm done listening to, you" self infatuated "lies! Hey mom! Don't you just hate it? When that kind of, stuff happens... I do!"

But since, my misclainious remark about, my images. Not having anymore than, a blue for a face Han left my mom "pretty much "dumbfounded" as, a result.

Just my having to, side out these circumstances "alone." Had given me more than, a "little time to, cross examine. The very "graphic mixture" of, events. My mother'd spent the past four years trying to, portray. As my unwilling like, mess.

All yea. When there's my "serious inability" to, except. Things as she'd saw them from "her perspective."

So before, I proceed to, continue. That mornings sequence of, events any further. I'd just like too, go on record as stating. That after this point in time. Almost anything mom said she'd witnessed after them.

Would basically, sound like, the adults do. On, "the" Charlie Brown" show. You know what I mean. "Wa, wa, wa, wa, Heather. Wa, wa, wa... wa, wa."

Personally, I'd already knew. How mom's "wa, wa" theory. Wouldn't hold up when I brought it to, her attention. But, I didn't care either!

Although, this was definitely, news. That mom hadn't "yet" grasped. I did manage to "accidentally, over hear. Someone trying to whisper my name to mom. In the same sentence as, the word "Epilepsy."

But since, I myself. Had absolutely, no idea as to, what that, word meant. Not to mention, they'd never made any efforts to explain it.

It apparently, left both, my mother and the hospitals employees. More than just a little less concerned. With how it's results looked in my world... "Amateurs!"

But, even though the truth it possessed. Would eventually, step up to proclaim it's freedom. It'd appear to be, a lot like, a lost fear to me!

One in which, my mom kept trying to, pretend. That people "didn't have" plastered all over their faces. Almost "every time" they'd so much as, "stroll my way.

Although, unknown, to anyone else preference of it's existence. I'd used the lame excuses mom'd invented. To both, ignores them and the wrath from it's sting.

I'd honestly, thought that, I'd destroyed. The aca of, all easy access to, the secrets it'd held.

That is, until mom attempted to, use them on me. In the ambulance that brought me there. But, hey! You know what they say. "Desperate times such desperate measures!"

Therefore, since both, them and my mother. Were literally, refusing to tell me. The truth about, what was going on.

I decided to, take it upon, myself. To casually, probe them for answers!

Which, had interestingly enough. Just ended up opening my mind. To an entirely different round of, even more questions.

But, with me being, such a nice lady and all. I wasn't willing to, let mom leave. Until, I'd opened her mind. To what the rest of, the world refers to as being." A little food for thought!

"Mother!" I remarked angrily. "As I'm sure that, you already know. It's your insistence to, not as any of, my questions. As, better yet. Even answer my comments honestly. That's made me so impatient. With your excuses to, avoid them!"

"Plus," I continued. "With that thought in mind. I really can't understand as to, how my request. Can actually, qualify as being, "too big, to fill!"

"Therefore, I refuse to listen. To anymore of, your immature excuses. Or perhaps, I should say. The ones you've chosen to, "Tap-Dance" around me. When you need to, leave me in, the dark without answers!"

"Because, unlike, yourself, for example. You "bull limp" just isn't good enough, to cut it for me anymore... dig?"

"So, just for fun. Be it, that, way or not! No matter how estranged they may seem. I'm willing to give you one "last chance. To mend the vices in, your interpretation.

"However, mother." I continued sarcastically "If you just "so happen" to, divide. That you are actually, willing to", listen to me. Not to mention, be straight up with me about, it. Instead of refusing my request to, try them, wise done?"

"In other words mom. I continued impatiently. Just in case, you haven't get, grasped. The depth of, the impact from this morning's events."

A lot of, seriously missed up factors. Have readily fallen into, play. Since it's all began. So, it'd probably be in your best interest to, pay special attention. To how much I choose to emphasize my words... during it!"

"All yea," I continued impatiently. "And we wouldn't want to, forget the fact. That I'm the only person standing, "right in the middle" of it!

"Then again." I remarked intimidatively, "since that's not exactly. What I'd call "unusual" for you. It makes me seriously wonder. If old habits really do, die hard... no pun intended."

"Heather Lynn!" mom remarked authoritatively, "I don't know whom, you thing you are. But, if you've trying to hint towards the idea. That whatever you think you've experienced. Has saved you. Then, trust me. I can relate!"

"Mom". I insisted curiously. "Tell me something. Is trying to grasp where this conversation creates the biggest problem. With "us" having it? Or, is it more along the line of being, you "not wanting "to?"

"As for me? Well, mom. It's like this. After all the things I've witnessed you doing during it? I remarked in intimidatively. I really don't as to, where you think it leads me. But, just so we both understand each other. A conversation "can't be" finalized on, stupid foundations. Such as, how "you" feel they should end!"

"Heather Lynn!" mom interrupted disapprovingly. "What gives you the right to speak to, me. In that, manner? Well, mom. I remarked determinedly. Let's just look at things from your perspective... shall we?"

"I mean, not that you've actually given me any say in this matter. Because, we both know that, you haven't."

"But, unlike yourself, for example. At least, I've never been too afraid. To step up an confront this problem at, it's "true" face value!"

Sure, my mom's main objective. May not've been any stronger than, the confession she'd created to trick me into, revealing. What she'd believed as being. An acceptable line of, questioning. To begin giving me an invalid line of, questioning. To an invalid line of, curiosity on my behalf.

"Mother!" I insisted. What the heck makes my asking you to, step past your self-denial act. Just long enough, to get you. To slide a little of your emotional feedback towards me? I mean,... My God!"

Well, even if I didn't have anything else to say to, her. At least, my last second comment. Had successfully given my mom a lame excuse. To establish solid sensitivity issues. As her temporarily get me out of, the way free card.

Although, personally. I didn't really care if my comment had offended her. Just so, I don't sound like, the bad guy here. I'd like to point out how badly. That moms stupid silent interrogation tactics "stood out."

But because, none of, them did me any favors. I should've probably, taken a few extra seconds. In order to make sure that, mom was as up to, date on the facts. As she'd thought she was before, I'd made my next move.

But, instead of being, thorough. I jumped in with "both" feet!

Which, curiously enough. Explains why mom started trying to ask me questions. That only she was interested in learning. The answers to!

"Heather Lynn!' mom remarked depicting. "What do you think your so called inquiring mind. Needs to know anyway?

"Well, mother." I replied seriously. "That depends really." "An what ???

"What do you think, I should do to take" you up. On your office? Mom remarked defiantly. You know, so I can slip up and lay my cards on, the table?"

"Well, mother I commented doubtingly. "Where should I start?" Besides, in case you haven't noticed it yet. You're not the one being confined to, a hospital bed. Without any reasons as to, why get." I am!"

"So, just for future reference. You know for sake of conversation." I insisted. "Here's how I see this issue" I remarked determinedly.

"Since God thinks that, I'm old enough, to side this out alone. Then if automatically means that, I'm good enough. To do so! Not to mention at least, hear the truth. About, what's going on with, my own body! After all, mother." I commented. You wouldn't want to question the "Lord's authority now, would you?"

"Well, mother" since you're the one. In whom, keeps refusing to, answer me. I guess it makes this your call. So, make it!

"Heather Lynn!" Mom jumped up disapprovingly. "What it goes. Is without saying that, the Lord thinks you're not maturely sufficient for it. But since that's already been proven." The insisted. "What makes you think you can handle. The as to, what it means part?"

"Newsflash, mother." I remarked angrily. "Just in case anything happens to, me with this. In which, I already know that, it has!" I remarked impatiently. I mean, I might only be eleven. But when you go out of, your way. To deny my ability to do so."

"All it does is to create nothing less than a complete insult. In which, you insist upon directing towards me!

"So, tell me something mother. I asked. Who do you thinks being, out of line now?"

"Heather Lynn," mom started out disapprovingly. "I may seek like I'm trying to ignore this conversation. As perhaps I should say, my discussing it. But, I'm not!" she insisted "I just can't find the proper words to explain it. Is that wrong?"

"Well mom". I replied impatiently. "It wouldn't be if you were just willing to tell me the truth. But, I know better!"

"Because, whether you like it or not mom. What you'd like me to be. Is nothing more than a lame excuse to, tell lies! "But," I continued. "Let's be for real... shall "we?"

"I mean, after all." I remarked. "If I can figure out as to, what words to use. Just to describe my point of view. On a first name basis. What you excuse to, not cooperate?"

Although, just as I'd expected her to. My mother thought that this was her excuse. To make me feel guilty for requesting an answer. I didn't feel sorry for what I'd said next!"

"Heather," mom readily insisted. As though, I was the only person at fault. "Why can't you just try showing a little respect... towards me?"

"Because, whether you like it or, not." She continued. I refuse to speak up about, your attitude anymore. Until, I at least, get an apology!"

"Well, mother." I commented doubtingly. "It be in your best interest.. To just not get your hopes up if I was you!"

"All yea?" Mom answered with her silent treatment techniques. Why shouldn't I?" "because, mother!" I insisted. "I wouldn't want you to end up disappointed! But, I know you will!"

Plus, since as, usual. It didn't take my mother very long to, change her attitude. To the entire extremity of the conversation at hand, I almost laughed right in her face. When she attempted to, ask. "So, Heather Lynn. Are you ready to apologize to me yet?"

"Hey, mom." I commented openly. "Perhaps you haven't heard yet." "Heard what, Heather Lynn?" That dreaming's free? Well, mom." I continued. I think if anyone here deserves an apology. It's me! "So." I continued. "Now that I've made you aware of, that part. Go ahead and give me your opinion. About, what happened... whenever you're ready."

"Heather." Mom remarked defensively. "I stood right there and watched it happen. As it was going on. But, rest assured. It was very real."

"Hey mom!" I interrupted sarcastically. "Nothing personal. But, I've been telling you, "that" part. All morning! So, did you see it's conclusion?"

"I mean, if you remember mom. You weren't the only one. In whom, felt it's wrath." I continued cautiously. "I was! So tell me mom." I asked curiously. "What makes you think that, I'm wrong? Or, better yet. What makes you that, I didn't?" Go ahead." I continued. "I'm listening."

"Heather!" mom exclaimed. Stop lying to me! "Mom," I asked. Are you trying to, call me. A liar?

"Yes, Heather." She insisted. "I am! But, who knows. Instead of just hiding your story. There could be a hidden story behind it. Not to mention, I may even find the solution. Who knows. Maybe by then. I could actually find it within myself. To believe you!

Although, nothing I'd said during, my remark. Had so much as, struck me.. As being of, the irritational side. I'd already knew how the thoughts from her inner mind. Had basically, worked.

Yea, she may've been trying. To hold back under stress. But, so was I. Just trying to, tolerate her sing and dance routine.

"Mother." I interrupted calmly. All I ask before, you rewrite our conversation. Is that you listen to, what I have to say. About it first, you know. In case you actually want to discuss the details from my side of, this fence. In a mature adult like, fashion."

Although, I can't pretend that, none of my experience with it. If you want to, call it that. Had so much as, came to fitting. The dictionaries definition of, the word "normal."

I really don't think. I could've rode out, my life's experience. Without learning the things I'd did, that morning. During the process.

Heck for as vague as, this experienced seemed. A lot of, it's terms had changed and they. Weren't about to tell me. Anything that I'd hadn't figured out. Through, "personal experience."

But since, I'd passed that, point. At least, a couple of, hours ago. It'd became more about. What I'd had to do to, survive it.

"Mom," I said "whether or not you were able to, see, what you think happened. Is irrelevant. If fact, they remind me of what, I watched through my dreams. You know, the one you didn't allow me to discuss."

"You should see how much clearer. That it'd all looked this time."

Which surprisingly enough, at the time. Must've been what let me shake. The "forbidden tree of, mom. A lot harder than, I'd thought.

Especially, when I tried to, stand my grounds on it. Before, mom decided to, back off.

"Well, Heather." Mom interrupted. "What you're saying, sounds all well and good. But, like get back. To what really happened. Shall we?"

No, I may've not been able to, figure it out. When my mom kept trying to, duck out. In the hallway at ER. But since, she did call "Aunt Carol" from there.

A few hours later. Here we were. But, I still didn't know. What was, going on.

Although, I'd had my own. I would've never allowed the look mom'd had possessing her face. On mine. I'd been the only one whom'd seem it's wrath. Amongst a building full of medical professional.

But since, my mother's level of fear. Had officially elevated itself to the next level. Which, since it'd happened to, me.

But, because, when Carol'd walked in. My mother'd jumped from her chair. So, she could meet her. Over by the door. Where they could speak freely about, it.

Or perhaps, I should say. From out of, earshot range. Thing got more complicated. Whether mom'd liked it. Or, not!

"Heather," Aunt Carol asked. When I'd explained. Why do you keep saying. That the medical professionals insisted. Upon taking a pow wow session. Out in the hallway?"

Yea, my comment may've struck her as being. Like another one of, mom's unexplainable questions. In which, she wasn't prepared to, answer.

But, when they were done with. The chatting session. After they'd exchanged notes. For about, five minutes.

Caro proceeded to, walk over by, my bed. Just to mention how badly. That she'd disapproved of, my behavior. Or perhaps, I should say. The one's I'd explained to her. Happened during my, "so called", scrapping session... with fate.

In order, to elaborate. The best I could. On it's facts. You know, the one's mom'd forbade me. To discuss two years earlier. Heck, I think I'd even suspected. To get in trouble. For doing something wrong. When, I didn't.

But, because. Unlike, my mother's concept of, how it worked. It really didn't bother me. Any deeper deeper than it'd had to.

I'd pretty much received the look. That'd come with it. More than, just a few times. Since, I'd been there.

Then again, to me. I'd just all seemed to be, a waist of, precious time. That I wasn't willing to, give up also. Especially, after all the time I'd wasted. Just trying to, figure out. All of, it's less than, interments details. By myself.

But since, I wasn't feeling up. To getting into, it's random after effects, with Carol or, mom. I guess, I couldn't blame them. For thinking that, it was real.

Besides, if I'd learned anything. From the "unwelcomed" experiences of, it's wraths chase. Especially, that morning.

It's how much you can learn from people. Whenever you're not trying to. Well, at least. That'd been "my impression," anyway!

As for, what I'd learn from my situation. Or, even how it'd end up fitting into, my life? Well, that was, anyone's guess.

But, it'd basically qualified as being, a hand that'd insisted upon holding a realm of strangers. Which, I'd never get over. ??? had on me as though, it. Was actually playing itself out. Right in front of me.

Which, according to those. In whom'd witnessed. Such as, my mother, for example. That couldn't reveal this opinions.

Without leasing mere "steady conclusions." About, what I'd been through that morning. But, even with all of, that... going on around me.

I'll never forget how. What I'd heard during, it. Almost didn't seem real.

Which, as far as, I know. I've always felt foolish about. Yea, I may've done my best to, play it out. That'd left me with a very complicated beat.

Besides, unlike, the others. I'd actually knew enough about it. To deliver your with it's conclusions.

The bottom line is, you can refer. To the likes of, that morning. As many times as, you want. But, it don't change.

It was the day that, time. Had actually, stood still in, my life. But, I can assure you. That in my mind. It was just the beginning of, many.

How would you explain it?

CHAPTER FOUR

"Untangling it's "mysterious,"
Web of last "dreams"

I'm going to, go ahead and begin. The chapter from my life by saying that I'd actually, be willing to, go. As far as, confronting a survey. On this particular subject as being, one serious pain in, the butt.

In fact, if I had survey it's "worth" altogether. I'd say that at least, 98% of the world's population. Would remark that they'd never even heard of, an "unwanted sidekick." Let alone, "dealt" with one!

But, win it they'd had. I can guarantee that their understanding of it. Couldn't hold a candle next to, mine! However, rest assured. Because, before this chapter is over... you will!

Heck, if I'd really felt. In the mood to, go that, route. I could probably answer that, question... right now! But, why take "all the fun" out of, it?

Especially, when it'd be a lot easier. Just to, let you disco your own conclusions towards, this subject. As we go along.

Although, just for records sake. I was still pretty foggy on, how. The rules to this particular game. Were supposed to, go myself. Well, at least, then I was. So, I could've also been wrong about them too.

I mean, along life's chosen path. It happens to, the best of, us. But, not this sound. No, this time, it hit me!

Heck, we since my newly acquired phantom friend. Had resurfaced after, lying dormant for four years. It'd downright refused to, just leave me alone. Which is exactly why I'd named it that, in the first place!

As far, when it'd decided to, just, come and go? Well, between you and me. I've never had any say, in that, part. But, if I did. I'd insist, upon, it being, never!

However, as I've said before. That part, just wasn't my call to, make. Which, made the concept of, trying to live my life. On what most people'd consider to be, a "normal basis." Became like, next to impossible!

Although, I personally. Will always stand true. To it's scariest parts. I think the one, that'd missed with me the most. Would have to, do. With the facts I'd drown from it. In what'd seemed like, no longer. Than the blink of, an eye.

After that, my entire life. Had actually, managed to, succeed. At turning itself completely, upside down.

Actually, since my mother was the one that'd told me. That I'd been unconscious for, right and a half minutes. Before, regaining consciousness. It's flickers and flashes will always seem way too short. To comment to, an actual memory.

Heck, I've never been able to, look at, myself. In the minor since! Now, "here's why."

Because, within the matter of, time. That'd lasted no more than, eight and a half minutes. I'd ended up performing. What was, our usual "Scooby-Doo" dance ritual. Until, it'd transformed. Into, me laying on a couch.

To standing ankle deep in, a creek bed. Which finally, ended. With me being, in a "seriously distorted," state of mind. Things had complicated quite fast.

Yea, it may've taken place last, 5/574. At 8:05 am. But, just for the record. I'd been counting every day since.

However, when it comes to keeping teach of, my phantom friend. You shouldn't be surprised. When you find yourself. Talking my mirage of, unsolved questions. With it "every time."

In fact, on the morning of, it's. So called, grand entrance ceremony. I'd honestly felt like, I'd stepped. Inside an, invisible "Time ripple." That'd somehow managed to, relocate itself. Right in the middle of, our "living room" floor. Which'd interestingly enough, had created it's mystic time ripple. In the middle of, it.

Things started to, get real interesting. Not to mention, that it'd actually last port hole, so to speak.

But, as a result. Instead of, my finishing myself. Trapped outside of, reality. I'd found myself being lost in, a huge spider web. With no way out. Until, it's predator. Acknowledged it's catch.

But since, what most people look at. As a still hidden key. In which, I'd needed to, unlock it's secrets. Had been dangling freely around me all along.

It'd made me feel like, I'd been trapped inside it. All along. Which, left me basically, feeling. Like I'd been trapped. With the chase of, trying. To unlock it's secrets.

Yea, just the memory of, what. It's actually like to, experience. Has haunted me ever since that, morning. By way of, my dreams.

Therefore, I may've done everything within my power. Just to keep myself from telling someone. To get it off of, my chest. But, my phantom friend never seized to, come back!

Then again, you can call me paranoid. All you want. But, before this conversation goes any further. Than it already has. You really should take care to, wonder why.

Besides, as I'm sure you're already aware. The fine art of, searching for answers to, questions. In which, you don't have the guts to ask about. Never comes off as being, mild.

Please, don't ask me as to, how many people. Had referred to themselves as being, doctors that morning. Because, as soon as, you have access. To the unwelcomed privilege of, it's "Grand Awakenings" after effects. Because, I'd stopped counting them. Somewhere in, the teens! But, that's only as, a result. That so far, not one of, them. Has ever been able to perceive me anything. To control it! Without my body immediately, rejecting it. With an allergic reaction.

Which, also explains why. That I'd looked at them. As what I like to, call "med-school" want to, he's. Just trying to, play along. With it's part.

But, relax. Because, it wasn't a total loss and I did. Manage to pick up a few things. That'd wild as, it was. Fill strictly under the category of being. From something. Called, "personal experience."

For example, when you find yourself trapped. Inside of, situations which require immediate answers to, step past. While your automatically bring, consumed by it!

However, when a search for it's answers. Isn't an issue. They never fail to be, no more. Than just "fingertip" distance away.

Of course, with that, specific failure. Now being, clearly in mind. You also need to remember. That once we've reviewed it's answers. There's a very good chance that, you might "not like" them. But, don't be surprised. When you get it's answers anyway!

Although, receiving it's secrets. Just means that, you'll get them anyway. If it bothers you to, this extent. Then, don't ask them, which, wildly enough. Just happened to be, my grandmother's. Favorite rule of, choice!

Yea, I may've been bodily led. To almost every medical facility. Within a hundred mile radius.

But, just cringing from the thought of, going. To another one. Had already created it's "own status," with me!

In fact, since my secret phantoms visitations first began I'd hadn't been able to, go anywhere. Without experience, my recognize of, it's wrath.

Whereas, the hardest part. Lied within the act of, getting my mother. To actually, discuss it.

No, I may not've figured out. How to, make it happen yet. But, mark my words. Because, it's real challenge. Held even darker secrets such as, the answers. That'd built it's mysteries around me.

But, just like, before. My mother'd spent most of, her time. Reviewing implausible answers. As she quoted stray bible verses for backup. As her "big solution" for, just about, everything!

I mean, don't get me wrong! Because, just like everything else, religion and otherwise. Holds in its place. It reminds me of, what a church possesses. On, Sunday's.

Besides. Since, most of, it's conquest. Only holds, one verse. Which is, "when the Lord closes a door. He opens a window."

It was, pretty apparent. That it'd held some kind of, significance. But, if I'd hadn't been with what. My mother'd insisted upon annoying the crap. "Completely" out of, me with. It probably would 've been "a lot easier" to, swallow.

Plus, if you really want my opinion towards mom's "stray quotes." I'd personally, would have to say? That my mother's quotes. Reminded me of, what, seemed much more like," unu8sed "fortune cookie" material. That'd not only, never made it's way outside of a bakery. But'd sounded as stupid. As allowing a calendar. To hold "hot water!"

Yea, I may've had more. Than just a few of, my own problems to, deal with by them. No, I have no idea as to, what I was thinking. But even though, I myself. Have never been of, the "religious prophet" type. Deciphering it's magic. Didn't qualify as being, one of them.

It'd made me even "more determined to realize. How, I'd known all along. That listening to, mother quote there "Bible Verses." Wouldn't materialize a "Good Solution." When it came to, solving this problem.

In fact! According to, all of my observations. Which, since my 5th, 1978. were very accurate. At, the time. It was, just mom. At a way to, hide her!

So even though, she'd spent 98% of, her energy. Awaiting, "Bible" verses my way. Not to mention. What they were worth at, "my" face value. I would've told mom at, an eye to eye stance. That, "riding it out. Was like being, doomed to follow. A long trail of, eggshells. For the rest of, my life.

Which ironically enough. Didn't end up being, far from, the truth. As, my pediatrician, Dr. Fisher. Gave me my monthly check up... as usual.

However, since, they'd really didn't seem to, concentrate. Towards "my health status anymore. It only made sense. When they got, "even more" complicated.

Therefore, I'd basically, made it's realm of, noise. Make me feel like, the only reason. I was there. Was to supervise, my mom's "spaz-out" sessions. Until, they reached their level of full climax.

The way, I'd seen it. The next six months. Got pretty interesting after my mother. Practically embarrassed the "crap" out of, me "so much". That I'd actually, thought. About, how wild it'd be. If I could, hide it's wrath. Under the carpet he'd had in his exam room. Just to, hide my humiliation amongst, the room.

But instead, it was just one more screening. Whether I'd liked it's conclusions... or not. As the result of, mom's repetitious "spaz out" sessions." During, the visit.

Although, this actioned made me more than, willing to reach it's soft spot "even more."

I'd grown significantly, tired. With small things. That didn't require me to, withdraw my emotions. So far, deeply inside me. That it, wouldn't even let "my mom" near it.

Because, judging from what I'd could read. According to her "Bible verses" for answers ritual. The wasn't ready to, face, it's circumstances, "yet"... anyway!

Which was, something. That'd definitely, required qualifying. As, that of, the "seriously," unexpected. Especially, when mom developed her problem with letting me. Grap it's reigns!

But, courtesy of, my mother. Things for as, strange as, they were. From, my side. It didn't take much to, realize how rapidly, things. Had started readily shifting to, my fence!

Then again, this may 'de been news to, her. But as I sat in, "Dr. Fisher's" exam room. Doing my best to time the wrath of, moms repetitious "spaz-out" sessions. The "wildest-thing happened.

But even though, it's cause was being, held, "Right across" the hallway from me. I did manage to feel the stin git showed me. With it's "wrath "repetitiously."

Yea, most of what they'd said about, my situation. Came out as being, below stupid circumstances.

However, I'd heard the doc. Refer to a place he'd called, "The "Cleveland Clinic" foundation.

Personally, I was just amazed that, the doc. Had actually, got her to, "shut up." Long enough, to get mom. To listen to, him. While discussing it's terms in piece.

I'd already spent it's stray time line in pain. But, after 6 long months of, shadowed Dr. Visits. It almost stuck me as, a calm. Before, a storm.

No! I don't claim to have understood it's purpose. But, according to, what I'd heard. So, as I eavesdropped in on, the details I could.

I created an understanding. No matter, "how vague." I started to, grasp an illusion. About, my impressing of, "what" It'd "supposedly," all meant.

Although, after I'd walked through hell in, the process. I couldn't get over how "pathetically." It was being, diagnosed. In, "the process." Well, here's what I'd learned "about, it" so to speak.

Apparently, the "Cleveland Clinic" foundation. Held easy access to, a certain test. That I'd never heard of, before, then.

Which, had been designed by, neurologists. To diagnose the amount of, activity In an epileptics brain cell's. I should call them the people exhibiting symptoms of, a "neurological disorder".

In fact, the way I'd understood it's procedures. It'd actually gave their doctors. A chance to observe it's patients brain. From what "Dr Fisher" called... the "inside out". Like, an x-ray... for example.

While the words, The "Cleveland Clinic" foundation. Held more than it's share of, supposed benefits to, investigate.

The first thought that'd ran through, my mind, was, "oh great!" Another hospital... Lucky me!"

Plus, since I'd already knew, that I'd just end up being, admitted. There really wasn't much. I could do to, prevent them.

As soon as, I'd heard "Dr. Fisher" bouch. For their "medical professionals success. I was convinced that, it was worth a try.

Yea, I could hear my mother's theory. That'd gave him the authority to, take things. Even "one step" further. So as he disappeared into, his office.

To avenge the very long stay it'd required. Just to make sure he'd had the details straight.

Heck I may've heard the word "Epilepsy" used. Several times during, the past "six months." But since, I'd still had no idea. As to, "what it'd accurately meant.

The time I'd spent. Only concluded. That in, my mom's eyes. It wasn't any of, "my" business!

I'm not going to, hard the secrets. I'd interrupted from, my brain. But, unlike, anyone else. That I'd met before, then.

I'd wasn't the least bit surprise. When it'd ended. With the suggestion of, having "more test's" done.

Besides from my perspective. It may 'de seemed like. Being stuck between another "each" and a "hard place."

But, thanks to, my step dad, and mom. The next seven days. Would become, more. Than even "I' could've anticipated.

Which, brings me to, another theory. Concerning my mom and step Father's opinion towards it.

Yea, I may've made my decisions. As to, what I'd felt their meetings. At the dining room conference table was, for.

But, once, you consider the "five feet." I'd' left between us, as, they'd liberally, discussed it's reign.

I was nothing less than, obvious. As to, how much they'd focused. The magnificence of, it's details. Towards, me!

All yea, and we don't want to, forget. This infamous repetitious "How dare you" glares. Or, even better yet. The depth of, their quest. To make me feel, like, I. Was just way, too "immature".

To know the overall truth. About, what kind of, terms it'd held. Until the "very end." As though, it's spiritual heart. Had consumed me!

Heck, I can't even tell you. As to what tastes it'd held. When it stepped up to, feel it's fire? But, I can remember each overly, annoying part. About, it. Every time!

Yea, it's true! I'd held numerous routes to test. But, if I had to. describe, as to, what it was like to, endure? Well, as I've said before. It's techniques, got old... "quite last!"

Besides, it was made more than, clear. How many mom felt with "her concept" of, what it'd meant.

Whereas, I'd. Held my own! No! I'd never expected her to understand it's worth. According to, my terrain of, thought.

But, when I'd evaluated. What I'd known from, "personal experience" itself.

The way I'd seen it. If the "Great Mastered" foresaw me as being, old enough. To ride this routine out alone.

It'd made the entire concept of, me. Being too young to endure it's wrath. Just sound stupid... "No, questions" asked!

I mean yea. My mom may've "thought." That she'd held the right. To voice her opinion towards it. When it made itself visible to, every one else.

Then, there was it's worst part. Such as, it's lacking towards emotional support... ect.

Yea, I'm sure if my mom. Could've understood the magnificence of it's depth. Things involving its terms. Would've portrayed it's worth of being, quite different. A of the way it was. Or, perhaps, I should say, portrayed itself. Like immediately, if not sooner!

But because, it's chosen method of, entry, was clearly, still too far over their heads to, grasp. To interpret the significance of, it's details... yet.

I knew, I'd end up having to earn the right. To retrieve it's secrets the hard way. All over again!

So, of course. With my self's refusal to bough down. To anyone else's foolish theory. That, I should just give up on finding. What I'd needed to, control it.

I'd had every intension of, giving them. A close-up as to, it's worth.

Yea, I may've held my own concept. As to, how it'd apparently, worked. From my mom and stepdad's reach.

But, when it came to, their lapsed concept. I really didn't care how they'd felt. Because, I knew why I'd acquired mine! It's called, good old fashioned "personal experience!"

Plus, whether everyone else cared. To hear it or, not. Was "their" business not mine. Making the challenge of, trying to, step past it's after effects. Sum like, an, even bigger problem.

Although, just between us. All I could really say. About, where they'd snatched their realm of information, was that, "I'd hoped they'd saved their secret." While acquiring, their foolish answers, was that, I'd hoped they'd kept their secret. So, they could return them!

That particular routine held it's own key. Which, unlocked a hidden door. I'd came across only, a few days earlier.

So, as I'd particularly sat there and counted. Every second until, it actually, did!

It seemed a lot more like, an uncharted realm of, my stories. I'd encountered "personally". No more than only, "two days" later. With me counting "every second in between them. For, person reference.

In hopes that, just it alone. Would unveil all of, it's still inconvenient mysteries. Amongst, the several that, were still tangled. In, it's web of, money.

Therefore, with the rules to, this mystic game. Being of neither, mom's, her husbands or, mine. It really didn't matter as to, whether or not. They'd cared for the charade it'd prevailed to protect itself!

Which, for sake of, conversation. Ended up turning into, a very big oops. On their part.

But, hey! I wasn't responsible for "everyone else's" problems! Just mine, own! Then again, I wasn't responsible for their problems, either!

No! I wasn't responsible for teaching them as to, how. This games routine was to, be played. So, shame on them for being, fools.

In whom'd ended up with egg rubbed. All over their faces. As a results of their own bad choice. In it's terms.

No, my mom and stepdad. Hadn't actually been made aware as to, what it'd meant, yet. That part, stood true.

Especially, when their discretely made "paw-wow" sessions. Didn't even qualify as, standing. In the same class as, mine.

Yea, they'd held strong to, their "shut up and take it line. That'd clearly stated how they'd felt. Towards protecting the lies they use to, portray.

But, after spending over four years' worth of, unspoken time. Listening to, their "It's none of, my freaking business" excuses.

Their so called, attitude problem. Just wasn't cutting it's course!

In fact, according to how I'd looked at, this endless quest. It lead my soul inspiration. Towards taking this plan forwards.' To, it's next level.

So, as usual. After I'd tolerated the days assortment of, "how dare you glairs.

All in which, I'd needless to say, Ended up having to take a literal bath. Just so, I could remove them. From, "my own" body!

Before, I could perform my own mirage of, investigations that'd highlighted it's behavior patterns. During, it's process, of, "conference sessions."

Which, also explains as to, why. I'd spent every day up in, my bedroom alone. So I could have the privilege of, looking up, the "true definition" of the word discrete definition. In my "Webster's" collegiate" dictionary. For future references towards. How I should handle it! Allow me to, explain further...

The definition of the word discuss. That the collegiate dictionary provided for me. Clearly reads...

"The ability to perceive the secrecy of, "prudent silence." Yea, it may sound pretty simple.

But, once you translate. This kind of, information into, "little kid" lingo. It'd basically meant that if my mom and stepdad. Or perhaps, I should say, "Me and Mrs." discrete.

Really felt that, strongly. About keeping their two bit, "paw-waw" sessions under wraps. That they could've pick a lot, "better than, our "dancing room." To make, them happen!

You know, somewhere like, In this bedroom... for example!

But, hey. This may just be one of, my. "Off-the-top of, my head guesses coming form what'd belonged in, an, "immature child's" head.

Honestly, yea. I'd tried to, voice my own opinions. About, how foolish. They'd insisted upon, treating "me". With their lame point of, view status. By throwing sarcastic remarks my way. Such as "Hello remember me? I'm standing right in front of, you made.

However, thanks to, their persistence. Towards wearing my piece of, mind. For their devote lack of, tolerance guiding it's identity status rates.

As they'd found undermining me. When it'd came to, this subjects self-worth. Well, let's just say it'd finally, reached it's end!

That'd rapidly evolved. Into, what'd now become. A serious battle of, wit's which, revolved around an even larger set of, standards. I'd had absolutely no intentions. In "missing out" on!

So, with the hardest part. Being, hidden sparring, beyond. What most people like, my "mom and stepdad", for example. Didn't have the ability to, decipher. Let alone, "acknowledge."

It'd created and episode from within itself. That'd made me feel as though, I'd been that "face first". Into, an unexplainable, situation. That they'd founded on, the theory of, me. Being, too young to, know the truth. In reference to, my own bodies "recent" past time."

Whereas, I'd preferred to, see things… "like so."

Their foolish and careless act to, hide. The truth about, it's circumstances. Or, at least, the ones, that they'd "thought" they'd knew.

Had changed the forum of, it's circumstances. Into, what'd now become, nothing less. Than an even biggest insult. That'd revolved "solely, around" me!

Yea, they may've done their best to, hide. Their overall surface problem with it's standards. But, if they'd actually, possessed. The glue it'd required to hold their ridiculous plan together.

You know, so it didn't start showing signs of, it's disintegration problem. It probably wouldn't've highlight various vulnerabilities. That'd belonged to, my mom's inabilities. Which, where naked to, the human eye.

Although, I do feel more than, a "little stupid." Especially, for not considering it a lot sooner. Then, I did.

But, whether my mom and stepdad's brain waves, were even worthy of, knowing this. Was irrelevant!

Besides. No, I may've felt any reason. To so much us, let "them. Know this, before then. But, I could figure out. What they "didn't want" me to find. Before, I'd even felt the single digits.

Although, in the real world. It's basically, just referred to. As, "Reverse Phycology" skills.

I could tell right then. That "Their" case of, the random hic-ups. was way over their heads. Correction... all of, our heads.

But, just between, you, me and the lamppost outback. I never did feel the need. To buy into, moms "I'm just being (overprotective) excuse."

Yea, up until, then. This trail may've held. It's more than, "extravagant circumstances" to, list. I'd still managed to do pretty good. At keeping the likes of, their circumstances. To, myself!"

Therefore, by the time that, "Wednesday afternoon's". Stare of, "less than informative" antics, called around. The rush of, exposing as to, what. It'd really meant in, my mind. Had turned into, a "must do" situation" ... "No, exceptions!"

While, she's obviously, hadn't picked up. On it's "over all vibe," yet. I was more than tired, of, sitting there until, I could play. What was still, "any much waiting around. For the perfect chance to reveal. What'd consisted of, my "ace in, the hole."

As for, whatever either, would. Or wouldn't. Come with it as, a result? Well, even though, the "so called" path it'd given me. Had it's own theory of, difficulties to examine.

My "key factor" towards, opening them up for further evaluation. Was only, based on, one thing. "My mother's "self-orientation" of, power. Towards trying to, keep this conversation from even "taking place."

No! I'd still hadn't had any time. To give any real thought to how. I'd end up having to, confront it's unknown difficulties. You know, in general.

Which is why, decided to go freestyle with it. By jumping in it with, both feet first, until it'd sent my mom's biggest. "Denial routine" powering. Straight towards, the "nearest corner" for protection.

So, with my main interest in the conversation. Being on, how I should keep it. At a mature adult level. Until, further notice on, my part.

Well, at least that was my goal anyway. I carefully stepped up to, the "dining room" table. To confront, my mother, with another "very delicate" line of, questioning. At, my house.

"OK, mom!" I began impatiently. I'm sick of, listening, to you go out of, your way. Just so, you can avoid answering my question concerning, a subject. That I've made us both, very much aware to.

Only now, I'm not leaving with conversation. At, what it is, until, you've given me my answers. Not just, some of, them! No, I want "all of, them!"

Yea, yea. I know what you're thinking. But, in my world. The act of, saying something and actually, doing it. Are quite clearly, based. On two completely, different things.

"In other words, mother." "Which, once translated into, my lingo I began "Basically, means. That, I'm tired of, pulling up, with your "lame excuses" for not being, "straight up" with me. About, what I've been dealing with. "Everyday." Just so, I can surface. The whims of, "your foolishness." Towards facing them. Not to mention, quoting empty "Bible" verses at, my expense for answers!"

So, since the rules to, round one "clearly stand." On your inability to, either, stop, your "I'm too immature to, know as to, what. Is now going on with "my own" body crap." I'm just going to drill you at, random. Until, I get what I want... feeling lucky?" I asked sneakily.

Yea, my oddball comment may've stimulated. One of, mom's "less than intelligent theories. Especially, when it came to how." She'd thought "I should handle it's "stray circumstances."

But, "as usual," when it came to this specific subject. Just as I'd predicted she would. My mom once again, attempted to, regain "stray control over the conversation. By coming back at it. With her "infamous," how dare speak to, me. In that, tone of, voice speak, young lady!"

Which, first between us. Had struck me as being, more than, a little inappropriate. Especially since I'd hadn't even raised my voice. "One decibel," diving, it!

I mean, who knows? Maybe in moms mind. Her spur of, the moment "save response" method. Had actually, made some kind of sense?"

So, needless to say. Since I'd myself, "immediately recognized" mom's denial defines. For what it really was. I wasn't in the, "least bit" amused. By the gesture she used to, portray it.

"Hey, mom!" I continued frustratingly. Since, I'm the one who's chosen to, honor this deal.

Before, I open up" my expectation. As to, "how" it works. It really be in "your" best interest. To try "practicing". What you preach. You know, just to be, different!

But, once again. Mom looked at me like, my solo request. Had taken me out of, line. When it came to, asking simple every day questions. About, my "own health status.

So, of course. I stood my grounds and redirected her reign of, brain activity. Back towards a unconfirmed talent that I like to, call. "Shaking the "forbidden tree" of, mom.

Yea, it may've only been six months. Since, all this "bull crappola" had started. But, other than it feeling as though, it'd taken. Around forever and a day. Just for, the cards themselves. To reach. What was now, my mother's "so called" home base.

I'd grown quite sick of listening to, my mom forbid me. To know anything else, "about it." So, this time. Instead of, just ignoring her stupidity in it.

I'd readily, took it upon, myself. To just step up and play each one out. For whatever they may've been worth. Like, they were nothing! Or perhaps, a much better comparison. Would be a "much better" description.

But, after about, twenty seconds of, dead silence. Which she'd humored with 2. "How dare you speak to, me. In that, tone of voice, young lady" lines later.

Even I wasn't' sure. What part of it. That I'd hated, the most. Let alone, where I'd heard then "first!"

But apparently, time has this ironic tendency to, fly even faster. When your "not" having "any fun. Which, I learned at, exactly 10 am. That morning. Like, it'd happened only, "yesterday!"

Then again, if for some reason or, another. Your finding yourself, "not interested." In how it'd turned out. You could at least, tell me now. Before I end up being, disappointed. As, a result!

Yea, I might've grown quite used to it. But, by then. I really don't think this part. Really mattered anymore either.

Plus, I may've grown quite used to, it. Over it during, these past "few years". But, once you consider. How "unexpectedly", new. That it really was to, me. It'd seemed a lot more like, it'd belonged. To a lost T.V. episode from, the 1970's. Called, "candid camera."

Personally, I'd really expected my mom's "next" verbal response. To come off "a lot louder." After I'd made my last remark. About, how'd "I'd felt," she'd been handling it.

But, instead of, getting. A valid response in return. My mom just sat there trying to, stare at me. Like she'd been struck with a "reality check". That'd held up an equivalence level. Which, held a 2.4 "slump rate."

So, before my mom. In whom'd as soon as, she'd the chance tried to shift it's terms back into, "her favor. By way of, silent intimidation techniques.

I took it upon, myself to being her up to date. On the ever-growing flaws and glitches. That where attached to, my "Rules of thumb." Towards them!

"O.K. mom!" I insisted stubbornly. "If you're really that, determined. To make a complete idiot of, yourself. When we're in, Cleveland. Just as you've "quit clearly" already, done. During, these "past six months."

"Then, hey! Go for it! But, do yourself a favor and don't forget. To remember this much! Because, as for, your "so called" rules. Well, life just say that "I." Have grown "extremely sick" of, following them!"

"In fact, just in case you're interested. I have been since, point A. Which, once translated. Basically means that, I, completely refuse to play along. Just so, you can use your "so called," rules. For even, "one millisecond" longer!"

Because, in case you haven't noticed, mother!" I insisted angrily. "Your theory, doesn't work in this situation! So, for the record. I continued frustrated. "Any form of, leverage. That you may think you've acquired. By the way of, "intimidation." Is, worthless... dig?"

"In fact, mother" I added sarcastically. "The way I'm seeing it. There's only, "two directions" that, this particular round. "Can" go from here!

1.) You can either, stop treating me as though, I. Am some kind of, immature child. When, I'm clearly, not even close. "AKA"/ Someone in whom, you think. Is too unworthy of, knowing. As to, what's going on with "their own" body.

Or,

2.) "Just don't talk to, me..." At all!"

"So, to tell the truth mom. Since, I've had more than enough, spare time. Between, round one and now to, "make" it happen! I've had more than, enough time. To figure out how to, prepare myself with it. Before, I'd even thought of, confronting you. About it, now!

Yea, I can "very distinctly remember. Exactly, what realm of defense. My mother'd attempted to, use. But, hey, as far as, I was concerned. She didn't need to, understand them!

Which, explains as to, why. She'd decided to step in to, perform. What I've learn to, consider as being, her." Last minute attempt at, a "save" routine.

Besides even though, I'd already knew. Exactly, what "she'd felt." Her "blowing all suspicions". Off of, herself routine was, "really worth."

Apparently, she wasn't convinced! Allow me to, explain...

"Heather Lynn!" Mom exclaimed ghastly. Why can't you first, shut up and try. To mind, "your own" freaking business for once?"

Yea, I know, "what" you're thinking right now! Because, it'd sounded more than, out there. To me at, that "particular time!" actually, I think "pathetic" would be. A much more "accurate" word of, describing it.

Especially, when as to, whether or not she'd believed it. Rested solely on, my business not hers!

"Mom!" I interrupted in hesitantly. "What the heck, is wrong with you anyway?"

"I mean," I insisted angrily. "I know as to, how much your so called, blind routine is really worth!

"Heather Lynn!" mom answered defensively. "Just, shut up! And mind. Your own freaking business" for once?

"Mom!" I continued impatiently. "I know one of your "more talented areas! But, just for fun. Let's try and keep this conversation. As much as, on the national side of, things. As, possible... shall we?"

"Besides," I continued doubtingly. Since, you've already went. So far, out of, your way. To sort this part out... "unsuccessfully!"

You've given me absolutely, no other choice. But to, personally trim. All of, your lame excuses to, even try. Are based on, your attempt to, waste my time. Consists of a malfunction, behind "these factors."

It makes the idea of, trying to hide them. Look like, it'd been founded. Strictly on, your, how to, "Prevent myself. From" looking bad" routine.

Which, by the way is a subject that,' stands solely. On you fears towards, "what." Or, even better, yet how. That "you'll end up facing them as, a result!

"Well, mom!" I insisted rudely. It's your call... make it

"Heather!" mom insisted accusingly. "Just, shut up!" No mom! I remarked defensively. I'm not going to, just shut up! I refuse!"

"You see!" I continued demandingly. Unlike, yourself, for example. I can't just cower into, the "nearest" corner. To satisfy, what's within the realm of, your wishes!"

"When you won't even consider humoring mine! However if you're interested in learning. About, "how" it plays itself out."

But, just in case you're interested in learning. The truth of, how I'm seeing it. Then, here's a little "News flash" for you!

When we get to the "Cleveland Clinic" foundation. I have "every intention" in learning. About, what's been going on. Inside my "own" body. Just don't be, "too" surprised. When, everything you've been trying to, hold "out" on me. Falls into, it's "correct place". Any questions, comments...ect?"

Yea, I may've already heard this line. At least, a thousand times. Before, then. During, just the past "six months" alone!

"Heather Lynn Jensen!" mom insisted angrily. "That's absolutely, no way to speak. To your mother!

But since, apparently. Someone had to, take care of, what anyone else. Had the guts to, "make" happen. I hooked it's details up!

So with myself being, such a "nice lady" and all. Not to mention, "still" of the unsure. That it, was, actually, over with.

I'd almost hesitated, my statis. When it'd came to getting up to, leave. Our so called infamous, "dining room table" zone.

Although, I basically, felt. My "next effort" as being, worthless. Before, I'd told mom. About my "first impression". Towards, his little "denial act." In which, she'd designed to make "her" look good! I strongly, advise you pay "very close" attention. To what'd unexpectedly, happened next.

"Mom," I'd insisted. I know this maybe, "a lot" for you to, grasp. But, just so we've both been made sure. As to, how this "next part" ends."

"I first have to, make sure. That you clearly, understand one thing. I really don't care as to, what. You either "can or cannot" except. About, what happens next with this subject!"

"Therefore," I continued impatiently. Since, this seems to be, the part. Where the "whole situation" itself. Gets "even harder" then, before."

"You might want to, remember that, in my world. Ignorance itself, never creates a solution for anything!"

"I'm fact!" I remarked carelessly. Since I personally, just don't seem to understand. You overbearing need to, hide. These problems, from yourself. Instead of, "escaping out" it's details.

"It only makes it even harder. Then it "already" has to, be!" Although, I was, hoping. It'd and "a lot better" this time"

Once again, my mother's reaction came back. In the form of what'd now. Just consisted of, extremely nauseating. "How dare you" glares.

Although, for as ironic as, it was, when it'd happened. My mother's next off the wall comment. Actually, seemed as though, it'd held. A definite side order of, "guilt" with it.

So, of course, with myself "Not being," in any interest. To want to, take the chance of, appearing rude. I'd decided that, my best bet. Would be to, portray. Her self-infatuated "good gesture". By, bringing her to, terms. With the rules from "my play book."

"OK mother!" I suggested patiently." You may not be fond of, my answer. But, as long as, we've managed. To get that, part out of way. Let's go ahead and review. All of, it's other details…Shall we?"

But since, all mom. Seemed to be, willing to say or, do. That'd so much as come close. To resembling an, answer. Was to, nod her head. As a form of, agreement.

Which, don't get me wrong. But, coming from "my mother". Was definitely what I'd consider. To be of, a "different styled" reaction.

I began doing what I could. Or perhaps, I should say. What she'd "listen" to. To try and enlighten her one track mind. On exactly what each ruled already proven. From my side of, it's fence.

Yea, I may've taken a few extra seconds. Just so I could make sure that, we. For as pathetically as, it was done. Were still. At least, partially working off the "same vibe." But, rest assured. It'd definitely, got interesting!

"Mom!" I remarked. No! I can't speak for you. In this specific case. But I really think. That before, "it". Actually, has the chance to, go. Any further. Than it clearly, has already gone.

I'd really like to make sure, that I've made the point to stress. How what I'm about to, say. Isn't just a lame joke! Allow me to, explain…

1.) The only people here. In whom, holds any rights "What-so-ever" to, confront. What you like to, consider as being, in my…"best interest." Is me!"

"Which, basically, means." I remarked sarcastically. That the stupidest part. About, my having to, say this. Is slightly, based. On the fact. That even with my supposedly, "overly matured, eleven and a half" year old mind. I'm at least intelligent enough, to understand it! What's your excuse, mom?"

So since, she didn't seem to, have. Any form of, comments to add. To her nature of being. A "mature, adult leveled" conversation. I'm not going to, try and claim. That, it'd went over. As easily as, I'd hoped it would.

But, that's OK. Because, if nothing else came from her frivolous effort. At least, I was satisfied. That her, attitude itself. Had finally "settled down" a little.

So, as I'd hesitantly, began. To explain exactly, how. All of, the unknown rules to, my playbook worked. Not to mention as to, why. I'd be the only, person. In whom'd held the sight. To call any of, it's "still unknown" shots. Which, were made available for our next. Round of, med school "want-to-be's."

"Mother!" I began impatiently. "In case, you're interested in what this means. Rule number, two. Is solely based on, what it'll actually take. To make sure that, we. Are made absolutely clear of, why. That we'll be using "my rules." Once we've arrived at, the "Cleveland Clinic foundation."

In other words, mother. I added intimidatively. There's no room left in your worthless intimidation game. For any element of, amateur to exist.

Therefore, if I was, in your position mom. I'd abandon them, right now. Because, if you so much as, can't restrain. Your "so called," spay-out sessions. When we're in Cleveland. Then, I won't hesitate. To just, walk out and leave you there!

"But, hey. Other than that. Feel free "to, do" your damage!"

First leave me out of, it...dig?"

"OK, Heather Lynn." mom interrupted. "Why am I no longer allowed. To decide, what's in your best interest "health wise" anymore?"

"Well, mom!" I replied bluntly. "that may be a stupid but, it's also, a very good one! One in which, I'm actually, going to take. The liberty of answering. In the exact same way that, you've done, mine. During, the past six months' time!"

"You, see! What I have to, live and deal with. On a "daily basis." Isn't about you! So, it's none of, you freaking business..."dig?"

"Besides, this game might've held more. Than a normal share of, mysteries. To start with!" I insisted. "But, at least, I don't possess the need. To laugh in someone's face. So I can make myself feel. As though, I officially, "won" this sound!"

Which, may've been a "seriously strong" remark. On, my part. Well, at least, it was. Until, mom tired her best. To slide in another one of, her. "How dare you speak to me. In that, tone of voice, young lady" speeches. For about, the "nineteenth" time!

"You see, mom." I continued impatiently. "It's like this! Because, unlike yourself, for example. My only purpose for having this conversation is to salvage whatever information that, I can "about, it." In the least arousing civil manner I can. Without causing any unnecessary suspicions that, I can't explain!"

"Then again," I'd thought. If I'd had just "a" penny. For every time I've already heard that line! Well, you get the "general idea"!

Heck, usually. I'd just ignore stupid remarks like that! Especially, when mom'd attempt to, slide them. In "my" direction for "whatever reasons."

Yea, I may've forgot to make, an actual "verbal reply in, return after that. But, at least, I'd acknowledged them. With the next words that, came out of, mom's mouth that morning.

"Heather Lynn!" mom insisted. Like she'd actually, thought that. I would even consider the idea of, supplying her with one. "I demand an apology!"

But, as far as, I was concerned. We'd both, new where this conversation was heading. Which was, nowhere fast!

However, since that, particular day. Didn't show any at, face value signs. To show suggestions of doing otherwise. I looked my mom "sight straight" in, her eyes. Just so, I could speak these words more intensely. Before drawing my next conclusion.

"Hey, mom!" I remarked even, more sarcastically. I wouldn't be getting your hopes up for an apology. Especially when it concerns you." "At, yea?" mom remarked snidely. Why shouldn't I Heather Lynn?" "Well, mom. I insisted impatiently I wouldn't!"

Besides. Even though, I've learned through good old "personal experience, what your self-infatuated false assumptions. Are really worth in, my world. You're the one who gets to, take. The wrath of, this hissy fit that, you alone. Well fly. Into as, a result thereof. I'm not afraid to, face it!"

Although, what my mother'd. Either, didn't want to know. Or, better yet. Just failed to understand in return. Was neither, my fault. Or about, it's usual miscellaneous styled, bull crap.

Which for records sake. Is why I was apparently. In this position itself…"Anyway."

The only difference, was. That, this time. I'd chosen to, base it's expectations. On my level of, impatient with her, "I can't see beyond my own "self-denial" attitude…even more!

So, with the focus of, it's "expectation date." Being the foundation of, this particular subject. I decided to base my "main interests". Towards making absolutely, sure. That my mom wouldn't end up finding an excuse. To put her half-wit denial act. Above, my "four years" long. Unanswered quest for "unproven" information. Concerning it.

So in interest of, her being able to, flip all of its hardships. Back towards her own best interests. Instead of, towards mine.

I'd found myself inside another position. That made me feel like. I'd been made part of, the seriously insulted…"Go figure."

I mean, yea. Maybe she was able to, insinuate It's terms as being, that way.

But, if I personally. Actually, had to, pick. Just "two words" to, describe. What I'd chosen to, except as being, my mom's. Choice of, overly repetitious request. Towards learning "my answers concerning it, since, "point A."

Then I'd have to, go with the words "annoyingly predictable."

Therefore, with these standards now being, exposed. I'm pretty sure" it gives you. A much better reason as to, why. It didn't give me the smallest hint of, surprise.

When I'd once again, found myself sitting. At mom's conference "table" silently dreading the use of, her half-witted remarks. Just so, she could perform. Another one of, her lame attempts to, retrieve. Unproven information towards a subject. Had very clearly been closed, "two years" earlier.

In fact. Since, just between us. I was her invalidated remarks. That'd successfully, found their way under my skin in, the first place.

It'd revealed how worthless that, useless vulnerabilities. Towards this subject…really were!

Plus. Since that, mistake. Even though it'd clearly, "not been" acknowledges yet. Rested solely on, her head.

Not to mention that, I 'the, had already voiced my general opinion towards them "verbally." I wasn't really. What I'd call, in any mood to, go for seconds!

But, just so, I can make sure. That what I have to, say about its terms. Don't came off as being of, the rude. Or, something like, that. I took extra care to, "relief her". On the realm of my "wisdoms input" towards it," first!

"OK mother!" I exclaimed frustrated. For about, the "hundredth time". Have it, your way!"

"I mean, after all. Right or wrong seems. To be of, the irrelevant in, this factor…right?"

"But, just so your aware as to, how far. The "bottom line" really rests at, this point. I refuse to suffer these consequence any longer. Just because, you don't have the guts. To live them out from behind. Your curtain of denial! In which "you" insist upon, using. To hide them!"

But since, you yourself really don't seem to, care. What I think or, feet about them. Not that, it really mattered in, the first place!

Heck, I was lucky if, I'd even succeeded. To get a total of, these more words. Out of, my mouth. Before, mom'd attempted to, slip back. Into, her infamous, "How dare you" mode.

No, that theory in, particular. May've not mattered much, either! By then, she'd managed to, make me. So, sad at, her that, I was actually, giving serious consideration. To hoofing my "own way" clear to, the "Cleveland Clinic foundation".

You know, just so, I wouldn't have to, put up. Or, even better yet. Tolerate her "stupid" remarks". All of the way there! But, hey after I'd tolerated round two. With that were so unpleasant breed of, torture… who wouldn't?

Besides. Since, whether or not. My mother's brain cell activity level. Was up to, my attention span quota. On my daily expectations potential. In ordered the act of, finding my "unwelcomed phantoms" potentials… not hers!

But, with my devoting extra care "not to," reveal. What secrets I'd literally watched happening. In the process of, these "part six" months. It'd given me a mild way of, dividing up. All of, the anger I'd felt equally. Between, both of, us.

Yea, it's true. That over half of, the anger it'd produced inside me. Was based solely on the grounds. That it's apparently, watched over. But, as far, it's other fifty percent standards. Well at least, it'd performed. Some kind of, stray significance in my life.

So as, the problem itself seemed as though, it'd been designed. By myself as, some kind of shield.

Besides, even though I'd managed to, reserve. It's so called, statis to, randomly avoid. Certain uncalled for moments such as, morning, afternoon and evening disagreements. Which, ironically enough. Were rapidly, becoming of, the more frequent.

For as wild as, it been to experience. I'd been the only one with, the capability. To since, it's presence!

In fact, if I'd had to, take a wild guess. As to why, I'd felt I'd picked up on, it's presence at all. It would be because, only I'd. Known exactly what it meant.

In fact. Since judging from my assortment of, past experiences with it. It basically, been feeling it needed to, talk. Just like it'd "did" any other timid we'd crossed paths.

I'd knew it's results themselves. Would have no other choice but to, turn either, for or against me. Yea, it may've sounded unusually, simple though. But, what'd really came next. Was even, better than that!

Heck, the way, I remember these details. Some of, them seemed kinda on, the iffy side...so to, speak.

Especially, once my mother decided that, it was time. To approach me with the details. That'd lied behind her "false assumptions". About, why we "were really", in Cleveland!

To tell the truth. Since, amongst my families state of, beliefs. It'd never really, been a big secret. That the concept of, flying in an airplane. At about, 37,000 ft. above sea level. Had even come close to being. Just one of, my mother's favorite "extracurricular" activities.

Which is also why, it'd caught me so "off guard." When she'd decided. Upon our way of, passage. To get, there!

Although, I admit that, most of, it's circumstances. Seemed to be, pretty much of, the predictable.

Especially when she'd chose. To share, this information with me!

Although, such things. As, how she'd expected me. To, except them. Wouldn't even come close to being, like mine. I really think it's safe. To list them as being, amongst the completely opposite. From the one's that, I'd chosen!

Yea, though I can't pretend that, there weren't. At least, a few things about, our trip. In which, I didn't really care for.

Not one of, them. Involved, "my mom's" over all fear for flying. So far, beyond the earth's surface…either! For example.

1.) There was the main part, where we'd had to, get up. No later than, "3:30 am"…sharp! Just so we could be, up at, the "Pittsburg Airport. In time to, make our flight!

But even though, I personally. Don't even think my mind. Had even found it's "going through the motions" mode. Until, after we'd actually, "boarded our plane.

I myself wouldn't've even gave any thought. Towards making a big deal over, our way of, passage!

Yea, all of, this! May've seemed like, it'd made sense to, them! When I myself, would've just immediately request for information. To give me an, idea of, how long. We'd be up there in, flight.

Just for the sake of record. Here's how it's side of, expectations which, I'd personally, hoped for. Had actually, played themselves out.

Which is, exactly, why. I'd made a point of, preparing myself. For something that'd quite clearly pack. Something that'd possess more of, a thrill side effect. Before, I'd even made plans to, leave home.

But since, the one I'd got. Only lasted for a whole 15 minutes taps. Not to mention, didn't even let us fly "upside down once. The whole time itself. Just seemed a lot like, a "big rip-off" to, me!

Heck, we couldn't've even been "in" the air. For any more than, 10 minutes. Before, the pilot came on over the loudspeaker. To totally, ruin my birds eye rush. By telling everyone there to, fasten their seat belts! Because, we were due to touch back down in Cleveland. In the matter of, "five minutes."

Like I'd said. Yea, it'd all sounded pathetically stupid. But, oddly enough, the realm of, our overly short flight. Didn't turn out as being at, a total loss!

Because, unlike them, for example. I did actually, manage to, snatch. A few bits and pieces of, stray information. That'd went on between, mom and the man. Sitting no further than, the "very next" seat.

1.) Since this particular dude. Was like, us. Also on route to, the Cleveland Clinic foundation." With the only difference being, his interest in, going there. Including, a "job interview."

Mom and him reached a agreement. To use the same taxi cab. Like, a "share the face type of deal.

However since, after that conversation was over. The only thing that'd seemed worthy of my attention. Until, we'd touched back down. Was the size of, the cities buildings. From 37,000 feet in the air.

Then, once we'd arrived at, "The Cleveland Clinic" foundation. I'd quietly, first stood and watched my surroundings. Until this dude and my mom. Had finished saying the cab driver his few.

So once, that'd been taken care of. The only thing that, mom and I. Had left to do. Was to, find our way to, the "nearest" elevator upstairs.

Until we'd reached the neurology department. Where I was to be, admitted for further tests.

Which is why, you can only imagine. How high my realm of, fascination with its surroundings really were. When I got on view of, it's make up. From the "inside out," so to speak.

That'd wildly enough, ended up a bit stranger. Within, itself! But, just for fun! Let me pick up my inside" explanation of, this experiences.

At the point where my mom and I'd. First stepped off the elevator onto, floor five...shall we?

I think the first thing that'd caught my attention. Was how easily, I'd noticed a man wearing, a doctors coat. Near the elevator were we'd got off.

But, to tell the honest truth about, it. His presence just didn't seem to connect. With why I was, there at, the time.

Although, I honestly, believe. That the only reason he'd even caught my attention in, the first place. Had to do with the fact that, he was standing close to, a nurses station...where I'd had to go to, check in.

Yea, my noticing. What type of, attire that, he was wearing. But, with my only being, there. For a matter of, ten minutes tops. His statis was still, very much on the "unconfirmed" side too!

No! I don't think anyone else noticed it. But, I'm convinced that, what'd pointed his presence out to, me didn't take place. Until a few minutes later. When only a few minutes later. That very same man. In whom, I was willing to, just blow off. Like, he didn't even matter.

Ended up being the "Cleveland Clinic foundations, Head Pediatric Neurologist, Dr. "David Rothner," the II.

Although I can't deny. That what'd first struck my attention. About him as being, unique. Had alot more to do. With how I'd prepared myself "ahead of, time. To just, end upcoming "face to face. With another one of those. So called, "Medical School" styled "want-to-be's. That's not what I'd found standing. On my side of, this rainbow.

Because, for as wild as, it may've seemed. He didn't even close to resembling. The way that, I'd pictured him. Allow me to, explain...

Yea, the real, "Dr. David Rothner II." May've only stood about, 5'4. I think the word, "short" accurately, describes. My first impression of, him.

He also had very neatly, trimmed medium brown hair. With a beard and mustache. In which were all tapped off. With what he'd referred to as being, a "Jewish prayer cap or yamica."

But even though, all of, these details. Had fell together as neatly as, they did. I think what'd stood out the most. About, him from my overall perspective.

Was how easily, he'd seemed to, have. This calming effect coming from him. Which, far as add as it may sound.

Had unlike, all the other med school misfits. In whom'd I'd already, crossed paths with. Didn't create, my "usual" paranoia. Towards what'd either, would or, wouldn't happen next.

Although, in all due fairness. No matter how hard I'd tried. To keep my own "personal enthusiasm" to myself. I'd been subjected to, my mom's several attempts. To loosely sway them back and forth…"All week!"

I can't pretend that I'd hadn't been anxious. To meet the "so called" man behind it's mystery. Ever since, I'd overheard "Dr. Fisher" mention his name. In his office that, day.

The silent note I'd made. About, being, sent to, another "medical facility. For another test didn't…yet.

Yea, I know. Your probably, wonder as to how. I'd managed to, scrounge that much, information together. About anyone or anything. When all I'd had was, a stray vibe. To, work with!

Well even though, most generally, you can't! Now that the topics been brought up. Once, you consider the true "neurological talents.

In which, as far as, "De Rothner" their capabilities went. Still remained to be of, the unseen. It did to, an extent. But all of, that, would change. As of, the "very next," morning!

In fact, far as weird as, it was. Even with all the distraction. That the nurses around as, they'd settled me in. I couldn't stop myself from looking over at, "Dr. Rothner. Without wondering to, myself. If him and his staff. Were really as good as I'd heard "Dr. Fisher" suggest.

So, as the nurses preoccupied themselves. With the chose of, getting me "All settled" in. To when I'd be staying while, I was there.

Which is why, I decided to, bring. My aura of, attention. Back towards Dr. Rocher's effort. To bring my mother's up to, speed. When it came to, the details. That my mother'd felt, she'd needed to know.

Especially those that sounded. Like just "extremely, good" advice, to me!

You know. Details such as, the "Ronald McDonald" house…for example.

Although, according to what I'd heard "Dr. Rothner" say. The Ronald McDonald" house. Had recently been constructed. Just right across the street from "The Cleveland Clinic" Foundation. To provide an acceptable, place for parents to stay. When they'd had children admitted there. But couldn't afford the cost of, a regular hotel room's fee.

"Mrs. Jensen!" I listened in discretely. "As, you can tell. The "Cleveland Clinic Foundation" isn't exactly located. In what's known as being, the best part of, this city."

"But even though, in all due fairness. I must say that, the Clinic's security guards. Do "their best" to, keep all of the cities "riff-raff." Away from gathering outside the buildings at, night."

"It doesn't keep some people from being, robbed of, both, their money and sometimes, their lives as, a result!"

"No, it doesn't happen a lot. But, it's not unheard of, either! Which, is why, I strongly advise you to, use. The clinics overpass at, night!"

Yea, this conversation. May've taken Dr. Rothner at least, a half hour. To complete. But once, my mother'd felt confident that, everything it'd concerned. Had sufficiently, settled itself down.

She'd headed over to the "Ronald McDonald" house next door. So, she could do the same for herself.

Which, in return. Brings me to, what "I feel". Was, the "best part" about, it!

While to, most people this particular routine. May leave them. With a fair share of, questionable doubts. I'd still had at least, four years' worth of, my own. To sort my way through.

So, as my mother went across the street. To take care of, her basic needs. Such as, stuff like. A shower, dinner and I think she'd even mentioned. Something about, taking a quick "Cat Nap."

I just couldn't help but to, find my mind. Trying to, recall the one sided disagreement. That mom And I'd had only a few days prior to, us coming here.

Heck, between you and me. I'd only need the assistance of, one finger. To count the total amount of, times.

In which, I'd actually succeeded at getting mom. To snidely sit down and discuss the details. That'd obviously, revolve itself around. The current "Health issues that came with it.

But even though the scariest part about, this confrontation. Always came back to, me. Trying to, shake information loose. From the forbidden tree of, mom.

I'll never forget as to, how close I'd came. To punching her right square in, the nose. As a result of, her overly persistent denial act.

Although since then. I've worked hard to dismiss the ill feelings and distrust. That'd piled up as, a result there of, it's aftermath.

Which, had "toned down" even further. After I'd met, "Dr Rothner", in person. I'd knew, he'd made a clear impression of, his intensions. Just by the way it'd made me feel. About, being there!

In fact, according to, what I could tell. From his aura of, confidence and concern. Which was something he'd apparently upheld. When it to, the "welfare of, his patients

Yea, I know it all sounds odd to, believe but, at least, it'd gave me a title assurance to support this round.

Honestly? I'd felt like. At least 50% of, it's burden. That'd been in the matter of, four year and 6 months' time.

Had managed to, accumulate itself from being, my phantoms "unwelcomed presence. To lifting itself up, off of my shoulders.

So it could replace its "dormant mode's" surroundings. With a "completely, different" type of, questions.

In which I knew from personal experience itself. Had existed only in my mind before, 5/5/78. As to, whether or, not. There really were such things as, miracles. That'd even favored "my World? Well, that questions answer. Was still, up for grasps!

Especially, when in my mind. Life hadn't ceased to spin around in circles since the first day that, "bull crapped began! But, now that, I'd had enough time. To consider, them more intensely. The thought of, their existence being, a real plausibility. Kept getting better by, the second!

No, it mayn't've lasted long enough, for my taste. But, after about, an hour and a half. The Act of my actually, enjoying. What "small amount" of, space it'd given me. To review everything I'd experienced these past six months. When it'd ended with my mother slithering back into, my room. Being an assortment of, various new questions.

Which, very strongly suggested. She was, quite interested in, learning. My first impression of, "Dr. Rothner". After, we'd met.

No, it wasn't the fact that, the question itself. Had even been raised. That'd made me feel so, hesitant. About, even answering mom's interestingly, devised question.

It was my recollection of, how. Only two days previous to my being, admitted there. Just the thought of, my being allowed. To voice my opinions towards this very same subject. Had seemed completely of, the insignificant. As far as, my mon was, concerned.

Then again. Since, my mother did make this request, personally. I just couldn't help but to, wonder. If this outcome hadn't triggered. Some kind of, unexpected impact. That'd actually been strong enough. To question the "various" amount of, stray flaws. That she'd left in, her "Chosen technic of, choice. When she'd entered the room.

But since, I was determined, "not to," show any signs. That'd so much as, surely hinted symptoms. That I'd had suspicions towards having them.

I'd only took my having a casual round of, twenty questions. To try and press a five minute round of, empty answers from me. Before, mom got tired of, dropping hints.

As a way of, getting me to, "unexpectedly" guess. Whatever answer that, she thought. She was hoping for at, her standards.

So, in interest of, my "not showing mine. With her first. Mom'd finally, just came out and asked. "Heather whom did Dr. Rothner, remind you of, when. You'd first meet? Anything or one in, particular?" She'd suggested, curiously. No, mom! He didn't remind me of, anyone at thing in, particular." I replied. Still unaware of, what she was trying to, suggest. "Why do you ask?"

Besides, with it already being, made "quite clear". That just, moms way of, delivering. What she'd considered to be, saddle hinting efforts. "Wasn't," working!

I guess, she'd finally, decided. That she'd reached a point. Where she'd believed that, her. So called, concept of, trying, to restrain herself from showing hers. Stopped being, a workable apion.

So, of course. In all defense, I think we both, shared a faint cheek. From that, image. Especially, after mom suddenly just, blurted out the words. "Heather, I think Dr. Rothner. Looks like, a leprechaun!"

Although, between us. I really think my mother, leprechaun theory. Wasn't meant to, be shared. With anyone else! I'd stayed that, way for awhile.

Which, brings me. To "my" description of, what Dr. Rothner'd explained to, me. Before he'd left my hospital, clinic room. On the "same evening."

While, I can't pretend that, our entire conversation. Wasn't tempered in, "certain areas" it'd pertained to. Before, Dr. Rothner'd walked from the room that, night. He'd made a point of, stopping and bringing it to, my attention.

That he'd scheduled a test. That he'd referred to, as being, a cat scan. In which, he'd scheduled for me to, take. On the following morning. At exactly, 5:30 AM..."sharp."

Well, other than, my mom and I having a very early start. Not to mention, the "leprechaun statement. She'd made the night before. I don't think that either, one of us. Were in, what I'd call. An exchanging notes, type of, mood.

Plus, once you consider. How Dr. Rothner seemed it up even more when we'd headed downstairs to, the "CT "lab." On the following morning.

This particular test, was specifically, designed to, give him. The ability to observe the activity, in my brain. From what he'd called, the inside out. Like, an "x-ray"...for example!

No. I can deny having sexual of, my own doubts. About, its "overall" capabilities. Especially, considering past experiences being as they were!

So, yes! It may've first been a result of, how farfetched it'd sounded. But after I'd spent all night preparing myself. For whatever diagnosis I'd receive. Once, everything I been said and done.

Or, at least, I should say. That after, tolerating "6 months" of, not being, allowed to know anything. Even though, I'd already did. I was, as prepared as, I was going to get. Before, facing it, one on one.

All I can really do. Is describe how, other than. Myself being, forced to, ride it out alone.

My mother'd basically, forbade me to, know "Anything." About, the habits of, my phantom friends. Spur of the moment visits. After it'd stepped up to flaunt it's "True Colors."

Which is why, I'd chosen to, commit. All my spare time. Where I didn't find myself. As usual, pricing together abstract factors. About, it, as, I'd awaited for its real answer. To swing my way.

While, someone else I'd knew but, shall remain nameless. Presented themselves as though, my efforts. Were wrong to, even think of, trying!

But, like, I've already explained. My mom was, "weird." So, of course unlike, her. Just the idea of, my cowering. Into, the nearest corner to, hide. To avoid facing the aftermath of, my denial. Didn't work as, a "workable solution" for me!

Therefore, since unlike, mom. I'd based my quest for finding answers. On more than a few stray and hypothetical questions. I'd had more than just, "unprovable answers" to, work with.

Yea, main question concerning it. May've been based on learning as to, why. That all this crap was, happening to, me.

Which, in return. Basically brings me. To the challenge of, trying to, live and deal with it after it'd been, identified and revealed "medically."

But, once we'd made our way downstairs to, the "CT" lab. As, Dr. Rothner, called it. I just, couldn't get over the place. Where I'd actually, be able, to observe this "infamous," inside out "theory…in action!

Heck, I could tell, just by the size of, medical equipment. That they'd used to, perform "the test itself. How much my main fascination with, its size. Had seemed to be, more absorbed. In whatever capabilities it'd held. Or, even better yet. "How" it'd been constructed in such, a "small area." Allow me to, explain further.

Since the room itself. Had basically, only consisted of, a "cement floor. Not to mention, a brick wall. That, couldn't've been any taller than, "4 feet" tops.

My immediately, noticing as to "how thick". That it's "plate glass" windows actually were. Ended up becoming, a big plus. Which, worked "quite nicely" in, my favor!

Besides since, the room itself. Which, was "partially made" with "plate glass" windows. They'd given me a "very clear view. As to what kind of, equipment. Was to be, used to perform this test.

Which is why, I'd directed my next unresolved answer. Towards trying to, silently theorize. As to, how something "that, size." Had managed to get in there. In the "first" place.

I mean, in my mind. It was like, just that, thought alone. Had been enough to, make me. Actually, consider, the thought that, it. Would've had to, have been constructed...Around it.

But because the wildest part, about, that test being, performed on me. Wouldn't actually, come into effect. Until, after I'd spent twenty minutes hanging out. Inside this machines "giant tube." So, it could take this infamous, "inside out" tests pictures.

Once, it'd been performed to, completion. A fellow staff member in whom'd, also worked in, the CT" lab. Came in to, instruct me to, wait. In the "very next" room. So, Dr. Rothner, could finish working on. What he'd referred to, as being, his "Neurological styled" magic.

But since, like it did before. This room within itself. Had "Several, plate glass windows in it. That'd automatically, gave me the ability to, watch, Dr. Rothner.

Not to mention, the contuse that; his facial expressions made. As he intensely, studied very little detail. That'd stood out about, my test results. Before, he'd reached his "official diagnoses" towards it.

Therefore. Even though it was based strictly on, my mother's call. I honestly believe, that if, Dr. Rothner hadnt've interrupted. What'd already became. About me wanting to, know its answer.

I would've first like, before. Never came close to, seeing or, knowing. Anything that'd answered these "test results". You know, for personal reference.

It was, something. That'd just seemed to, give me. A couple more discreet reasons. That 'the, rest assured. Just end up making "this sound" of, medical tests." Turn into, what I'd thought for sure. Would end up with, my mother trying to, turn it. Into, another "complete loss" on, "my part."

No, I can't pretend that, most people. Like, my mother, for example. Would've probably, just "spayed-out" from, the "impact" alone." That'd came with finding themselves being, asked, to wait alone, in a room without answers!

But, if I had to, draw a rational conclusion. That described it from strictly, my side of this fence.

I honestly think that, the only thing. I'd had to, keep myself calm as, it went on. Was my determinate desire to, know it's truth.

So, once you consider the amount of, time. That I'd either, spent or, thought I did. Just watching and waiting for, Dr. Rothner. To reach his "still unconfirmed" diagnosis towards it. Ended up working, "quite well." In my favor.

Besides, I've always felt heavy about, sharing this. The twenty minutes I'd spent alone in that, glass room. Gave me the "more than", needed silent ability, I'd needed. To scarf together.

What I considered to be, my own "personal emotions." That'd not only, let me feel and come to, their terms. Without knowing the whole truth about them.

Which judging from my own personal incites. I'd made to, except it's consequences. Without being plagued by mom. As she'd "loomed" over me. To inform me that it didn't hold. Any information that, was, of, my business".

But, since, my mother'd already. Went out of, her way to, "force me". To walk around in circles "blindly," for the past six months.

I've never so much as, "found" the stray opportunity. To actually. Sit down long enough. To mentally prepare myself, for his "final diagnosis" conclusion.

Although, during this "20" minute wait. I ironically enough, did observe "everyone" of, Dr. Rothner emotional or, physical moves.

The "Plate Glass" windows that'd separated us. Didn't seem to, have anything to do. With "how" it'd experienced all of, the "anger and denial".

It was more like being, bottled up inside a "miscellaneous element" of, captured nervousness. But, then again. Under those type of, circumstances. Who wouldn't know that?

Besides, since, most people. Would with "my mother" holding point A. Would've probably, spayed out" from the "very same" fear!

Whereas, I'd for examples. Had actually, managed to, find. A small element of, piece. Within my sudden realization jolt. That I'd finally, found myself dealing with.

Thanks to, a faraway "neurological" doctor. In whom, wasn't afraid of, revealing. My diagnosis findings with me. Instead of, just mom.

Which, just for sake of, record. Is what'd convinced me that, Dr. Rothner. Was indeed, a "highly intelligent" man.

So as soon as, Dr. Rothners finished reviewing. The test results to my diagnosis. He'd turned around and called me. Right back into, this room of, "plate glass" windows. So, we could review his diagnosis of, my problem. Just so I'd have the "right to, hear them.

In other words, let's just say, that when, "Dr. Rothner'd" turned around. To signal me back into, this room for "further investigations I didn't "freaking hesitate" to, "oblige" his request.

Heck, between you and I. I don't think I'd even made my way. Through the door that'd separated. His room from mine. Before he'd glanced over at, me and asked, "Miss Jensen," do you remember when we'd "just discussed." The "major advantages" this "CT" scan gives us?" Or, even better yet. How well, it'd worked?"

"Yes Dr. Rothner!" I replied attentively. "I do! In fact "I added patiently, "I can remember the "exact words" that, you used. In order to, explain it accurately!"

"Please feel free to correct me Sir. But, I believe you described the "Cat scans" abilities. By stating, how it gave you. The ability to observe me brain from the inside out. Like, on x-ray...for example!

"Yes, heather," he replied confidently. However, I've been, watching your emotion reactions "closely." As, I did this couldn't help but to, notice my own…too!"

"however," he continued. "Before I can explain what these results really mean. You know, in the "neurological world."

I'd like to, take a few extra minutes, just so, I can learn about, the things you've witnessed. Or perhaps, I should say what you've learned through, your wrath, with it's personal experience observations… first!"

"Plus," he continued persistently since, you seem to be, "quite aware of, how it works, ect. I'd like you to, look at this screen and attempt to, tell me. What do you see, Miss Monroe?" he asked calmly.

So, after I'd "quickly glanced" at the screen. I turned back around after about, ten seconds and replied. "Yes, sir! This is a picture of, a brain. I explained patiently, "But, hey!" I continued sarcastically. "Everybody knows that! Right?"

No. I didn't think most people. Or perhaps, I should say, "Children". Would've been able to, read "Dr. Rothner's" "unusual" response. Once, I'd actually voiced that, comment.

When, for as suddly as, he'd expressed them. His facial features hinted towards the "vivid suspicion". That my answer. No matter, how off the wall it'd sounded. Had "obviously", caught his attention.

"Heather" Dr. Rothner, replied positively. "This may be, a picture of, a brain. But, it's not just of, "anyone's" brain. This, is a picture of, "your" brain! So, tell me. What do you think?"

"Dr. Rothner, sir. I'm aware of, who this brain belongs to!" I remarked patiently. "I know this because, if you remember correctly." These are, my "CT" results!

"Besides, doc." I continued calmly. Shouldn't you be, the one describing "this part" to, me?"

So, after "Dr. Rothner nodded his head. In agreement, with me. He began trying to, explain to me. Why, my answer. No matter, "how dumb" my mom tried to, portray it's worth. Had caught, his attention.

"Heather," the doc finished confidently. "Yes! You're right about this. Being a picture of, your brain." But!" he pointed out." When it comes down to, everyone. In whom, knows that, answer? You're wrong!"

Yea, I may've acquired a few questions. Concerning as to, what his last comment meant. But he didn't give me any chance. To actually, mention them. Before he explaining to, me why. He'd already began reviewing. His need to, even bring, it up.

Only, this time. I'd struck me as being, a little more in depth! "Heather, Dr. Rothner'd explained. I've been the "head pediatric neurologist". Here at the "Cleveland Clinic" "Well," he interpreted. "For quite a while now!"

But, I want to, explain, that during, this amount of, time. I've made it my business to, ask this same question. To several of, my patents. Over the years."

Therefore, other than the worst part. About it being, that, most of, them. Will end up having. Absolutely, no idea as to, what it's telling them.

In fact, I'm convinced as to, what'd impressed me. The most about, them. It's the idea that, you. "Very well" could and you're how old? Eleven and a half?

"Well," Dr. Rothner continued. "Your age itself, may be irrelevant under these circumstances. But, I'm definitely impressed, by your answer!"

"Especially with you not even having to, stop "long enough." To so much as think about it first!

"Which as, a result. Leads me "straight towards" my next question! How come you know this answer? When most people can't even guess?"

Yea, I was just as curious as, they were. Especially, when my usual agenda, didn't cover his questions. But, as a last resort, so to speak I answered.

Well, Dr. Rothner, sir. I was just thumbing through my science book one afternoon. You know, between class! So, of course. When the part about the, human brain. Just seemed to, capture my attention towards it."

"So as an attempt to, satisfy. My "quest for answers", curiosity. Well, sir. I continued "I chose to, investigate them!"

Although, I'm judging this next input, that I'd noticed on, "Dr. Rothner's face. Did have the tendency, to throw me off guard a bit. I'm pretty sure that, it was safe to assume.

Which is when, I think is, when the doc first realized. That he, wasn't just dealing. With "my" IQ. Level.

I mean, yes, this assumption, may've been good enough to handle. Those of, an eleven and a half year old teenager's abilities. I believe my next comment concerning it. Had pretty much confirmed my suspicions.

Because, for at least, the next "10 to 25" seconds. Dr. Rothner'd just stood there listening to, me!

That is, until, his sudden curiosity raised itself...even further!

In fact, I continued. "As far as, I'm concerned. His next statement "pretty much," confirmed it!

"Heather," Dr. Rothner pointed out calmly. I want you to, understand. That juts because, I'm curious. About, what else you can tell me. I'd like you to examine these test results first. So you can tell me "what" if, anything. Captures your attention the most about, them.

"Dr. Rothner, sir." I replied curiously. "I think I understand your question "clearly" enough. But, how do you expect me to, clarify it. When you still haven't answered mine?" Don't worry, Heather," he insisted. "I will!"

No! Dr. Rothner, didn't quality as being, the type. That you'd ordinarily, hear under these circumstances. So, I decided to, play along. You know, in hopes of, scrounging together. A few "stray details" of, my own. At, the same time.

"Dr. Rothner, sir." I interrupted. "With all due respects. I have absolutely "no, problem". What-so-ever. With the thought of, answering your request. But, shouldn't you be the one. In whom, is telling "me" these answers?"

"I mean, let's face it. You are the doc!"

"You're right, Heather. I am! So, I should be the one. Who's saying this to, you. But, I'd like to, hear your impression first. What do you think they mean?"

Heck, I could definitely say one thing about, "Dr. Rothner's" request that, morning. It'd definitely, held a tough bargain. But, in interest of stepping my way past. His "you show me yours and I'll show you mine" routine. I'd open mindedly, went for it!

No, I'm not going to, deny. That it'd took me a few extra seconds of silent evaluation. Before, I'd glanced towards my "CT" test results and replied.

"Dr. Rothner, sir." I began nervously, although, the first thing I'd noticed. Is when it comes to, these test results. The first thing that'd caught my attention. Was that, unlike an, x-ray. The "CT" results, were done in color."

"Which naturally, gives me no other choice. But to, reach the conclusion that, each shade. Somehow signifies, the "different levels of, activity. In my brain! Is that, correct, Sir?"

So, when "the Doc" didn't answer me. I glanced up at, him until, he'd stated as to, whether or not. I was, even close to being, correct.

Therefore, with there being a difference. Between, looking at me and saying nothing to, answer. I decided to, recreate my next observation. That'd concerned, his "still unknown" test results.

"Dr. Rothner, sir. I continued. "Although, it didn't capture my attention at first. There seems to be, a color chart. Located in its upper right hand corner."

"In which, even though, I could be wrong," I pointed out. "I believe is to, show levels of, brain activity. That each one, represents. So, doc! I asked almost sure that my answer.

CHAPTER FIVE

My eight grade discovery

Although, other than my daily experiences with it. There really wasn't much I could say about, facing it's wrath.

These brief moments they'd taken place on that, afternoon. Had almost seemed like, they'd belonged there.

The only difference was that, this time. It'd also give me the opportunity. To actually test my mother's "not" stepping up theory.

Which, in return. Would also give me the chance to experience. What she'd made the depth of, her shallow minded brain cells. Or perhaps, I should say, what they were really worth.

Yea, Miss "Tonya Banks" may've attempted to, portray herself. As being just like, any other student. In whom, I'd had no other choice but to, silently tolerates she'd may've gotten away by, walking. What I'd considered to be, an extremely thinning line. Especially, on my part!

So since, my overall concept towards her unwanted presence. Did include the concept of, her heading straight downward. My biggest chore involving the usual method of, choice. While trying to, push her over it mentally. Had portrayed itself as being, a fantization.

But even though, I myself. Was just surprised that, I'd hadn't already done it. It wasn't enough to, keep me from wondering why.

There was really only one problem that, needed fixing. Because, until I'd made an effort. To actually, give my unwanted sidekick the sight! To step up and make it's big move towards, stopping her ignorance. All I could really do was to, watch the schools hallway, until, she'd created her plan to pull it off.

Heck, to most people. Miss "Tonya Banks", was just humoring her "Daily Rush." One which, just couldn't be surfaced. Until, she'd made a "complete fool" out of, me! Or, someone else. Before, 1st period had even started.

The day itself, had started out like, any other!

One second things may've came off as being, peaceful enough. But, as soon as, I'd started going through my school locker. In search of, the answers to, a science test. You know, so I could have the chance to, review them more thoroughly. Before, going to class!

Whereas, the next. I'd find myself practically standing nose to, nose. In the middle of, the hallway with Miss "Tonya Banks." In whom, was literally demanding an explanation. That'd provoke her malfunction, which, she'd insisted was solely directed towards me!

The only difference was, that this time. It'd came fully equip with a stupid expression. That was clearly, plastered "all over" her face. Instead of mine! Which, needless to, say. Spoke for itself!

I mean, yea! I my mind it may've held more significance. But apparently, it'd held no it significance to hers. Because, as soon as, she'd realized. That today's effort had left her at a loss of, words. She'd almost immediately decided to, relocate her attitude. A bit further down the hallway.

In fact, I'll even make the effort to, say. That she'd struck me as being, a little faster paced than usual. But, I knew she'd be back after she'd worked out the flaws. That'd belonged to, her "so called" big plan to, enforce it.

However, with all due respect intended. She wasn't the type to, just leave her audience hanging either. Especially, when it came to, me!

While, my first didn't really hit me. Until, I'd had the privileged of, watching her. Proceed to, slither off in, her chosen direction. I just couldn't help but to, notice how oddly, she'd reacted...towards it!

Besides, if I was able to, get this reaction from her. By just getting into, her mind "emotionally." I couldn't stop myself from wondering as to, what kind I'd get. After I'd decided to, pounce on it! But, I guess it's after effects. Where meant for future investigation."

So, in all due fairness to, the situation at hand. Not to mention, the part, where I had to watch her walk away from it. I couldn't help but to, feel as though, I. Had formed a bond. With my "unwanted sidekick" buddy.

Although, with myself still being, heavy of it's circumstances. I wasn't prepared to, show my immediately found information. Well, at least, not yet anyway. I would "a lot quicker" than, I'd predicted!

"Don't try to deny that, you're hooked on heroin!" She remarked as, she'd made her way down the hall. "Everyone knows it! "yea," I thought to myself. "Everyone but, me!" How convenient!"

Heck, I was still in the process of, putting these comments together. When she decided to, start on me again!

"You only come to, school for one reason fuck! " She remarked angrily. It's so you can get high! Don't try to, deny this freak. I know the truth... ha, ha, ha! I can tell that, by the look on your face! That's why you're always passing out at school!

"Shut up Tonya!" I replied insistently. You don't even know what you talking about!" "Yes, I do!" she remarked in return. "You just want everyone to, feel sorry for you! So, you can feed your problem!"

I swear that, in my opinion. Miss "Tonya Banks", thought she'd knew the answers to, everything. You know the type. A regular Einstein on a stick...so to speak.

Yea, Tonya may've been a little bit on the stupid and selfish side. But, I have to admit. She'd basically, lost me. Right when she'd mentioned the word Heroin.

But even though, I'd never heard this word before, in my life. Let alone! Knew what it'd meant! I kind of, felt. Like my lack of knowledge.

So, once Tonya tried to, regain my attention. By switching my train of, thought. Towards what I'd considered to be, a twenty questions mode. Things got even more interesting!

"What's the matter freak? Don't you know that, you're a disgrace to, everyone. Who comes here?" she insisted.

Which is when, Miss "Tonya Banks" stepped well past. The point of, no return! Plus, since I'd been waiting for the perfect opportunity to arrange. This woman's so called, big and bad attitude for a while now. I'd really didn't expect my wish to, come true.

"Tonya!" I commented frustratingly. "Apparently, it's time for me to, show you, what I call, the error of, your ways.

So, when I decided that, just for fun. That I should try to, humor her a little bit. Or at least, make an effort to figure out. Whatever she'd felt she knew.

"I guess, you're a little up to, date. On these facts, Tonya." "You better believe it freak! I know exactly, what I'm talking about!" she insulted.

"Here's the thing, Tonya." I pointed out frustrated. "I may not be as, intelligent as, you grade wise. Which, explains my need to, ask you this."

"Hey, freak," she insisted. "You just can't help it that, you're stupid! So, just ask your stupid question and get it over with?

"Tell me something, Tonya." I remarked in an angry tone. "Did it take you all night to, think this bullcrap up? Or, did it just come to you. Like an inspiration...for example?"

"Personally, it really doesn't matter either. Because, I myself wouldn't even have mentioned it. If you'd hadn't forgot the most important thing."

"Ah, yea!" she remarked angrily. "What part did I forget about, freak?" "Tonya" I interrupted "It's the part where I, kick your butt as, a result. Watch, I'll prove it!"

Heck, before I even realized that, I'd moved. I'd found myself just sitting on her chest. While I indulged in my "long-awaited" fantasy of, kicking her butt. Right in the middle of, our schools hallway.

Besides, even though this was, still news to her. I had to let "Tonya Banks realize that, she. Just wasn't the one who called it's shots.

Yes, she may've been stupid enough, to fall for it. But, with myself basically, playing it by ear. It'd seemed to be, a lot more like, playing it by ear.

However. Since, I'd not only managed to develop. What was now, my own method of, handling this situation.

After about, every six or seven steps towards the office. I would just casually, stop. So, I could turn around to, scope my perimeter out. But, once I was satisfied. I'd just stand there for, the next 10 seconds. Then I'd double check my path towards the office.

No, Toya couldn't've been any more. Then at least, ten feet behind me. When she'd decided to, come off with her "2nd" big daily outburst. "Hey, freak!" she'd proclaimed. Which is when, things started to, get even more interesting.

"Tonya!" I'd insisted. "Do you have any idea as to, how sick. That I am of, hearing your selfish remarks? So, if you like the idea of, keeping your health. You'll get out of, my face. Like, immediately if not sooner!"

The only difference was that, this time. It'd "finally" came true!:

But, after that. I think that, everyone had come out of, their classrooms. In hopes of, learning as to, exactly what. All the hallway "hoo-ha". Was really about.

Which is when, "Tonya" herself. Began yelling out phrases such as, "They're going to throw you out of, school freak!"

It was like, "Tonya," herself. Had insisted upon, proving exactly how ignorant her comments really were. To almost anyone who'd listen to them!

Which, also explains as to, why. I'd just humor her by playing along with it. "No." I remarked angrily. They won't! Because as you've already stated. I'm just a freak...remember?

"Besides, Tonya," I continued "These were your words, not mine!

"Then again, didn't you also mention that, I was hooked on something that, you called...Heroin?

But because, I'd had absolutely, no intensions. In just using words to, describe this. Things went even one more step further.

In fact. Even though she wasn't aware of, it yet. After she'd made her last off the wall comment. She was basically, lucky that, I'd managed to keep myself. From coming straight up off of, the office chair after her!

"Tonya," I remarked insultingly. "Do you even have any idea as to, how sick I am. Because of, your ignorant remarks towards me?"

"In other words, Tonya. If you like the idea of, keeping yourself in good health. You'll get out of, my face and keep it that, way!"

"What are you going to, do about it freak? She remarked debatingly. "Beat me up...Ha Ha Ha!"

But since, by then. My temper had already escalated itself. To what I refer to as being, its slow boil mode. Of course, I'd had to, reply.

"Actually, Tonya! I've seen this "particular episode" coming for a while now. Just consider this as being, my last effort. Towards officially, trying to avoid. What I already know is, inevitable.

But before, I start to describe how easily that, it. Can truly be arranged. I want you to, look me in the eyes. Then, if you still think that, you. Still have what it takes to, step up. Then, please. Feel free to make my day!"

"Hey, freak!" she insisted. "I have a lot more guts than you're willing to, give me credit for. Not to mention, how I plan on making your life. Into, a living hell in the process!"

Heck, all I could do from, there. Was to just stand there and laugh. At, the thought.

"In case you haven't noticed Tonya. Everyone else has already tried to, beat you to it!"

"I don't care either, way freak! She remarked. "I refuse to leave this spot until, everyone who goes here.. Knows what you're really about!"

"OK, Tonya." I insultingly commented. "Since, you think you're so update. About, what's really going on in my world. Then, please... enlighten me!"

Heck, I'd barely even got the words out of, my mouth. Before, I'd looked over at Tonya. Just to see that, she'd had the exact same expression smeared. All over her face earlier.

"Tonya, I've waited for this moment to, get here. Far way too long now!" Yea, I've always known I'd love it's rush. Well, I guess that, there are things in, this world. In which, just don't go away!

But, by then. I think that, even Tonya was well aware. That her usual realm of, pathetic comments. Just weren't working anymore.

Therefore, Tonya made her "so called," last minute attempt. To reach an intimidation level. When she'd decided to, kick the stakes up, a couple of, more notches.

No, I've never had any kind of, problem. With the thought of, speaking for myself.

But since, as usual. Mr. Allison started his next lecture off. With another one of, his lame lectures. On the consequences of, fighting at school. It's safe to, assume that, I. Just wasn't in any mood to hear them... again!

However, once Mr. Allison had finished his boring speech on, the woe of, our ways. He'd actually, gave us an option.

We could apologize to, each other. Which allowed us to, go back to class. Or, face the mandatory three day suspicion it'd held.

Personally, no I couldn't believe that, Mr Allison, was actually, ignorant enough to put those options. On the table like, he'd himself expected this issue. To just be, resolved right there.

Plus, there wasn't any way that, even I. Or, anyone else for that, matter. Would so much as, give him. The privilege of, hearing those words pass my lips.

Whereas, just in case the school "hadn't noticed. I was the victim of, not them!

Then again. Since, the more I'd thought. About being suspended for, the next 3 days. The better it'd sounded. So much as, try.

Tonya, insisted on running her clueless, mouth at me. But even though, she'd apparently, didn't care. As to how stupid she'd made herself sound.

I'd just turned her ignorant behavior. Into, a pile of, smoking ash right before, her eyes. It was almost as though, she'd never even seen it coming!

So, once we'd reached the office and sat down. I attempted to, amuse myself. By sitting there and watching the clock. As it'd ticked away each second. Until, my mom arrived to, pick me up at school.

But, instead of, letting myself get loud. I made the decision to, make my so called, scrapping partner. Quite aware as to, exactly where she'd stood.

"Hey, Tonya!" I mentioned calmly. "If you're ever feeling the desire to, finish. What you've already started. Then please, bring it to, my attention. I'll hook you up!"

Personally, I'd at least, expected to, hear. One of Tonya's usual smart else remarks. But, when all she gave in return. Was a glare that, had. The words, "How dare you speak to, me smeared all over it.

I honestly, think that, even she'd. Got a firsthand taste as to, how far. That I was, willing to, go. To shut her up.

No, she still just couldn't bear. The idea of, taking these moments seriously.

Yea, today may've started out like, any other. But since, I was now being, forced to absorb. All of, it's daily events. From a chair in, the office. It really didn't require, a "college education to understand. Exactly what, was going on!

Heck, all you had to, do. Was to, look around!

No, they mayn't've known it, yet. But, the tables them self. Had "quit" turning and they knew it! Tonya, just didn't have enough guts to, admit it.

Although, as for, Mr. Allison. Well, he was prohibited by, school rules. To refrain from discussing his verdict of, this scrapping session. Until, our parents showed up.

He was also limited to, giving Tonya and I assigned seats. Which, were located outside the secretary's office. Until, further notice

I was just sitting there by my own business. When I'd heard, Tonya, come off with the words, "Well, freak! I hope you're happy now. Because, you've managed to get us both, in trouble...this time!"

Heck, Tonya was just lucky that, I. Didn't just come up off of my chair right then...Amateurs!

Although, if it hadn't been for my assistance. I would've sworn that, I'd never got any exercise "what so ever. I'd always "refrained myself" from letting their level flaws. Be enough to, lower myself down. "To everyone else's level of, "pathetic words".

Tonya, decided to try and make herself look good. By trying to literally, standing up to handle this situation. With the means of, a supposedly "sincere apology.

Which, with her bring, someone. In whom, would say just about, anything. In interest of, keeping herself. Out of, trouble.

But, I guess, she just couldn't bear. The mere idea of, taking this seriously.

Yea, the day may've started out like, any other.

Which is, also probably why she'd. Once she'd filled his head up with worthless bull crop. In interest of, defending her actions. Mr. Allison, looked at me like he'd actually, expected. Me to do the same!

But unlike, Tonya. I wasn't just willing to, say these words. Like, they were my own. I just shook my head no instead.

Plus since, unlike, Miss "Tonya Banks." You'd never hear me apologize, for saying as to, what I'd knew. Trust me, I meant my words.

Building, you have to, remember. I was just a teenager. All I could really do, was to make, the effort to, explain myself.

OK. I admit that, my word choice. May've seemed a little bit insulting on, her part. But, at least, my words were true.

"Mr Allison," I commented calmly. Before you either, say or do something else rather stupidly. You might want to, remember that, Tony's ignorance. Is why we're here in, the first place.

"Tonya," I remarked angrily. "There will always be someone there to pull me off of, you. That is, when I'm at, school. But, there's really a few things you need to, know about me!

"Oh yea, freak? Tonya remarked defensively. "What's that supposed to mean?"

"Well, Tonya", I commented clearly. "It's like this in, my world."

1.) Don't start what you can't finish. It's bad for your health.

2.) I will catch up with you outside of, school. But, when I do and trust me. I will. I'm going to finish it off some more.

"In other words, I'd watch my back if, I was you. Because, I will be there and in the real world. That's "not" a luxury but, a gift! Who's laugh now, wimp...Ha, ha, ha!"

"Mr Allison," I'd insisted. "Heck, starting they second leave my house every morning. My having to tolerate this rude crap doesn't stop. Until, after I get back home.

Yes, my mother may've told me to, just report these things. To, you! But every time I've tried to, mention this subject. You've purposely, stood right there and let people. Just do it, anyway!

Not that, you actually, care. Because, if you did. You'd stop trying to help everyone else pass their blame. Off on, me.

I refuse to take anymore of, this bull pucky. From either, you or anyone else! But, hey! If this is what you expect me to, say, then, you're expecting way "too much" from, the "wrong person!"

Personally, I really don't care as to, how many times. That she's tried to work with you people. Because, the only thing you're worth is, making false promises.

In which, none of, you people. Has ever intended on keeping!

I'm done with the idea of, trying to, handle my life. In the manner that, everyone else. Thinks it should be done!

The only difference is, Mr Allison. I'm handling this round in, my way. But, hey. I insist!

Since, Mr Allison did seem to be. At a loss of, words. Not to mention, act like, he'd just been insulted.

I glanced Tonya's way. So, I could lay down the current circumstances for her.

As for you, Miss Tonya Banks. Just consider yourself for being privileged. Because, the next time we have this conversation. It won't be held at, school!

"When I'm done," I continued persistently. "You'll be lucky to, just walk away. Under your own power!

"In fact, Mr Allison," I remarked angrily. "There's only one fake in, this entire room...you!

"Why do you say that?" Mr Allison asked after his office door swung open. Which is when, Tonya's parents came stealing out of, his office.

Although, at least, now. I know where she'd learned to, walk like that.

Just judging by, their facial expressions. Once I arrived neither, one of, Tonya's parents. Seemed to be, in the best of, moods.

Yea, as Tonya got up to, leave the room. I tried to, keep my mouth shut. I see", did! But, if it hadn't been for her trying to stand here. As, it'd happened.

"If you would've done your job, Mr Allison. We wouldn't be having this conversation! Now, would we?" I insisted angrily.

"I mean, after all. It's not your fault that, you're a self-centered jerk!" "Miss Jensen? He interrupted. "If you can't find it within yourself. To restrain your attitude problem and I mean like, immediately! Then I'll have to contact your parents!"

"Mr Allison", I replied insultingly. "I hate to be, the one. Of whom, bursts your little "authorative" bubble. But, according to you. This has already been done..."Correct?"

"However," I continued. Just for records sake. I do have something else to, say. Before, I leave today.'

"Just in case, you haven't been paying any attention, Mr. Allison. Your worthless threats don't mean "anything" in my world.

Whereas, everything and every time that, you resort. To calling my mom. You're actually, doing me a favor!

"In fact, Mr. Allison." To me, you're doing this, does look a lot more like, a gift. Now, just to prove that, I'm a good sport. I'm actually, going to, do one for you!"

Then again. Since your job as, an authorative figure. Is clearly, more important than, your students welfare. I'll just wait on my mom. From your secretaries office. After all, I wouldn't want to be, the one. Who's responsible for inconveniencing. Either, you or anyone else for that, matter. Have a nice day!"

Yea, I'd glanced at both, Tonya and Mr. Allison. Before, I'd even left his office that, afternoon. But since, neither of, them. Seemed to have anything intelligent. To, add to, the overall conversation. I'd made it "my business" to, laugh in their faces. Before, I'd left.

Since, the school rules them self clearly, stated. That our parents couldn't take us home. Until, they'd actually, spoke to, Mr. Allison.

I'd found myself sitting alone in, the secretary's office. When I'd first noticed the school's "main doors" opening.

Which, sure enough, was caused by "Tonya's" parents. Heck, I could tell that. Just by their so called, heading towards the office routine!

Then, after they'd informed the school secretary that, they were there. They'd sat down beside, "Tonya". Until, Mr. Allison, called them in his office.

Although, personally. I'd heard all I could take. Especially, when it came to, "Mr. Allison's," pathetic exercises". To why he'd hadn't done his job. To last anyone at least, two different lifetimes...If not more!

However, while "Tonya's" parents. Were in, "Mr. Allison's" officer. In order to hear his version of, what'd taken place.

With myself being, such a "nice lady" and all. I proceeded to, brief Tonya. On all of, the facts that, she'd just opened up.

Yea, I may've only had two words for her to, remember. While we were on suspension. But, even with them being not enough. To turn around and slide another smart else remark. Before. I'd finished my statement with, the "rattle rattle" part.

Then again, that's life in my fast lane!

CHAPTER SIX

"Talks the easy part

Yea, exactly three years ago. My epilepsy/unwanted sidekick, had made it's first "grand entrance into, my life!

Which, as a result. Had left me just, standing there and watching. As my "entire world," turned topsy-turvy right in front of, me!

It was as though, I'd spent the past three years living through an, episode. That'd made everything in its path reach "warp speed." Without any chance what-so-ever of, turning back!

But, if that, alone had been enough to, deal with. I'd also found myself learning. The "several new" adjustments that came with it. They were ones which, I'd both. Have to come to learn and understand. To live with its wrath!

Therefore, according to, the Webster's "Collegiated dictionary." Was the act of, making "immediate change."

What this definition doesn't explain. Is how or, why the doing so, requires the use of, two different things.

1.) Bring able to, recognize all of, ti's errors and flaws. When you see them. While at the same time. To try to, sort them out before, they were over. Which, in my case. Were still in need of being, ironed out.

Although, I can't pretend that, at 13, 14, ect. I'd had a hard time excepting either, school. Or, the world as being, the education experience. That everyone claimed it supposedly was.

Tell me, how could I. When everything around me. Was trying to move at, the speed of, light?

However, in my opinion. Just the idea that, I was being forced to, go there, had more to do with, making me mingle "amongst the wolves."

In those days my mother'd invested most of, her spare time. Trying to invent "new ways and methods. To get me out of, bed so I'd go!

Yea, I'd hated it that, much! But since, by then. It'd grown pretty clear as to, how much. My mother and I'd shared the emotional impact that, it. Had now held on "both" of, our lives.

In which, needless to say. Neither one of, us were prepared to, bare. Heck all I'd have to, do. Is think about it and I'd be nauseous.

Besides. Since, after mom'd finished "throwing me" out of bed. Things usually, went pretty smoothly! Well, at least. Until, I'd crossed paths with the other kids along the way. Things would go OK.

I'd mainly preferred taking the alley routes myself. But even though, they'd only let me avoid the problem for a little while.

At least, until we'd cross paths at, the other end of town. I was basically, on my own!

But even though, to me. This walk always seemed a lot more like, these. Once we met back up. I'd have no other choice but to, listen to their pathetic remarks. For the rest of, the way!

Plus, because they'd always followed the "exact same" routine. Like it was, some kind of, creepy made up ritual. They'd secretly, acquired knowledge of, at home.

Of which, they'd obviously pick up from their parents and within minutes. Would never fail to, escalate. Into, something that'd sounded like, lost reruns from the "twilight zone." It got interesting…so to speak!

No, back then. I mayn't've appeared to be, mature enough. To understand their overwhelming desire to make a "big deal." Out of something that, I'd had no control over. But, I'd figure it out, "eventually."

Besides, why couldn't they understand that, this. Was my problem to understand. Not theirs!

Yea, they may've been like my mother. Too shallow minded to, see it, yet. But, those immature idiots. Not unlike, their childish comments weren't worth "two dead flies." To a spider in, my world!

No I mayn't've and wouldn't be aware of, it myself. Until, that, year was completely over. I couldn't just, turn around to, observe it's impact on me. From a third person's point of view. Until, it was!

Besides, what made it stand out. Wouldn't have anything to do. With how it'd started. It's what happened in between then and now. That'd make the actual difference! Allow me to, explain...

While, most of, the kids. That I'd traveled back and forth to, school with every day. Did due to, it's circumstances. Acted pretty cool around me.

I mean, sure. They may've seemed to be, a little on the "paranoid side. About, what they'd seen happen with me at, school. But, when you're put in that, kind of position. What do you expect?

Yea, sometimes I'd catch them glancing. My way from the corner of, my eye. But, I'd never gave it a second thought. Unless they felt the need to, make. A "big deal" about it.

After all, it takes a lot to walk with someone! Especially, once you've stood there and watched. When something like that, happens to someone you know. Not to mention, only 13.

Besides, my real problem was with those, whom felt the need to, insist. Upon making my personal hell. Into, their personal ritual...not them.

Heck, everyday I'd attempt to, report their behavior. To our school principal, Mr. Allison. But, the only thing he ever did to, stop them. Was to laugh in my face. Like I was supposed to just stand down and take it! Before, he'd roll his eyes to, blow me off and walk away.

Then again, when it came to, maintaining a good work environment. Apparently. All of his efforts. Laid strictly within "his" fantasized boundaries...not mine!

I guess the idea of, stopping it. Seemed a lot more of, an "inconvenience" to him. Well, at least, this was the impression he'd always given "me."

In fact, since during the time this took place. I'd honestly, "believed" that, the only person who'd found any form amusement. In his lame sense of, humor. Was...My mother.

I've always thought that, the hardest part about, this epilepsy situation. Would consist of, learning to live and deal with it! When it was really based on, the support that, I'd need. To psychologically hold myself together in, the process!

Although, there are two things about, my mom. That it'd never permit me to, forget.

1.) How her words of, wisdom. "Never" calmed me down.

2.) His concept of, inner strength and persistence. Which, in her mind. "Never" burned up.

My inner drive to, learn these answers. Was the source that, drove my motivation. When everything else would appear to be, at its worst!

Yea, I know this was just her way of, doing her best to, keep her lack of knowledge...from me.

But, I've never had any doubts. That my quest to, learn the right answers. Was weighing just as, heavily on her. As they did me. Which, says a lot! When I was the one "riding it" out!

Although, most of the kids I knew and went to school with. Would literally go out of, their way. To either, convince me and anyone else that, I'd deserved. To be treated like, "white trash". As an attempt to, justify their two bit actions.

They never failed to, twist the truth of, these words around. Until, they'd make it all sound. Like I was, the one at fault!

Which explains why, this empty theory. Would always draw me back to, the same question!"

"What kind of, psychopathically infested moron. Would feel this random need or, desire. To put themselves in that, kind of position. For the "sole purpose" of, gaining attention?

Although, when it came to, the physiological part. I'd already came to, my own terms with the fact that, my "unwanted sidekick." Had become, a "permanent fixture" in, my world.

Physically, I'd figured that, my best bet. Would be to, let the doctor's doodle with it for awhile!

After all. That was, what they were being, paid for...right?

Whereas, when it came to, halting. The worthless comments I'd received from home to, school? Well, I was working on it!

Because, no matter how my mother felt, about, trying to get me to, discuss. How I'd felt towards them...emotionally.

I'd always manage to, push her away from the subject.

I mean! It's not that, I didn't want. To talk about, how I'd felt towards them. Because, I know that, I did!

It was more about being, along the lines of, how!

All yea! Then there's that, other part. Where once I did. I couldn't even walk away from it. Without wondering in whom. She was actually, trying to convince of, them...her or me!

Heck, if I'd had to, describe. How this mess had made me feel at, this point. Then I guess the word would've been...terrified.

Especially, when the only thing I'd really knew about, 5/5/78. Was that, one second. I was sitting down to, breakfast with, Walt and Hanna. Whereas, next I'd have. What I'd later come to, known as being, my "unwanted sidekick. Literally, jumping up and down on, my forehead!

While now, thank God for small favors. I'm thirty four years older and a lot of, things in my world. Have changed since then.

Yea, then I may've felt confused and emotionally vulnerable. But, this isn't a story about, now. It's about, what happened them! Not to mention, what it'd took to, fight my way through it!

So, let's get back to, the facts...shall we?

"However," I continued. "If I wasn't at school. The next best place to, look for me. Would be in my bedroom. AKA/ the place where I'd taught myself the Art of, playing the guitar. But, if you still, can't find me.

Then, check down by the banks of, a small creek. That wasn't very far from, where we lived...remember it?

For as shallow as, it may have seemed. These were my only, "real memories. I'd had left to, sort out. From the morning "whatever happened. Between the time I'd went into, my first conversion and when. I'd came out of it.

Everything else was, just black! Like, it'd been erased from, my mind!

As for, whatever happened after that. Seemed like, it'd consisted of, various flickers and flasks. From a "bad nightmare come true. Of which, I'd had as to, no concept of, how. To, piece together!

After that, it'd found myself hiding. Down by, the creek!

Which is why, whenever I'd go there. I'd let myself step into, a "special place. That I'd reserved in the back of, my mind. Where only, I knew of, it's existence!

So now, every time I'd find myself needing a place. Where I could resume my relent house search of, words. Or better yet, just a chance to think. About, "what" it meant. That's where I'd go.

Eventually, I'd find the words I needed to, describe it. All of which, would ironically enough. End up having nothing to, do, with it's still "undeciphered answers".

But, then again. They never did! Well. At least, they'd never seemed to, anyway!

But, if I'd even had the slightest chance. When it came to, getting all of, this bull crap off my chest. The first thing I'd require. Was the talent to, "make" it happen.

Therefore, in hopes that, it. Could help me get my "so called" words past my lips to, describe them.

Which, at my age. Wasn't the easiest thing in, the world to do. Just discussing this touch and go technique. That I'd not yet acquired. Took its share of, tolls.

Heck, just trying to, get me to talk. About this specific topic. Was challenging enough, within itself. But, as I've said before. The Act of, watching it play itself out repetitiously. Was another! For example...

Every time I'd attempt to, discuss it with mom. She'd instantly begin pacing back and forth. Through whatever room we were in!

That is until, she'd finally, just throw her arms up in the air. In hopes that, it, would help her fill in, the blanks!

Although, making empty questions and comments towards it. Was her usual, method of, choice for handling it. She'd most generally, start asking questions such as,

1.) What kind of, teacher, allows a student to treat people like, that. But, does absolutely "nothing." To report them for it?

Whereas, other times. Her remarks would sound more like, a statement!

1.) Heather, the teachers at, your school. Aren't even intelligent enough to, know. What the word "epilepsy" even means!

It was, something my mother referred to as, "thinking out loud."

Personally, I really didn't care as to, how. She'd chose to, phrase it. As long as, it'd made sense!

Yea, they may've been "Well made" conclusions. But, no matter how I'd look at them. Neither one was, worth anything. Without some form of, solid reasoning. To back them up!

In other words, I was basically, in search of, something rael. That'd held room for foundation.

But, just between my, you and the lamppost outback. I'd always managed to, get lost in it. Somewhere after. I'd asked my questions and my inability to, figure them out.

So, if it hadn't been for that lame remark. I probably, would've understood mom's explanations perfectly!

Or, at least, a lot better than, I did anyway!

Yea, I have to, admit. That, my mother's grasping at straws theories. Were a "tad bit" different from, Dr. Rothner's.

Right before, she'd finish explaining her state of, logic. No matter, how weird it'd sounded during, her speech. They'd seem to, somehow make sense! Especially. After I'd compared hers to, mine.

I'd knew all along that, my mom. Would always act like, she was right on the verge of, making. A "big" break through." But, I didn't know the when and where's.

No, I can't remember as to, how many times. That I'd worked to, throw a useable solution together. To, explain it.

But, with what little facts. That I'd had to, work with "without" success to, back it up. It'd gotten tough!

Which, meant. I'd have to, hear myself saying these words out loud. Before, mine" would make any sense!

Whereas, if it didn't. It wouldn't!

It's a theory that, made me notice, "how it'd elevate. The "tone change" in, mom's voice pitch!

To most people who witness something like, this. Yea, it'd probably strike them as, odd. But, I didn't!

Because, to me. It was like, looking into," a mirror. Without having one at, my disposal. But, it'd never seemed to, bother me! Well, "not much" anyway!

I'd grown "quite familiar". With the word, strange and that, it'd held a pattern. On my emotions towards having, "epilepsy."

I'd "never" brought myself to, admit this before now. But, I'd had numerous reasons. To avoid this area of, conversation over the years.

Yea, this may've only been "one" of, them. But, then. I'd had several to keep them to, myself!

Heck, they might've been my own. But, I'd been made to, feel. Like everything I'd been forced to, live with as, a result. Was solely, my fault!

Especially when once a week. Just like, "clockwork." My mother would find herself in, Mr. Allison's office. So she could hear his complaints. About both, students and various teachers attitude. Towards my "supposedly" uncooperative behavior. With my "newly found" problem.

But, instead of, using their brains to deal with it. They'd preferred to, ignore it!

Because, if "Mr Allison" didn't do everything he could. To prevent having to, face these facts. To protect his own self-esteem. He'd also have to come to, terms. With the fact that, his students. Weren't the only ones responsible for innighting all the "bull crap" lies. About, my "non-existent" sidekick.

Although, the teachers themselves. Were just as, guilty for it's unruly existence. If, not more!

They'd had this habit of, standing out in, the hallway during, class intermissions. So they could laugh at, me.

While, they'd knowingly, let their students. Try to mess with my head about, it...for fun!

Now, don't get me wrong with this insinuation. Because, they'd didn't all. Insist upon, conducting themselves like, brats.

Whereas, most of, it's "so called," teachers. Wouldn't even recognize my epilepsy as being, a problem! Just, a "fantasized" obstacle. In which, they'd needed to, "step past!"

But, even under those circumstances. I can still name at least, five. Whom insisted upon, taking it...even further!

Heck, all of, my life. I've been listening to, people. Say that, kids can be cruel and, to an extent. They're right!

However, teachers are supposed to be adults. Not to mention, expected to, act like, one.

Therefore, when they choose to, conduct themselves, as otherwise. The only way to, explain their behavior is, ignorance!

Yea, they may insist, upon pawning themselves off as being, an authority figure. But, they're easy to, pick out. Because, in the "real world." Or, at least, in mine! When it's time to, step up and "prove" their worth. They're nowhere to be, found!

So, the very next day. I decided to, change my path to, the second floor. By detouring it up the main stairway, past, Mr. Allison's office. Which, as I've explained. Took you through the buildings main entrance.

But, just as, I'd started up. It's second flight of stairs. I got this sudden urge to, glance outside. Just in time to, notice my mother coming in.

Sure, it may've caught me a little "off guard" at, first. But, like I've said. I've noticed "worst" situations.

Although, from my perspective. This only meant one of, two things.

1.) She was either, these to receive invalid information. About, something I'd hadn't done.

Or,

2.) Was, telepathic.

I was personally, leaning towards number one. So, of, course, when she looked up and saw me walking through the hallway. I'd thought I was, in some kind of, trouble.

No, I didn't know as to, why. Yet. But, I was half right!

Yea, it may've been mom's time to, give the principal. His weekly update that'd consumed. Specific teachers conduct towards, my epilepsy.

Which once translated meant. She was pushing this issue. In order to, make sure that, something was done. To, stop them from portraying it.

I knew I'd witnessed the results of, her mental chain being, rattled. Which, never seemed to, end well for anyone! Especially, when it'd concerned my "epilepsy" situation.

But, just like, before. She couldn't confront him. About, the conduct of, certain teachers working there. Without him doing his best. To dismiss these accusations as being, nothing more than lies.

No, he didn't have what it'd took to, fool me. It was just another one of, his "last minute" saves.

In which, he'd foolishly conjured up. To make the stupidity of, his staffs actions look innocent. To protect what he'd felt belonged to his "job obligation". Not the welfare of, his students.

Heck, to hear Mr. Allison's side of this story. The only think I'd found interesting at, school. Was thinking up ways to, use my epilepsy. As a way of, causing unnecessary problems for, his loyal staff! So, just the act of, trying to prove it. Didn't require any assistance from me.

However, since just the concept of, having to deal, with unnecessary problems at, school. Wasn't exactly on, my daily "things to do" list. My main problem basically, fill. Within the grounds of, my getting home. With my morals, dignity and self-respect. Still being, intact.

I mean, maybe the rest of, the world. Wasn't capable of, seeing through their behaviors. But, I was and wasn't going to, just take. Their foolish disrespect from it.

In other words, if that's what they were expecting to create. Then, they were expecting way too much. From, the wrong person!

Then, again. Since we're both on the subject of, tolerating teachers. Of whom, took it upon, themselves. To purposely make my world harder than it already was. Miss Gorrel was the worst part at, the top of my list of, things to do.

Although, for her. It'd appeared to be, more of, a personal quest. Than it was, anything else. Allow me to explain...

"AKA," Miss Goral. Or, as I like to, call her. Seemed to have a real gift for getting on peoples nerves. Especial, she compared her theories to, my mother's.

I don't think there's a number that, can accurately explain it. But, I just wanted to turn around and hook up. Her concept of, home accessories. With a reality check from my side of, it's fence.

So, she could get a clearer view. At what she'd found so easy to, condemn. But, if there was a way to, explain it. No one bothered to, tell me.

However, if you were ever curious as to, whom or why. I have it from a very reliable source of, my own. That she'd possessed keep of, it's golden shovel.

While, my mother, for example. Always told me that, I was to, handle this situation. In one of, the following three ways when confronted.

1.) To just ignore their ignorant comments

2.) Hold my tongue

Or,

3.) Walk away.

Yea, she may've always made a point of, reminding me. That it'd took a bigger person to, walk than step up. But, that, was before, I'd noticed my life. Taking a very relevant change while doing so.

Only this time. Instead of, hiding. I'd be there to welcome it's demise.

Because, according to, my observations. Miss Gocullo real aura of, expertise in teaching skills. Didn't seem to, fall beyond boundaries. That humored "Home Economics or, "physical education" class.

With, "home economics" not being, a required class. I did manage to get out of, it. Whereas, "Phys. Ed.". I was basically, stuck with!

In fact, we'd no more than show up at, the girls locker room. Before, she'd start waving her "Miss Goodie two shoes" act around. Like, she'd alone, held all the cards.

Yea, I'd tolerated that, part. But, that was only because, I had to!

Although, I could've used it, a few times. I've never allowed myself to, receive special treatment. Based on the grounds that, I was, epileptic. Because, to me. It'd never been anything more or, less, than, an insult.

Actually, just the thought of, taking gym class. Didn't bother me at, all. What missed with me, was the fact that, I couldn't even step on the gym floor. Without having every hair on the teach of, my neck. Stand strait up like, she was sending me this vibe. That she was on, a personal quest to prove something. The big question was, "what?"

So while, Miss Gorrell, basked in the luxury of, investigating. New ways to, drive me crazy during, "gym class. I decided use mine for something. That'd fell a bit more on, the constructive side...so to speak.

But even though, each piece to, "my" plan of, action. Was being assembled, right in front of, her. She was bound to, get the faust of things sooner or later. Because as, I've learned the "hard" way. Somethings in life, just weren't meant to be, avoided!

Sure, I'd bought "Miss Gorrells less than professional attitude. To my mom's attention for, the fourth time. Since that school year started. After I'd got home that, afternoon.

Plus, although, I'd had my own personal pinions towards this subject. In return for Miss Gorrells, less than adult like conduct. Mom decided to confront her the very next day at, school. About, how stupid her conduct as, a teacher..."Really was."

Heck, ever since, my "sidekick first showed up. I'd watched my mother do everything she'd "claimed" she could. To not only worth with the school. But, to do what she could. To reach a reasonable solution towards handling it.

Yea, the only they'd either, done or put forth. Was to create a constant refusal to, cooperate with it.

Thanks to, Miss Gorrells, "worthless efforts. I'd spent the past three years of, my life feeling. Like, I was running around in circles. Inside this, giant rot maze.

But, every time I'd find my way past one obstacle. Another would pop up to, take it's place.

No. It never seemed to, matter. What path I'd take to, avoid them. Because they'd all bring me face to face. With another brick wall.

Besides, my grandmother may've always said. That desperate times, seek desperate measures. Whereas, my instincts, told me, that I was right on the verge of, understanding as to, what it'd meant.

Which is why, when my mother found herself standing. In Mr. Allison's office the next morning. She'd came well prepared. By demanding to speak directly to, Miss Gorrell in Mr. Allison's office. No later than, "10:30 am" the very next morning.

Yea, he eventually gave her the OK for their meeting. But only, if they agreed. To have a media present at, all times.

Therefore, once I'd been handed a note from the office. To report to Miss Gorrells classroom for a conference "before" lunch. I couldn't keep myself from wondering why.

After all, we are speaking about, the same woman. Who practically, needed a shrink. Just to deal with the thought of, having me. In her gym class every other day. So, it didn't require a genius to, figure out. That it wouldn't be about, my grades!

Although, I'd basically, perform the same routine every day. My first order of, business during lunch hour. Was to report to the office for my 12:00 meds.

Then after that, I head downstairs to Miss Gorrell's classroom. So I could find out what'd rattled her chain enough. To call "me" in, for a meeting.

Plus, since by that time. I'd already spent the past hour and a half. Just trying to, imagine the expression that, she'd have on her face. Once, I'd showed up...Talk about, you "Kodak" moments.

Since, I could tell she'd had her classroom door shut. Before, I'd even made it "half-way" down the hallway.

Out of, respect. I just knocked on her class room door and waited. Until, I'd heard her give me permission to, enter.

Heck, the first thing I did when I came in. Was to walk over by her desk and wait. Until, she'd signaled to me that, it was OK. To come in and sit down.

But since, the "first words" she'd mentioned to, me. Concerned the meeting she'd had with mom that, morning. Her opening choice of, lines. Even stuck me as being, a little odd.

After all, she couldn't've called me in. Just to give me the "unspoken details" to it...right?

So, after I'd sat in her classroom for at least, ten minutes. Just listening to, her various attempts. To casually, shift the topic of, conversation towards my epilepsy.

I could tell from her behavior. She was appearing to be, intimidating me for signs. That she'd held the upper hand.

But, once she'd realized that, it wasn't working. Her real reason for having me there. Become pretty much obvious.

Therefore, as soon as, she'd started showing signs of, nervousness. Her "Miss Goody two shoes act. Automatically, kicked in and out so called, meeting. Began to get interesting.

Yea, she'd accused me of, making false accusations to, my mother. About, how she'd conducted herself. When it came to, her dealing with my being, epileptic.

Which is when, her line of bull crap. Started coming right back at her through my remarks. Even though I couldn't prevent myself from laughing in, "her face" in return.

But, it especially became apparent that, she wasn't amused with my reply. When the next words out of, her mouth. Were, "Miss Jensen! If you feel you have something to add to, this conversation. Then it would be in your best interest. To bring it to, my attention. Before, this meeting is over!"

In other words. Not only was, she flaunting her interpretation of, the B-word. But, now. She was just being, pushy!

No, I mayn't've been all together sure. About as to, how she'd expected me to, respond. So I calmly shrugged my shoulders and asked. "Like, how? With an apology?"

No. I didn't expect a positive response. But, I didn't really start to, get upset with her. Until, she'd tried to insist that, I'd. Owed her an apology for lying to, my mother about it.

"Miss Gorrell!" I'd insisted. "I don't really care as to, what you think of, me! Because, I'm my own woman!

"But." I continued. "If you think that, you. Can intimidate me into, believing otherwise. By calling me in during, lunch hour. Then, I'm not the one with the problem. You are!"

"Because, after these years of, putting up. With your behavior towards this subject. You'll never hear anything coming from me. That even sounds like, it's in your best interest! So, don't get your hopes up. Because, you'll only be disappointed!"

Yea, I'd expected her. To either, say or, do something in reply. But, the only response I'd got from her. Was this gasping noise like, she'd been insulted. With the expression that, was followed. By her infamous, "how dare you speak to me like that, look. Written all over it!

Which, was immediately, followed with a reply. That'd sounded like, this. "Miss Jensen! When I had the meeting with, your mother this morning. I told her that, you. We're trying to, use your epilepsy. As an excuse to cause unnecessary problems. For everyone else! Especially, teachers!"

But, rest assured. She wasn't the only one in, the room. With choice comments to, share! Because, I'd had several of, my own!

In fact, whether she'd liked the idea or, not. I was now, bringing them to, her attention!

Yea, she may've just sat there like, she was daring me. To say something in return. Which is, how I'd knew right then. That it was, my turn to, approach the subject. From a "completely different" angle.

"Miss Gorrell." I remarked. "You're supposed to be, a teacher, correct?"
"Yes, Miss Jensen." She replied snidely. "But I don't see how it. Would have anything to do with, this conversation."

But before, I waited any more of my time. Just listening to her bull crap. As she proceeded to, dance around "the subject." I decided to, take a quick breath. And request permission to, speak freely.

So, once she'd agreed that, it went without saying. That I didn't hesitate without trying to collect my seize.

Which included her, I'm "Holier than thou" speech. That'd already haunted me through. What'd felt like, at least, two life times. Made it my turn to, talk.

"Miss Gorrell!" I interrupted. "Do you even realize that, you. Have been strutting around this school for three years. Just looking for ways to, use "my epilepsy" either against me. Or, as an excuse to miss with my head. In any way "you" could invent?"

Therefore, I'm going to tell you that, everything changes...right now!

Yea, she may've still been sitting smugly at her desk. When she brought up her next question.

Which was, "Tell me something Miss Jensen. What make you think that, you. Can stop me?"

"Well, Miss Gorrell. It just so happens that, I can! "I replied angrily. "But, just in case you haven't been paying any attention, to this "so called," conversation we've been having. Your job consist of, "you" pulling the wool over people's eyes. So, you can keep yours!"

"In other words," I continued. There's only one person in this room. Of whom, is worthy of, an apology..."Me!"

Which is, probably why. She attempted to, "casually" laugh at me. Before asking, "Miss Jensen." What makes you think that, you're the one. Of whom, deserves an, apology?"

Well, in case you haven't been keeping up. With the latest set of, current events, Miss Gorrell. Maybe it's because, I've been the one taking the rap for, your ignorance! Or, have you "already" forgot that, part?" I remarked defensively.

In fact, I would've left her class room right then. If it hadn't been for her next comment.

"Miss Jensen!" she insisted defensively. Who do you think your mother will believe? You or me?"

However, if she really wanted to, play "that game." I had absolutely, no problem. With the idea of, arranging it's terms.

Besides, since she'd already layed. Her concept of, the cards. On the so called table. I had no problem with, playing along.

"Miss Gorrell!" I replied. "Whether you like it or not. Is irrelevant! Because, I have no intension of, leaving this room. Until, I drawn you. An accurate picture as to where. This conversation. Is, leading!"

"Go ahead, Miss Jensen." She remarked snidely. "Just speak your piece and leave!"

Which is when, I'd began began painting a more realistic picture. To describe it's facts from, "my perspective."

"Miss Gorrell." I remarked determinedly. Just so, we're clear as to, how this works. I guarantee that, this conversation. Will be brought to, my mother's attention. As soon as, "I" get home!"

No, she may not be happy about, it! But, I plan on making her. Aware of, every word that, was said during it! Not to mention, every gesture made. As, it took place!"

"Miss Jensen!" she asked defensively. Are you threatening me? Because, that's the impression that, I'm getting!"

"No, mame!" I replied angrily. "I'm not!" But since, you feel the need to ask."

"Unlike, you. I'm also not the kind of, person. Whom goes around making them. Towards innocent children either!"

I mean, it's just "not" my mo. dig?" I'm the kind that, makes promises. With every intension of, keeping them!"

Well, Miss Jensen! It sure sounded like, one to me!" she remarked. "Which is exactly, how "I". Intend on, reporting it!"

Although, I must admit. When it came to, intimidation tactics. Or, perhaps, I should say trying to, enforce them. She'd definitely given it the "old college" try…no pun intended.

After "everything else" I'd experienced. She was going to, have to, do alot better than. Just to scratch the surface of, my "emotional boundaries."

Besides, unknown to, her. I'd had a much better idea.

"Miss Gorrell." I remarked upon, exit. "Since, I've taken all I can tolerate. As far as, this worthless conversation goes.

linda

you can tell those worthless morons whatever you want! You will anyway … right?"

"Miss Jensen!" Miss Gavelle insisted foolishly. "If you leave this room without my permission, I will go straight to the office to report that you've threatened me!"

"Miss Gavelle." I added calmly. "I really don't care as to what you do!" But trust me. "Before this years over, I'll make you regret that decision!"

"Do you have anything else to add in your own defence young lady?" she insisted.

"Well, Miss Gavelle." I answered provokingly. "Now that, you ask. I do have a few questions to slide your way. Before I leave the room and you know it's rules. Turnabout is, fair play!"

Just ask your questions and leave, Miss Jensen." she insisted regretfully. "Well, Miss Gavelle." I requested curiously. "If you have "so much" confidence in what you're saying, then how come you "won't" look at me in the face, when "you're" saying them?"

Although, needless to say, I never did get an answer to suffice my curiosity, she did signal me to leave the room.

No, she may've "not" figured it out, yet. But whatever she was thinking was "irrelevant" to me! Because, no matter what, she couldn't pretend that her hands weren't "more than full now!"

Yea, she could try to bury herself in the world of denial all she'd wanted. But, the truth that, controlled it has never failed to make itself known... No exceptions!

Especially, after she'd chosen to rattle "my chain," without counting on me to rattle back!

Yea! To her I may've seemed like just any other kid which is why, she'd expected a child's reaction. But, that was her mistake. Not mine!

Besides since by that time, I'd had plenty to think its rules out. They'd seemed even clearer to me.

"Expect the unexpected at "all times"..."No exceptions!"

I'd always known that this day "would come." But, until I'd showed up at Miss Gavelle's "room that day, I'd never thought that "I" would end up being "so nervous" ect.

I guess, it's outcome had even succeeded at surprising me! What'd caught me off guard even more didn't come from "Miss Gavelle", until she'd found herself at a sudden loss for words.

No, I've never seen it happen before then! But, apparently there's a first time for everything.

While, what'd seemed to make their conversation so messed up! Did start in "American History" class.

Which is where I was when I'd received "Miss Gavelle's" request to show up! It was "the one that would either begin or end. Before, I'd even left her classroom with less answers than, when I'd come in!

Then again, from what I'd knew. Yes, it may've felt like I was experiencing what my mom considered to be her "thinking out loud" mode.

But, one thing was definitely clear about it, I'd had no reason to question towards her level of trying to "intimidate me."

Heck, she'd obviously set her level of expectations way too low for my taste, which does explain why it didn't work.

After I'd stepped back for a few minutes, to evaluate everything that was said ... "more thoroughly."

I started making my way to the "school cafeteria."

Although, once I'd found an open table. What I really needed was a little space. So, I could "sort out" these facts in peace.

It didn't matter as to how many times I reviewed them because they'd always led me to the same place.

If you're asking me "my" concept of it. What'd seemed to have the biggest impact on me wasn't the evidence I'd now possess towards having to hold these angry emotions in. But, how easily they'd poured out.

Either way, I'd said my piece. All I had to do now was to wait for its verdict to come in. The only bad part was "not knowing," what to expect as, its result!

Although no more than twenty minutes ago, I was seriously wondering if I'd even had enough self-esteem to win some close to pulling it off. Now, all I'd felt was "pride!"

Personally, I'd never even knew that I'd had any fight left to give!

But since Miss Gavelle's "happy go luck" attitude has never failed to give me the impression that she'd enjoyed presenting this vibe.

In order to make everyone believe that she was "all that and a box of chicken, I guess she hadn't been made aware that it...wasn't included!

Apparently, I thought I'd lost part of myself somewhere amongst the battles I'd fought and belonged to my sidekick and I.

But, I was wrong because, I'd find them again!

No. My unknown sidekick would never leave me so I'd never lost "anything," it'd concerned. It'd just decided to stand back so it could observe its shadows for a while.

However, just the gossip alone had already proven itself to be a completely different ball game. One that, I'd loved to "play rough."

No, it couldn't just sprout up by itself without having a fertile source to feed it.

So, evertime I'd make a quick glance towards "Miss Gavelle's" room when I'd pass by, it was pretty obvious that she'd believed. That she was on a personal quest to prove something to me. The real question was...what?"

Besides since my mother always did feel that she couldn't reach her "best conclusions" about me until she'd had time to read my "facial expression."

I think it's safe to say that, she'd felt like she'd been blessed with this specific gift. Or, at least, one close to it anyway!

No, my mom never openly insinuated it. But, I'd knew her plan to keep tabs on the current situations of my teachers at school.

Then again, you know what they say..."You can't fool moma!"

In fact, since the first thing I'd noticed when I'd woke up the next morning, was that I'd only had fifteen minutes to do both, get dressed and have breakfast. Before, I'd even left for school.

I'd no more than got a chance to head downstairs. Before, several images from the previous day would start replaying themselves in my mind.

Plus, since, I could hear her cruising around from "my room," I'd knew mom was already in the kitchen!

Yea, this may've been her usual procedure, for preparing my "mandatory" co. co. what's breakfast. So, it'd be ready and waiting when I'd reached the dining room table.

But, I didn't care! Because I'd already knew she'd have "several questions" to ask. As soon as I'd sat down to eat it, all of which, she'd be expecting "me" to answer.

Heck to anyone else. It may've seemed like it was any other dining room affair, but, I'd knew my mother's conference table well!

Besides, I've always known that this particular subject was eventually bound to step up and take its place.

So eventhough the conversation itself was of the unavoidable, I did manage to have at least one advantage working on my side.

"I was there when it'd originally played itself out!"

Yea, my main interest at the time. May've revolved solely around my quest to find out whatever lies "Mrs Gavelle'd" told my mom. During her faulty efforts to power its details up.

All I had to figure out before going downstairs. Basically, lied within my ability to explain them.

But, after I'd avoided the subject for as long as possible. The morning's present events became all about facing it's music.

There were exactly 20 steps that led from the top of the staircase to the bottom. But even after the many times I'd traveled them, I still believe it was longest it'd taken me to reach the "living room."

Then, just to be, on the precautious side, I'd even made a point to peak around the corner. In hopes that my brief gesture would give me just enough time to evaluate. What to expect one I'd got there.

Although the only thing you'd be able to see from this spot were it's cupboards and countertop. If you really wanted to evaluate our "kitchens" actual size, you'd have to be willing to walk over by its doorway and look in.

I honestly think what'd caught my attention the most that morning involved mom's "ironically styled" fashion of calmness.

However, once you overlook the fact that our stove and sink were located on the opposite sides of the room. The act of evaluating its overall diameter...got easier.

Which brings me to how uncomfortable I'd get just by watching mom's weird facial expressions. Everytime she'd stroll past it's door.

Yea, she may've wanted me to be the first one to bring it up, I used whatever amount time that I'd still had left to spare in a "more productive" manner such as, reviewing my opening line...ect.

There was really only one way to put it! For example...

"Well, mom." I suggested nervously. "Yesterday during, "American Studies" class, I received this note stating that I was to report to "Miss Gavelle's" room. Before, I'd went to lunch. Which, needless to say ended like this..."

"No, that'll never work!" I thought Heck, it didn't even sound right to me and I...was there!

Then again, maybe mom's "room length" absence gave me a "much larger" advantage than I'd forseen. After all, she'd hadn't got in my face about it...yet!

Which, fantasy to popular belief. Usually meant that, I'd still had a slim chance of having this round. Go, my way!

Yea, I may've tried to act. Like this was just any other morning. When my mother'd brought breakfast in and sat down. The only problem was, that this time. She didn't sit with me. In the same manner that, fit her normal sequence.

In fact, if I'd have to, describe it "my way." It'd almost seemed as though, she was testing its grounds. So, she could "quietly observe the standards it'd held. Over by the side window, a few feet away.

But, it didn't last long. Because, after five minutes of silent interrogation. She'd realized that, I wasn't talking about, what'd happened. Unless, she'd mentioned it first.

"Heather Lynn," she began casually. "I heard that you and Miss Gavelle had a "small misunderstanding" yesterday and I was just wondering if you'd care to discuss it?"

"No, mom." I replied. "I don't." which in turn, she answered with "Heather, I've already heard Miss Gavelle's version of this story. But, I can't decide how I should handle it. Until you've given me yours." Mom insisted calmly.

Yea. I could tell she was frustrated about something. The only difference was that this time. She didn't appear to be, directing it… towards me!"

Which explains why she decided to rephrase her question in a manner that didn't suggest that it was on me.

"Heather," she asked curiously. "Do you feel the need to share anything she said or did during this conversation?"

So, in interest of figuring out why, Mom'd felt this need to catch me off guard. I figured it'd "probably" be in my best interest. Just to lay all of its cards out. In the same manner "Miss Gavelle" offered me.

Because, at least, that way. I'd be able to atleast, get everything out. So, she could sort them in the open. Instead of trying to usuange. What little she didn't know concerning its real terms. Instead of trying to hide them "inside me."

"Hey, mom." I remarked doubtfully. "Personally, I'd like to avoid the consequences. Of which, judging from past experience in this case. Can't be done."

"But, now that, it's already been brought up. You can ask me as many questions as you'd like. About, yesterday's series of events…I'll answer them!"

Just don't expect me to apologize for them! Because, I refuse to take so much as one worst of it back! Let alone, everything the responsibility for, someone else's actions…dig?

"Heather Lynn" mom implied patiently. "Just calm down for a minute! Since, you "obviously," don't care to discuss this topic. Will just start at, the beginning. So, we can go through what "really" happened step by step"…OK?"

"Just remember." she continued. "I've already heard "Miss Gavelle's" side of this story. But, I'm not buying "one word" of it!

"In other words." she insisted. "I need you tell me every word and gesture that was made. Between the point you came in the room yesterday. To the time you walked out and… I want details!"

"Mom." I interrupted curiously. "May I ask you a question before saying anything else? Because, I seriously, "doubt my words will even matter!"

"I mean, let's just face it, shall we?" I know what I'm telling you is true. But, I seriously don't see them even caring! Let alone, doing something about i! Especially with Miss Gavelle being, a teacher!"

No, I didn't see mom answering me. So, in interest of avoiding. The wrath of another dirty load. I started filling in the blanks in farther. The way I'd watched them go down.

"Mom." I replied frustrated. When I just received Miss Gavelle's note. I reviewed each word step by step. Until, I'd left "American studies."

Once, I'd finished going over. All the details for the "second time." I glanced up to check her reaction. Then, to my extreme surprise. Instead of her denying my words. We both just started laughing hysterically at the image she'd conceived from it.

Yea, this may've been a first time thing. Especially, when it'd came to this subject!

But after she'd finally, quiet laughing. About the image she'd drawn from my words. I began explaining the how's and why's as to where. Miss Gavelle, thought her "apology theory" fit into her lecture.

"Mom." I began hesitantly. "I'm quite aware that, "Miss Gavelle." Has practically went out of her way. Not to mention, insist that I liked to you. About how she'd behaved. But, I'd no more than started laughing in her face. Before she'd straight up demanded an apology and explanation for it!"

"Therefore, since that thought alone. Just made me laugh "even harder." I almost couldn't believe it. When she'd actually had the nerve. To stand there and act like I'd insulted her!"

"Heather," mom continued. "Tell me. Did she do anything else offensive. While this went on?"

"Mom," I continued angrily. "I may've given her "my vision" of the straight up faces, as this went on. But honestly! I don't even think she'd took me seriously. Until, I'd mentioned, "Dr. Rathner's" name.

"Then, almost immediately, after that. She started acting real nervous and shut up!"

"Yea!" I insisted even more. I may've called her a liar before I left!

"Besides," I finished discussed. " think the only reason she'd tried to play this out, was that, she'd couldn't the truth to Mr. Allison or you. Without "literally," humiliating the crap out of herself. In front of everyone else!

"So, since I didn't have anything else to say. That hadn't "already, been said ... I left!"

"Heather," mom remarked curiously. "Would you like to know. The version that, "Miss Gavelle," portrayed?" "Yes, mom. I would!" "Well," she began. She told me that, you "uninvitedly" walked into her classroom during lunch and literally threatened her! "Mom, that's a lie! I've never threatened anyone!"

"Heck," I continued. "I wouldn't've even been there. If I'd hadn't received her note to show up!

"Heather." mom interrupted patiently. "Just calm down for a second."
"Mom," I replied insistently. "I knew the second I'd saw the look on Miss Gavelle's face. That she was living. I just can't figure out why!"

"No, Heather." she remarked arguing. "Miss Gavelle, didn't have any right to call you on. Unless, she'd had my authority to do so."

"However" mom replied deviously. "This time, unknowingly to, to her. She's backed herself into a corner. That she can't possibly get out of, without abetting her suspicious. To how large of a mess she's made!"

"Heather." she continued angrily. "Just concentrate on your grades. I'll handle Miss Gavelle!"

To tell the truth about Miss Gavelle's attitude. During these past three years, I've probably heard. About, every excuse she could create. Along, her so called, quest to turn my life. Into, her own private joke that, wasn't!

Only, now. Instead of just freely flaunting her ignorance. She was about, half of a nat's eyelash away. From having her actions backfire. Right in her lap! "Who knows," I thought. Maybe miracles, "really do" exist!"

No. I can't remember how long my "unwanted sideck's" been right there beside me. But, ever time my life's thrown a challenge "my way." I've never denied it's presence.

Yes, alot of things it'd consisted from. May've changed since the year of 1978. Only, this time. They were all just, standing there in front of me. Like, it was waiting to see. My next move as a result.

Personally, I don't know as to how many hours. I'd spent struggling with the fact that, it was all real and not just a phantom. That would literally come and go. At it's own "free leisure."

Now, if I could only figure out a way to talk "it." Into giving me a little advance notice before it showed up! I'd be in business...details!

Although on my way to school that morning, I just couldn't stop thinking about our little "before school" table talk. I'd never expected it to play itself out. To easily, once I'd got there. But, still. Nothing was that definite!

Plus I may've promised myself that, I'd never let someone else's opinions keep me from living my life. When it'd came down to it. I couldn't ignore that mine. Seemed to be the only one that mattered.

A good friend of mine once described this as being her "Rose colored glasses" theory. Allow me to explain...

According to my understanding, there are those living amongst us. In whom'd rather spend their entire lives hiding behind them.

Because apparently. Just the thought of having to see life for "what it really is, when it reveals it's flaws. Or, perhaps I should say, "true colors." Just terrifies the "crap" out of them!

"Why do you ask? Well, I guess just the thought of it's truths scares them! So, they attempt to bare the impact of reality "behind" them!

No. At thirteen years old I may've had no concept as to what this meant. Not to mention, "wouldn't!" until, at least, twenty five years later.

Just the thought of her rose colored glasses people of whom were the kind of people that'd required them to follow a daily diet. Which feasts on innocent people's flaws as though it's a delicacy. The image just altogether ... creeped me out.

Especially with them being more than comfortable with the concept of them stealing an innocent person's morals, dignity and self-respect to satisfy their "disturbing" craving other than earning them fair and square.

It's like suffering an addiction. They never seemed to show any interest in quieting. Until, it backfired in their face."

Which brings me to "my" definitions of the word "violence."

Although no matter what language you use, it speaks for itself. It basically consist of a person. In whom takes it upon, themselves. To hurt anyone! For nothing more than elevating or boasting their "own" morals, dignity or self-respect... No exceptions!

With the point being. If your definitions of the word "extra-curricular" activities. Includes the thought of "literally" pushing people around. For the sole pleasure of saying that it. Is something that, you did. Then, sooner or later. You "will" get pushed back! That part, you can "count" on!

No! I don't know as to how anyone else felt about all of this violence crap floating around. But I'd been planning my next move for a while. That way, when it came back, I'd be ready for it!

Heck, math may've been my "least favorite" class to attend, but, with the big test I'd had coming my way. I'd figured it be in my best interest to prepare myself for it, while, I'd still had the time.

Yea, I may've went straight to my locker when I'd arrived at school that morning, but, as I was getting my books together I couldn't help but to overhear two girls in the locker beside me exchanging rude comments about the events from the day before.

Although my mom seemed to be right about the supported threats I'd made towards "Miss Gavelle" being everywhere.

When it'd came to my unwanted sidekick, I'd only had one rule in which, I'd absolutely "refused" to break!

"As long as nobody got the "overwhelming" urge to jerk my chain about its existence. I wouldn't feel any need to knack them on their lame birth as a result!"

In the real world, it's known as mutual respect. But just like anywhere else, you'll always into those idiots, who'll do whatever they can to prove it's worth wrong.

Then again, I know they thought they'd held all of its top cards. But they weren't seeing this world from my perspective, either!

While, I can't deny that most kids in whom I'd attended school with, would "putty much" just mind their own business.

There were also, those who'd just thought that their "bull crap" didn't stink!

Yea, they may've believed that the planet Earth. Only revolved around "their" lame bagonza beans. But since scientific evidence had already proven otherwise. I've never trusted their kind.

Heck, I wouldn't even have made an attempt to open my locker door without checking behind me first. Until I was satisfied one of them wasn't lurking nearby for me that just wasn't an option. Some people even referred to me as paranoid! What they so easily dismissed as paranoid, I considered scoping out my perimeter. Better safe than sorry!

Looking back on those days now, the name Tamera Wells still makes me cringe. Every morning before first period sked slither past my locker in search of her daily rush. As soon as she see me the next two words out of her mouth would be, "Hey freak!" and I'd immediately have to restrain my sidekick just so it wouldn't indulge itself by jumping on her as soon as she'd stroll by.

However, during the past few weeks I had the privilege of witnessing a lot of change taking place in my would and I had a strong hunch I wouldn't have to tolerate things being that way for much longer. But any farther than, I could slobber!

In fact, for the sole purpose of describing. Exactly "how far" the area of this depth went, then, between you and me.

I wouldn't even made the attempt to open my school lockers door until I'd felt completely satisfied that one of their kind wasn't lurking nearly!

In fact, psychologically, I personally, was that, I'd hadn't already done this. But, the word patience in my world wasn't a virtue but a lie!

However, if I'd actually felt this subject to be in any way worth of pushing, then, I would've been the "perfect" person to prove it!

The only problem was that until I'd felt safe enough to give my side kick the job. All I could do was to observe "patiently" from the sidelines to contemplate my "unspoken theories" of every move it made.

I've always had a hidden madness to my method of doing so. But no matter how large or intense it's words grew, I'd had no other choice but to watch them silently fester.

Because at least, then when I'd release it to do it's damage, there'd be no doubts as to why. But until then, all I could really do about them was to reevaluate its factually details!

Yea, maybe some people had been successful at convincing all of the school idiots to blindly follow them into their battle against me. But, I've had this attitude pegged all along.

Although, for as unusually as, it seemed, this specific meaning did come off as being creepily quite. It'd basically, consisted of, my instincts incites speaking to me!

Then again, since the concept behind my newest plan of action towards defending this problem has always revolved around devising a resoluting to defend it.

My intensions to do so have never failed to lead it's idiot like followers in the wrong freaking direction. But, that was their problem ... not mine!

In other words, my idea to overcome the difficulties they'd arouse was developed to make them feel like they were the one's calling the shots.

Which basically, meant that, I'd have to play them all "by ear."

Heck, I'd already knew that they were "definitely," stupid enough to fall for it. Or, they wouldn't've been there in the first place! So, to me riding it out was a lot more like going through its motions.

What they didn't seem to understand was that I could pull them off in my sleep!

Then again since somethings in life just don't change. It didn't keep them from thinking that they were like Einstein on a stick either!

Heck, If I would've been like anyone else, I would've probably even got "a lot more" upset about their foolish accusations than I did!

But, other than that, their excusive type of idiosyncrasies made the view from my perspective look pretty awesome!

It was just too bad that my mother wasn't there to enjoy it! Ah, well, you know what they say, you can't have everything!

Which is also why if someone were to come up to me today and ask if I'd had any regrets about how that day played itself out. I'd have to say yes!

But because it didn't require the a college education to understand the extent of what this meant, I'd knew the tables themselves. Had readily turned!

Besides, since by this point, there wasn't even enough many on the entire planet to lower me down to their level of thought, I couldn't be broken, by their mere "pathetic" use of words anymore!

Ok. Maybe my choice of words do seem like they're more than just a little forward. Especially in this case! But, at least, they're true!

Yea, I guess when 'that" year started I'd felt like my entire world was "caveing in" around me. But, when I stop to think about how much it's changed since then, I'm dumbfounded by the visual every time!

Heck, my "Aunt Carol" may've always told me to let people's actions speaks for themselves. But since her words are just as clear now as they were then.

I guess I'd never really understand as to what they really meant until the day I'd found myself standing face to face with them. As they literally, screamed the words "talks cheap" back at me!

No, I may've had absolutely no idea exactly how significant this year would be during my life's path but even though its impact would have nothing to do with either, the beginning or end.

It's what'd happened in between that'd make the difference. But after I'd finally found these answers, I've never had any doubts that they were the one's I'd "never" forget.

www.ingramcontent.com/pod-product-compliance
Lightning Source LLC
Chambersburg PA
CBHW021424070526
44577CB00001B/41